FRANK WILLIAMS

Other books by Maurice Hamilton with Jon Nicholson

RACING STEWART:
THE BIRTH OF A GRAND PRIX TEAM

INSIDE FORMULA ONE

POLE POSITION:
THE INSIDE STORY OF WILLIAMS-RENAULT

FRANK WILLIAMS

MAURICE HAMILTON

MACMILLAN

First published 1998 by Macmillan
an imprint of Macmillan Publishers Ltd
25 Eccleston Place, London SW1W 9NF
and Basingstoke

Associated companies throughout the world

ISBN 0 333 71716 3

1 3 5 7 9 8 6 4 2

A CIP catalogue record for this book is available from
the British Library.

Typeset by SetSystems Ltd, Saffron Walden, Essex
Printed and bound in Great Britain by
Mackays of Chatham plc, Chatham, Kent.

Contents

1 Motor Mad
1

2 The fun of it all
21

3 On the point of collapse
35

4 Can this be true?
56

5 The first is the best
80

6 Double top
94

7 The end of an era
112

8 Stumbling across another champion
122

9 Here's Nigel
140

CONTENTS

10 Upside down
148

11 Slipping through their fingers
162

12 Nigel: gone today, here tomorrow
181

13 A champion's fast farewell
199

14 Working towards a nightmare
216

15 1 May 1994
232

16 Pressure everywhere
240

17 The Boy Damon
257

18 The trouble with speed
276

Acknowledgements

I owe a debt of gratitude to many people who took time to reminisce and provide such a revealing insight, without which this book would have been infinitely poorer. My thanks to Ann Bradshaw, Ross Brawn, Michael Cane, Iain Cunningham, Derek Daly, Walter Hayes, Damon Hill, Alan Jones, Andrew Marriott, Neil Oatley, Viv (neé Orriss) Woods, Keke Rosberg, Denis Rushen, Tim Schenken, Bob Torrie, Ken Tyrrell, Jonathan Williams and Peter Windsor. I must also thank Peter Foubister (publisher of Autosport), Jane Gorard, Alan Henry and Richard Poulter (director of Hazleton Publishing, publisher of Autocourse) for their assistance in various ways.

There has been much enjoyable delving into a variety of publications. References have been gleaned from *Racers* by Doug Nye (Arthur Barker), *Nigel Mansell. My Autobiography* (CollinsWillow), *Damon Hill's Grand Prix Year* (Macmillan), *Life at the Limit* by Professor Sid Watkins (Macmillan), *The Death of Ayrton Senna* by Richard Williams (Viking), *Driving Ambition* by Alan Jones and Keith Botsford (Stanley Paul), *Faster* by Jackie Stewart and Peter Manso (William Kimber) and Alan Henry's *Damon Hill. Hero to Zero* (PSL), *Williams. The Business of Grand Prix Racing* (PSL) and *Williams. Triumph out of Tragedy* (PSL). Newspapers, magazines and annuals

ACKNOWLEDGEMENTS

consulted include the *Guardian*, the *Independent*, the *Observer*,
Autosport, *Autocar* grand prix specials and *Autocourse*.

Finally, I must make special mention of *A Different Kind
of Life* by Virginia Williams with Pamela Cockerill (Double-
day). I have unashamedly leaned heavily on this most moving
account, but by no means have I been able to do it justice.
To do so would have been to intrude too deeply and
insensitively into a uniquely personal story. Nevertheless,
I was grateful for the opportunity to learn so much from a
book which cannot be recommended highly enough when
attempting to understand another side of a remarkable and
sometimes controversial man.

Preface

At the time of gathering information for this book, former properties used by Frank Williams – on Bennet Road in Reading and Station Road in Didcot – were derelict. Outwardly at least, there were no indications that the nucleus of a racing team which would become the best in the business had passed through. Both buildings looked forlorn and shabby, silent indicators of the various recessions which had done their best to embrace a mercurial man in love with motor racing. Each time, Frank had shrugged off the various set-backs as he ducked and dived, driven on by enthusiasm and incredible self-belief. There was no doubt – in his mind, anyway – that he could win races. He would not be satisfied until he had.

More than 100 Grand Prix victories and several World Championships later, he is still not satisfied. Now he sits in the understated opulence of an imposing headquarters in Oxfordshire. His circumstances have changed, almost beyond recognition.

The marble-floored reception area alone would accommodate the small workshop, located between a bingo hall and a pub, which had provided the launch-pad for his ambitions in 1967. The purpose-built factory and wind tunnel, which adjoin the administration block, would have been beyond his wildest dreams. But Frank does not see it that way. The thirty-two-acre site at Grove is not a status symbol. It is a necessary tool to allow Williams Grand Prix Engineering to win in the nineties and keep on winning into the millennium. Or, at least, that is the aim. Williams knows it will not be easy. Today's success is all very well, but it is tomorrow's victory which really matters.

That has been the fundamental constant within a company which has expanded at a prodigious rate. This driving ambition may account for the relentless search for technical excellence but it also explains Frank's ability to overcome problems of a more personal and potentially devastating nature. The changes to his circumstances are not confined to business. The former fitness fanatic and marathon runner is now a quadriplegic, a prisoner within a body which was almost fatally broken by a road accident in 1986. Frank's ability to cope with the appalling consequences of the crash is matched by the achievements of a company which barely seemed to break its stride. Indeed, the team itself has provided Williams with a stimulation which no amount of medicine and rehabilitation could match. It is, you might argue, his reason for living.

Despite the massive changes, both physical and material, Frank Williams remains more or less the same person who embarked on his Formula One mission with Piers Courage in 1968. Since then, Williams has experienced overwhelming lows, first with the loss of Courage at Zandvoort in 1970 and, more recently, the death of Ayrton Senna at Imola. But his love of the sport and its top performers remains steadfast. As does a refusal to accept that his personal achievements — as opposed to those of his team — are anything special.

Books such as this have no place on his agenda. When notified of my plan to write his biography, there was no approval forthcoming. But neither was there any formal objection even though Frank thinks such a project irrelevant, puzzling and mildly irritating. There is, therefore, no direct input from either Williams or his close friends, since such a demand would have placed them in a difficult position.

I have relied on interviews conducted with Frank during the past twenty years, most notably an amazingly candid insight when we spoke twelve months after his accident. The choice of former associates as subjects for interview is vast and doubtless the reader may feel that certain key characters have been omitted. That may be so but I would like to think that the contributors to this book provide a wide-ranging view, particularly since many of their voices have not been heard before. Whether he likes it or not, Frank Williams is one of the most poignant and frequently misunderstood figures in British public life. The aim has been to reveal far more than the familiar and misleading television image of an intense and gaunt figure hunched in his wheelchair, watching his beloved team at work.

Maurice Hamilton
October 1997

CHAPTER ONE

Motor mad

During the first week of September 1996, the paddock at Monza exuded its traditional ambience. It was the heart of Italian motor sport, a place where waves of passion poured through the wire-mesh fence and threatened to engulf everyone inside the hallowed enclosure. The Ferrari fans and local Formula One fanatics – the tifosi – may have been locked out but they were as knowledgeable as the privileged members of the Grand Prix circus parading within.

The tifosi communicated their enthusiasm with a day-long barrage of banter from the fence. Their finely tuned antennae were alert to the matters of the moment. On 5 September, they spoke of two things: Ferrari's chances in the forthcoming Italian Grand Prix; and the latest extraordinary piece of decision-making by Frank Williams.

The progress of the Ferrari team is common currency in the bars and cafés south of the Alps. The fans, fed by pages of daily newsprint, felt qualified to discuss every nuance associated with the Ferrari headquarters at Maranello, about an hour's drive from Monza. Frank Williams proved infinitely more difficult to understand. The owner of the British team remained a mystery not only to the Italians, but to observers at home. Williams may be one of the most successful Formula One entrants of the past decade but his wish to maintain a low profile is frequently contradicted by controversial decisions which automatically propel the Englishman into the lime-light. Thursday, 5 September 1996, was a case in point.

Eight days previously, Frank Williams had told Damon Hill that his services as a driver would not be required in 1997. That was Williams's privilege; he was responsible for hiring and firing. It was, after all, his team. But it was the logic of the decision, as well as its manner and timing, which had brought a stunned reaction, not least from Hill.

There seemed no good reason why Hill should be dis-missed in such a peremptory fashion. He had been with Williams, first as a test driver and then as part of the race team, for five years. He had carried the team in the difficult aftermath of Ayrton Senna's death in 1994. He had won twenty Grands Prix for Williams and been in the running for the championship three years in succession. Hill had yet to claim the world title but he was favourite to do so in 1996 after the competition had boiled down to a fight between the Englishman and his team-mate, Jacques Ville-neuve. As far as Hill was concerned, he was happy to stay with the company which had given him his big chance. Negotiations had been opened concerning a contract for 1997. On 28 August, Frank Williams had telephoned to say he did not wish to take discussions any further. Seven days after that, Frank announced that Heinz-Harald Frentzen, a twenty-nine-year-old German driver whose best result had been one third place in 1995, would be taking Hill's place.

The judgement appeared to lack either logic or compas-sion. That was no surprise, given Frank's reputation for ruthless pragmatism. This was not the first time Frank Williams had caused controversy by failing to keep his world champion on board for the following season. In 1987, he let Nelson Piquet go despite the Brazilian driver having given Williams the title for the first time in five years; five years after that, there was uproar in the British tabloid press when Nigel Mansell failed to agree terms not long after he had won the crown with Williams; in 1993, Alain Prost felt he had no alternative but to leave despite having given Williams yet another championship. And now this. It was the talk of the paddock and those pressed against its wire-mesh border.

The Thursday preceding a Grand Prix is a day of preparation and settling in. The trucks, each carrying equipment and cars worth £1m, arrive on the Wednesday and, by the time the rest of the race team flies in the following day, the garages are laid out, ready for the mechanics to commence work. The drivers and the media also arrive on Thursday. Since there is no track activity (practice starts on Friday), this is an ideal time to catch up on the latest stories and canvas drivers for their predictions for the weekend. On 5 September, however, the race was the last topic anyone wished to discuss. Sensing the avalanche of questions heading his way, Hill decided to hold a press conference on neutral ground, away from the Williams motor home.

In many respects, he was simply going through the motions. He explained the sequence of events but, since he had not been offered an explanation for the decision, he could do little to answer the most pressing question of all: what had possessed Frank Williams to do such a thing? Hill's preoccupied look portrayed a mixture of bemusement and simmering anger. His innate sense of manners and dignity prevented him from expressing his true feelings.

An hour previously, Frentzen had given his side of the story. He could offer no clues to the reasoning. Not that he cared particularly. His permanent smile spoke volumes about the opportunity of a lifetime which had been thrown his way.

Frustrated by the absence of fresh evidence, the journalists made their way to the media centre located on the first floor above the garages and overlooking the pit lane. Attempting to question Frank Williams was not an option. The team owner had yet to arrive and, even if he was present, he would be unwilling to talk. Twenty years spent working in the front line of such a politically motivated and secretive business had allowed Williams to turn evasive answering into an art form. Ask Frank the time of day and he would hesitate before replying. With pressing deadlines, journalists wisely decided not to hang around the Williams motor home. The boss's eventual arrival was typically low-key.

Apart from essential equipment such as motor homes and transporters, vehicles are banned from the Grand Prix paddocks. Not even motor cycles or bicycles are allowed to enter. The one exception is the car carrying Frank Williams. The bending of the rules has nothing to do with Williams's status in Formula One; given his way, he would be delighted to walk in with everyone else. The plain fact is that Frank Williams no longer has any choice in such matters. In March 1986, he crashed and overturned his hire car while driving too fast on a minor road in the south of France. Williams has been a quadriplegic ever since but he does not express the least bit of self-pity. He will admit, however, that he was fortunate to survive.

Although he does not say so, there is the strong impression that Williams Grand Prix Engineering and the passionate and thrilling world of Formula One has given Frank the will to carry on living. With his emotions bouncing between exceptional extremes in the course of a single day, it is small wonder that Williams cares little about what people may think about his decisions. The fact that he is around to make them renders outside opinion irrelevant.

That, at least, is a reasonable excuse. The truth about Frank Williams is that chilling and sometimes quirky behaviour was part of his make-up long before he drove his last mile at the wheel of a car. His life has hardly been mainstream, almost since birth in South Shields on 16 April 1942.

Frank's father was flying Wellington bombers in the war and Britain was plunging into a state of austerity. Apart from coping with life's difficulties in the industrial heartland of Britain's north-east, Frank's mother had to care for him single-handed, almost from birth, when his father left home. They lived in Jarrow and Mrs Williams worked hard to ensure that her boy had a decent upbringing and education, a fact for which Frank, who would undergo difficult times himself thirty years later, would always remain grateful. Their relationship seems to have lacked an intense warmth. On the one hand that was surprising, since his mother worked with children; on the other, it was understandable since she gave her time to teaching sub-normal and backward kids, a vocation which perhaps made it difficult for her to relate to a perfectly healthy son. In any case, she saw very little of Frank.

He was cared for by his grandparents for much of the time and then spent three years at a convent school near Liverpool. After a further year at day school in Jarrow, Frank was sent to Scotland at the age of seven, his mother having scraped together enough money to find him a place at St Joseph's Roman Catholic boarding school in Dumfries. It would be a tough and demanding regime, one which would shape Frank's outlook on life. 'It was hard,' said Williams. 'The emphasis was on attainment and that rubbed off on me during ten very formative years at the school. There were 320 boys, split almost evenly between English and Scots since we were pretty close to the English border. At first I couldn't understand a word some of the Scots were saying but I quickly developed a pride in my nationality which I would never lose.'

Dormitory talk of sporting conflict was encouraged by a battle within the world of sports car racing. In the early and mid-fifties, the Le Mans 24-Hour race was just as prestigious as the Formula One World Championship, perhaps more so in the United Kingdom because British sports car teams were dominating the leaderboards. Jaguar was the key player and the motor manufacturer was represented by a works team, operating from Coventry, and a well organised private entrant known as Ecurie Ecosse, based in Edinburgh. With the works team winning Le Mans three times between 1951 and 1955, and the Scottish privateer taking stirring victories in 1956 and 1957, the battle lines expressed within the school quadrangle were clearly drawn. This division of loyalties gave Frank his introduction to the racing side of motoring, a world in which the youngster had become totally immersed.

By the age of ten, Frank could recite the specification of almost every road car listed in *The Autocar* and *The Motor*, weekly publications which, when he could lay his hands on them, he would devour from cover to cover. The fascination with motor cars was fed by the regular appearance at the school of the latest models driven by well heeled parents. Frank's mum would arrive by train. Knowing the hardships she was enduring, Frank felt no bitterness, but the experience made him aware of the prestige value attached to fine cars and heightened his longing to ride in them.

The father of one of his school mates was a bookmaker from Glasgow and the family's prosperity was marked by the purchase of a Jaguar XK150S, unquestionably *the* sports car of the day. When Frank was taken for a drive in this stunning machine, he admitted he was 'virtually speechless with excitement'. Now he was hooked irrevocably by the world of fast cars. They meant everything to him. He would hitch-hike rather than travel by train, not to save money but simply to experience the thrill of movement in a motor car.

School friend, Francis Holmes, came from a family of motor traders. Mrs Holmes took Frank under her wing during half-terms, bringing him back to her home in Newcastle-upon-Tyne, where Frank would immediately investigate the latest range of cars in the company's stock. Some of them were bought at auction in Glasgow and Frank discovered that, if he went along for the trip, he could ride back to Newcastle in the passenger seat of the most exciting purchase of the day. He loved every minute of it. During school holidays, he would hitch-hike overnight from Nottingham – where his mother had moved following her appointment as headmistress of a small school in a village ten miles from the city centre – tidy himself up in the washroom at the Newcastle Central railway station and present himself at the Holmes's residence, ready for the trip into Scotland. All for the pleasure of sitting for three hours on the return trip inside a decent motor car. Then he would hitch-hike back to Nottingham.

Williams also used his thumb to travel to various motor race meetings in England, and the more he saw, the more determined he became to take part. The problem, of course, was money, a shortcoming which would be his constant companion for the next decade and more. It cost nothing, however, to drive his mother's Morris Minor 1000 around the grounds of her school and, as soon as he was able, Frank passed his driving test at the first attempt. He left school at seventeen, with no idea about his future, hopeless at mathematics, but accomplished in Latin, French, German and Italian. The only certainty was that he did not wish to go to university. He had had his fill of the academic life. Motoring had to be the priority from now on.

In 1960, Williams entered a management trainee course with a motor car and commercial vehicle distributor in Nottingham, a decision which would introduce him to the less attractive side of the automotive business as he lay beneath trucks, up to his elbows in grease and transmissions. It was not really what he had in mind. Of more interest was his mother's offer of a cash contribution towards the purchase of his first car. Typically, he bought a racing car. Well, a racing car of sorts. It was actually an Austin A35, a dumpy little car with two doors and a noisy exhaust. It had been tuned for racing by Speedwell Conversions, a company owned by Graham Hill, a leading British racing driver who had yet to win a Grand Prix or the first of two world championships. On 17 September 1960, Hill had become a father; to a son, called Damon. Frank would never have believed in a million years that their paths would later cross in such a spectacular fashion.

For the moment, he was only interested in being the fastest driver in the business. This may have been a modest start to his career as a racer, but Frank was thrilled to bits with his car as he drove it home from London. Despite the racket from the semi-racing exhaust, the car was street-legal and Frank used it as his personal transport around Nottingham and as a means of driving to and from his first race, a minor club event at Oulton Park in Cheshire in April 1961. He finished the race – something which would become a rare achievement in the months to come – but, on his way back to Nottingham, the transmission broke, leaving Frank to revert to the use of his thumb. The car was towed back the following day.

Williams was earning £3 10s (£3.50) a week. Since he was living at home, every single penny was spent on the car and his racing. On Sunday, 2 July 1961, the cash flow of Francis Owen Garbett Williams was about to take a hefty knock. Frank entered the race for saloon cars (up to 1,500cc) at the Nottingham Sports Car Club's meeting at Mallory Park in Leicestershire. It was a filthy day but the treacherous conditions caught out surprisingly few competitors in the first three races. That soon changed when the saloon cars came to the grid. Reporting in the weekly magazine *Autosport*, Francis Penn wrote: 'As the cars lined up, the rain stopped; first away was P. Eva (Mini Minor), only to lose the lot at the Lake Ese. He continued, trailing a damaged exhaust pipe . . . Spins in this event were plentiful, the worst being F. O. Williams . . .'

Frank had crashed into the bank at Gerards, a bend which had also accounted for Jonathan Williams, another keen young amateur intent on making his way as a racing driver. Frank joined his namesake on top of the bank and struck up a conversation as they waited until the end of the race. Despite the mishap, this would be Frank's first very small step down a long road to international fame and fortune. When they returned to the paddock, Jonathan introduced Frank to a tall, handsome Old Etonian who was accompanying Williams that day. This was Piers Courage, heir to the brewery of the same name. He and Frank would become inseparable friends in the years to come, their relationship beginning and ending at a race track.

The following week's issue of *Autosport* carried an advertisement for a Speedwell Austin A35. The proud owner, who lived in London's Kensington, said the bodywork was unmarked and the asking price was £400. In the light of the damage sustained at Mallory Park, Frank's model was worth considerably less. But he hadn't quite finished with it yet. After straightening out the bodywork, Williams fitted a Weber carburettor, a state-of-the-art performance improvement which would have set him back £20. It was a last-minute job and Frank had only four hours to make the journey from the tuning shop in Wiltshire to Oulton Park, where he was entered for a race later that day. The car had never felt better but, in the middle of Salisbury, Frank's enthusiasm got the better of him. Failing to take his semi-bald racing tyres into account, he accelerated too hard on a wet road and the A35 spun backwards into a lamppost. The car was a write-off.

With help from a friend, he dismantled the wreck during the winter, saving parts from the engine and installing them in the shell of a larger Austin, the A40, in preparation for a season of racing in 1962. One of his main rivals would be Jonathan Williams in a similar car. They engaged in furious battles in club meetings throughout the country, Williams J. having the better car and usually making the most of it.

Generally I had the upper hand, because I tried to avoid spinning off! Frank was very clean to race with; very fair. But he was a daredevil and, unfortunately, he had no self-control. I don't think any of us had any race craft whatsoever in those days – you just went fast! The trouble was, Frank didn't know when to stop.

At the Crystal Palace circuit in south London, Williams F. O. made the pages of *Autosport* once more. Reporting on the British Racing and Sports Car Club's August bank holiday meeting, Michael Kettlewell wrote: 'Mike Young (Ford Anglia) had been dicing heavily with Frank Williams's Austin A40 until the eighth lap when the BMC car spun and bashed in its front. Both drivers established a new class lap record.' In fact, that record would stand for at least two years but, in the meantime, all Williams had to show for his trouble was another damaged car.

He had built on his friendship with Jonathan Williams and Piers Courage and would frequently travel from Nottingham to London to spend time in the flat they shared in Lower

Sloane Street with Sheridan Thynne, scion of the Marquess of Bath's family. Thynne would later – much later – become commercial director of Williams Grand Prix Engineering but, at the time, he and his flat mates enjoyed Frank's company and were amused by his antics, as Williams J. recalled:

When we first met at Mallory Park, I remember watching him driving and thinking he was a right lunatic. But when he joined me on top of the bank, I could tell straight away that he was just like the rest of us. A perfect fit. We were all mad on motor racing. We would rather not have eaten if it meant going somewhere and racing something. We couldn't wait until the next Sunday before we could go and do it again. We always felt there should be races on a Wednesday as well. We hadn't got much money – and Frank had even less than that!

It would not be uncommon for Frank to race at Brands Hatch in Kent, park his A40 outside the flat and then hitch-hike back to Nottingham (he couldn't afford the petrol) in time to start work on Monday morning.

By that time, Frank had been fired by the motor dealer for not attending a day-release course. It was not that he disliked the technical training. He was fascinated by the nuts and bolts of the trade but he objected to being forced to undergo a course in rudimentary English when he already held an A-level certificate in the subject. His employers did not share the opinion that it was a waste of time and therefore worth avoiding. Frank found a job as a filling station attendant before moving up-market and becoming a trainee sales representative for Campbell's Soup. This brought £10 per week, a Ford Anglia company car and a bowler hat which he had to wear while visiting storekeepers in Yorkshire. He was reasonably successful but his mind was continually on other things.

The lifestyle of his more wealthy friends in Lower Sloane Street was infinitely more appealing. In 1963, he decided to abandon the pretence that he wanted to do anything other than be a member of the motor racing world. He forsook the delights of Scotch broth and cream of tomato, left home for good and moved to London to become Jonathan Williams's 'mechanic' – in the loosest sense of the expression:

I went to see Frank in the team's motor home at the Monaco Grand Prix a few years ago. He never forgets the old days, which is super. He called out to Damon [Hill] – who was busy doing something at the far end of the motor home – and asked him to come down. He said, 'Damon, this is Jonathan. I used to be his mechanic!' It was a very nice thing for him to say. But it was quite untrue. He didn't know a piston from a piece of tin. He was hopeless. He would pick up a spanner and, if you were lucky, he would go to the correct end of the car.

Frank had become a good friend and he would come down to my home in Colchester at weekends. He became very fond of my parents. He would always ask my mother to come and say good night to him after he had gone to bed. She used to make fruit cakes for him and give him a slice when he was off to London; Frank would make a point of saying he would stop in a lay-by and eat it. I got the impression the relationship with his mother was not particularly close. I remember once Piers and I called in to see Frank in Nottingham. His mother took one look at us and disappeared. There didn't seem much warmth there and, in a way, I think my mum became a sort of surrogate mother to Frank.

Jonathan – financed by his father, a Squadron Leader in the RAF during the war and then a headmaster of a private co-educational school in Essex – had taken the major step from saloon car racer to international driver in Formula Junior, a single-seater formula which was recognised as being the proving ground for future Grand Prix talent. If Frank barely knew one end of the car from the other, he was at least good company for Jonathan as they joined this gypsy-style life, racing every weekend from the beginning of May to the end of September and earning enough start or prize money to see them through each week. Jonathan bought a Merlyn and a Volkswagen pick-up as a means of transporting the racing car to race tracks scattered across Europe. One weekend, it might be Sicily; the next, Sweden. They more or less lived in the Volkswagen, sleeping on the rear platform, under the canvas cover and either side of their precious car. Once a week they would allow themselves the luxury of sharing a hotel room in order to enjoy a proper meal, bed, breakfast and shower.

We slept on two lilos between the wheels,' said Jonathan Williams. 'It was pretty brutal, not very comfortable. But we were as happy as could be. Delighted! We didn't feel deprived in the least. It was a great life and, at the end of the week, there was a race! It was hugely convivial and Frank loved every minute of it. Mind you, I put him to the test during the weeks following a race in Monte Carlo.

Jonathan received a knock on the head when he crashed during practice for the supporting race to the Monaco Grand Prix. He later replaced the badly damaged Merlyn with a Lotus but, while that sorted out the mechanical set-back caused by the accident, the driver suffered delayed concussion. Frank became a minder more than a mechanic.

It tells you how stupid we were in those days. When two other Merlyn drivers entered for the race at Monaco suffered identical suspension failures, it never occurred to me that the same thing might happen to my car, which was exactly the same as the other two. I simply thought of it as having those drivers out of the way, two I wouldn't need to worry about in the race! The next thing, I woke up in the Princess Grace hospital.

Nobody seemed to know much about concussion then. I could remember everything about my life, up to and including the crash. But I couldn't remember what had happened a couple of hours ago. It was so frustrating to find that, in the evening, you hadn't a clue what you had been doing in the morning. Little by little it caught up – but nobody told me not to go motor racing. And Frank found he had to stop me from wandering off and getting lost. Why he didn't go insane, I don't know.

The big thing in our lives would be the starting money – usually about £100, £150 if you were lucky – from the next race.

'Where are we going next, Frank?' I would ask.

'Rheims' he would say.

An hour later: 'Where are we going, Frank?'

'Rheims, Jonathan!'

Jonathan's money eventually ran out and he returned home. Completely absorbed by the fun and camaraderie of a carefree existence with an element of risk and excitement thrown in, Frank found enough work to allow him to continue on the European trail, acting as mechanic and helper for various drivers, one of whom would figure prominently in his plans fifteen years later.

Earlier in the season he had visited a track in East Germany, where he met Charlie Crichton-Stuart, from the family of the Marquess of Bute. Frank had been impressed by Charlie. Despite a privileged background which permitted purchase of the latest racing equipment, Charlie was a 'good bloke'. Frank discovered that Crichton-Stuart shared a ground-floor flat in Pinner Road, Harrow, soon to become one of the most notorious addresses in the junior ranks of motor racing. In late 1963, Frank moved in.

His bed was the sofa. Occupying the regular sleeping accommodation was an assorted crowd from various rungs of the social ladder – but all devoted to motor racing. The flat was shared at different times by Charlie Crichton-Stuart; Jonathan Williams; Piers Courage; Charles Lucas, the son of a wealthy businessman and land owner; and Anthony Horsley, an entrepreneur who went under the name of 'Bubbles'. Frank Williams may have been as poor as a church mouse, particularly in the midst of such comparative wealth, but his bubbling enthusiasm made him instantly acceptable even though his rental payments for the sofa were invariably late.

Frank was living a hand to mouth existence. Nothing was too much trouble when it came to earning 'a couple of bob'. Aware of his willingness to accept any bet which was half-reasonable, Charlie wagered Frank ten shillings (fifty pence) that he would not run, stark naked, outside the house when, the story goes, the congregation was emerging from the local church. Frank accepted. He darted outside, but on his return found that the door had been locked. With the occupants of the flat watching from the windows, Frank called their bluff by returning to the middle of the road and thumping his chest in a demented fashion before answering the plaintive calls to get back inside. There was no argument that he had won his ten-bob note, a small fortune for someone who had difficulty scraping together half a crown (twelve and a half pence) for a plate of egg and chips and a cup of tea.

In 1964, Formula Junior became known as Formula Three. The name may have changed and the mechanical specification may have altered slightly but the attractive nomadic quality of racing in Europe remained. The beauty of the series for hard-up but enthusiastic racers was the proliferation of events. It was not necessary to compete against the better organised and more financially sound teams in the important meetings. The promoters of races at remote circuits in countries such as Czechoslovakia or Denmark would pay starting money to whoever made the effort to turn up. Today, Formula Three is more rigidly organised, a handful of countries running their own championships with contestants rarely straying beyond their national boundaries. The annual budget for a Formula Three entrant in the nineties would quite easily have taken two Formula One teams through a full season of Grand Prix racing in 1964. For Frank Williams and his mates, with barely enough in their pockets to buy petrol for the journey, the priority was living for the moment and taking each race as it came.

Frank teamed up with Bubbles Horsley. Cashing in a small legacy, Bubbles had acquired two Formula Three cars, one of which, a Brabham, had been rebuilt after an accident. The arrangement allowed Frank to race this car in return for his services as mechanic and general dogsbody. Horsley raced a brand-new Ausper but Frank was delighted with the deal, even more so when he discovered that they would have an elderly Morris van in which to live and sleep, a significant improvement on the back platform of a Volkswagen pick-up.

The diesel van, formerly the property of the Hoover company, provided reasonable service as a tow vehicle for the trailer with its two racing cars but, halfway through the season, the diesel oil infiltrated the living quarters and gave the occupants a mild form of dermatitis. In fact there seemed to be more oil outside the engine than within and it was decided that the vehicle would not make the trip to Sicily for one of the best-paying races of the season. Bubbles acquired a 1955 Plymouth from Piers Courage. The racing car spares – such as they were – were thrown into the boot and the trailer hitched onto the rear. They never made it to Sicily, but the journey encapsulated the precarious nature of their existence.

The two would-be Grand Prix drivers found they could just about cope with hopelessly inadequate brakes as the wallowing American machine struggled to restrain its load on the mountain passes. But there was no answer when Frank left a wallet containing what little money they had on the roof of the car at a service station, failing to retrieve it before the pair drove off. Since they were more than halfway down Italy, it was decided to press on in the hope of borrowing money from other racers as they waited to board the ferry to Messina. The Plymouth, its brakes next to useless, trundled into the empty square at the port of Reggio di Calabria. The ferry had departed.

Frank and Bubbles had no alternative but to park in the square and live on a diet of bread and water for three days while waiting to borrow £100 as competitors returned to the mainland. On the three-day non-stop journey home, the exhaust fell off, the battery failed and the power steering packed up. Tired, penniless and close to asphyxiation, they crawled off the ferry at Dover, the Plymouth having been started with the help of jump-leads. When a customs officer waved the combination and its seedy inhabitants to one side and ordered them to switch off the fuming, unsilenced engine, it was the final straw.

Horsley, still furious with Williams over the missing wallet, was seriously demoralised. Frank was just plain tired. Once they had finally cleared customs, the rig was left in the car park and Frank hitched a lift to London. After forcing entry to a friend's flat, he slept like the dead and awoke ready for whatever the day had to offer. The only certainty was that he wanted, more than ever, to be a racing driver.

His progress in the Brabham had been erratic, a number of promising performances spoiled by incidents as he flew off the road. Horsley did not fare much better, handicapped as he was by his considerable bulk which the Ausper could just about accommodate. 'Poor Bubbles,' reflected Jonathan Williams. 'He came back to the flat from doing something one day and there was Charlie and Frank, sitting side by side in this single-seater! Bubbles was cut to the quick. Very unfair.'

Horsley and Williams competed in a few more events that year but the partnership came to an unfortunate end at the Nurburgring south circuit in Germany. Frank, who revelled in the challenge of this twisting and difficult track in the Eifel mountains, made a bad start. In his over-enthusiastic climb through the field, he lost control and lodged the Brabham halfway up a grass bank. When Bubbles rounded the corner not long after and saw half of his worldly goods in a mangled state, with the driver grinning inanely from the top of the bank, he became so furious that he lost concentration and crashed at the next corner. Unlike his partner, Horsley was winded by the experience and, into the bargain, lost his spectacles during the impact. In a confused state, he was loaded into an ambulance but quickly regained enough composure to realise that this could cost money. When the ambulance stopped at a gate, Horsley opened the rear doors and made his escape, a move which caused huge consternation at the local hospital, when the ambulance arrived without its passenger. The police, instructed to find an overweight racing driver without his glasses, gave Horsley a severe dressing down when they eventually located him bumbling around the paddock in search of his team-mate.

Frank did not have two pennies to rub together. The situation reached such a state in the autumn of 1964 that, on occasion, he could not even afford to rent the sofa in Pinner Road and resorted to sleeping in the Morris van, for which Horsley had been unable to find a buyer. For some time now, Frank had made use of his exceptional ability with languages. The majority of the Formula Three drivers from abroad raced cars and engines which were manufactured in Britain, but they found great difficulty in arranging the supply and delivery of spare parts. The language barrier caused problems at the switchboard of, say, Lotus in Norwich and, since this was in the days before credit cards, the business of raising bank transfers proved time-consuming and complicated. The racers were desperate. Williams saw the opening and became a straightforward conduit between the two parties. Tell Frank what you needed and the job was done. He would turn up sooner rather than later with the necessary part – having added a small financial margin for his trouble, of course.

Williams gradually moved up the scale and began to buy and sell racing cars. He made enough money not only to allow a return to Pinner Road but also to afford the luxury of a decent bed and a telephone line on which to do his trading. Frank was not particularly sharp in his business practices; the secret of his success was enthusiasm. Nothing was too much trouble. If a customer wanted a set of wheels for a Brabham, Frank would find and deliver them, perhaps taking a gearbox in exchange and moving that on elsewhere in return for a steering rack and cash. And if that required a journey from Southampton to Aberdeen to Harwich, then so be it. The reward for his efforts was the purchase of a second-hand Cooper for the 1965 Formula Three season.

It was not a good car. It had been bought from a reputable team and the deal had been satisfactory, but that was the extent of Frank's knowledge on the subject. His inexperience was such that he could not cope with the car's unusual handling characteristics, in addition to which the car was not fitted with the most competitive engine. These engines were hard to find and, in any case, a price tag of £600 meant they were beyond Frank's means.

As the season went by, Williams got the hang of the car

sufficiently to register his first international result of consequence when he finished fourth at Skarpnack in Sweden on
5 September 1965. Shortly afterwards, he sold the Cooper to
a Swedish driver and considered himself lucky to have made
a profit.

The aim was to buy a better car for 1966. To that end,
Williams hurled himself into the business of selling new
Formula Three Brabhams and Lolas which he had bought
direct from the manufacturers with borrowed money. Along
the way he secured a new Brabham for himself and set off for
Europe. Again, his fervour got the better of him and he
crashed frequently. One particular accident in Portugal,
when he lost control on a level crossing and destroyed the
front of the car against a gate post, brought the realisation
that perhaps he did not have the necessary qualities as a top
driver. Then, on 28 August, at the wheel of another new car
(the repaired Brabham having been sold), he won a minor
international race at Knutstorp in Sweden, thus rekindling
the hope and self-belief all over again.

He continued to find it difficult to make ends meet. This
time, he vowed, he would spend the winter building up his
business in order to buy top-rate equipment to permit a
proper job of racing in 1967. His stock was stashed in
various garages and lock-ups around Harrow. He placed full-
page advertisements in *Autosport*, offering racing cars for sale.
Business took off, so much so that he put his plans to
continue racing on hold for a year. In fact, although he
didn't know it, his career as a driver was over. A different
but equally demanding trade lay in store. Frank Williams
was about to become an entrant and team owner.

CHAPTER TWO

The fun of it all

Frank Williams (Racing Cars) Ltd became a presentable business in the winter of 1967/8 when the proprietor found a small workshop, with a flat overhead, situated between a bingo hall and a pub at 361 Bath Road, Cippenham, near Slough. Frank did not drink and he would never take a financial gamble on anything over which he had absolutely no control. But the location was symbolic. The pub was part of the chain owned by Courage and that name was about to become a central part of his life for the next two and a half years.

The friendship with Piers Courage had grown since their first meeting at Mallory Park in 1961. Courage's career as a racing driver had developed rapidly and Williams had become aware of his natural talent at the end of a Formula Three race at Caserta in Italy in which they had both taken part. For once, Frank had brought his car home in one piece, and it was during the slowing down lap that he was suddenly overtaken by Courage. 'He came past on a wildly bumpy section of track and I realised just what a natural talent he was,' said Frank in an interview in 1969. 'That was confirmed a year later when I saw him in the wet at Silverstone. He drove fantastically well. A good driver is always best in the wet and he had the most wonderful reactions. I could see he was very special.'

Not everyone agreed with that assessment. Courage had won a number of races while working his way into the leading role with the works Lotus Formula Three team in 1966. The following year, he was offered a drive in the semi-works BRM Formula One team but progress was punctuated by spins and accidents. The general conclusion was that the rich young kid was in over his head.

In fact, Piers was not quite as wealthy as his detractors imagined. Relationships with his family had been strained when he failed to pursue accountancy studies which had been seen as the necessary precursor to a move into the brewing business. The lure of motor racing proved too much, and in 1964 he was persuaded by Jonathan Williams to leave college and go racing in Europe. His only income came from a modest trust fund which he had inherited after turning twenty-one the previous year, and much of that was spent on having a wonderful time with the motor racing mavericks from Pinner Road. During the course of his adventures, he met Charles Lucas. At the beginning of 1965, 'Luke' inherited a sum of money which he was persuaded to spend on a fleet of Formula Three cars for himself and his friends Courage and Jonathan Williams. Courage's success in the Lucas Brabham led to the role with Lotus the following season, by which time he had become engaged to Lady Sarah Curzon.

'Sally' Curzon was no stranger to motor racing. Her father, Earl Howe, was a pioneer of the post-war motor sport scene and president of the British Racing Drivers' Club. With her new-found experience of both ends of the motor racing social scene, Sally loved the enthusiasm and vitality of the motley crew operating from Pinner Road. 'They were,' as she was to recount many years later, 'magical days.' She had no hesitation in becoming Mrs Piers Courage and, a year later, her husband became a Grand Prix driver for BRM. But not for long, judging by his erratic progress and the race reports which, although genteel by today's withering standards, damned Courage with faint praise.

Frank Williams remained convinced: Piers could do no wrong, either in or out of the cockpit. Frank saw a means of reviving Courage's career by offering him a drive in a Formula Three car in an important race at Brands Hatch at the end of 1967. In some respects it would have been a backward step for Piers but, since Williams was now an agent for Brabham cars, this brand-new machine was, in fact, a prototype for 1968. On a circuit made even more difficult than usual by rain, Courage waltzed away from the rest of the field. It was a dazzling performance which went some way towards redeeming his reputation, not to mention sending new clients to Bath Road, Cippenham. It also gave Frank food for thought about becoming an entrant.

That germ of an idea suddenly took serious shape when Williams found himself with an unsold Brabham Formula Two car on his hands due to a last-minute cancellation at the beginning of 1968. Almost before Frank knew it, Courage had persuaded him to enter the European Formula Two Championship which, at the time, was the next best thing to Formula One. It cost Frank about £10,000 to set up his team. He was not entirely sure where the money would come from, but he pressed on regardless. The original purchaser had ordered the Brabham in dark blue and that automatically became the team's official colour.

While all of this was going on, Courage was racing in Australia and New Zealand in a championship known as the Tasman Series. As far as the Europeans were concerned, the Tasman Series was the perfect excuse to get away from the miseries of winter. The racing was serious enough but the time in between was spent water skiing and hosting barbecues on the beach. Most of the leading Grand Prix drivers attended, more for the fun and camaraderie than anything else. For Courage, however, the trip had serious intent since he needed to continue rebuilding his reputation. Driving a Formula Two McLaren he had bought for the series, he scored a very impressive win at Longford in Tasmania. All told, he had done enough to earn another run with the semi-works BRM in Grand Prix racing, a commitment which would take priority over his Formula Two effort.

One such date clash occurred in June when Courage had to race in the Dutch Grand Prix. Frank Williams asked his namesake, Jonathan, to drive the Formula Two car at Monza:

The team consisted of the car, Frank and a Kiwi mechanic called Johnny Muller. Both Frank and Johnny were meticulous. I have never sat in a car like it, before or since. I had been racing for Ferrari the year before and they were junk compared to this. I don't think Muller went to bed; he just guarded and worked on the car twenty-four hours a day! It was beautiful. Anything you wanted done, was done. To drive a car like that was a pleasure. It was an indication of Frank's commitment. He figured out earlier than most that if you polished the wheel rims, it wouldn't make the car go any faster but it would *look* fast. Frank has never fielded a tatty car.

Williams, an expert in the art of slipstreaming on this very fast track, gave Frank his first victory as a team owner:

He was delighted. But he was very mean. He gave me half the prize money and bought me dinner that night. That was it! I had to get myself there and pay all my expenses. But it was great fun. Even though Frank was now a team owner, he was no different to the Frank I had known for six years. He wasn't intense and he wasn't critical, particularly after I had a bad practice. But I knew I could win. It was a track I could drive with my eyes shut and it was a hell of a good car.

Courage did not win a race for Frank in the Formula Two car but his performances were quick and consistent. In the autumn, the organisers of the forthcoming Tasman Series, keen to have Courage on the 1969 entry list following his popular win in Tasmania, offered Frank £6,000 to make the trip. Williams accepted.

The Tasman championship was run for the equivalent of Formula One cars, but with slightly less powerful engines. Williams bought a chassis which Brabham had used during the 1968 F1 championship and then ordered two Ford-Cosworth V8s to go with it. The Ford-Cosworth V8 was the engine to have in Grand Prix racing. The beauty about this unit was that it could be reduced from three-litre, which was the limit in F1 at the time, to two-and-a-half-litre capacity, as required by the Tasman regulations, and then be converted back again, if necessary.

If necessary Frank was sitting in his office in Cippenham, thinking about this latest turn of events. In effect, he had the nucleus of a Grand Prix team taking shape in the workshop downstairs. He had a Formula One chassis, a couple of F1 engines, a very promising driver and most of the paraphernalia necessary to go racing. Thinking aloud, he said to his secretary: 'Why don't we go Formula One racing next year?' It was a rhetorical question. He had more or less made up his mind on the spur of the moment.

Courage was easily persuaded to go Grand Prix racing with Frank. As ever, the problem would be paying for it. Frank talked to Dunlop, with whom he already had a working relationship, and arranged a tyre deal which would also bring in £10,000. A further £2,000 came from Castrol, these arrangements being made with trade suppliers since sponsorship, as we know it today, was in its infancy. Frank, always alert to new ideas, was about to discover the potential of commercial support from outside motor racing.

As often happens, some of the best deals arrive out of the blue. One of Frank's mechanics, Bob Evans, had been to a party and met a man who was involved with machine tool manufacturers. And *he* knew a man who was interested in Formula One. It was an unlikely story, but Frank followed it up. Through the contact, he met Ted Williams, a motor racing enthusiast who owned a company called T.W. Ward. There was an element of personal indulgence in providing support for a Grand Prix team but the company was keen to promote its name through the sport. Ward wanted a return which would go beyond simply handing over money and having a small sticker placed in front of the windscreen on Courage's car. The involvement would give the company's sales force a unique talking point when dealing with customers. It was a bold approach which brought the machine tool business in touch with a glamorous sport. The company brought guests to the races. Everyone was delighted with the arrangement. Ted Williams would remain a staunch supporter of the team until his death in 1979. Frank, in turn, would quickly become aware of sponsorship's enormous potential. But, first, there was much to be organised as 1968 raced towards its close.

Frank Williams (Racing Cars) Ltd placed regular advertisements in the sales columns of *Autosport*. Under the company's insignia – a winged arrow – Williams would list a variety of hardware ranging from second-hand racing cars (around £2,000) to engines (£425 for a Formula Three example), transporters (£995 for a 1966 Bedford van), trailers, wheels and the occasional highly tuned (and, as likely as not, thoroughly thrashed) road car. Elsewhere in the magazine, road tests would praise the latest Ford Capri (from £890) and Mercedes-Benz 220 (£2,440). For enthusiasts wishing to follow the Grand Prix scene, Page & Moy offered a five-night trip by British Caledonian Boeing 707 to the

Monaco Grand Prix for forty-five guineas (about £47). Part of the attraction would be watching the dashing Piers Courage at the wheel of a Williams Brabham, a classic British tale of the underdog taking on the works teams. First, though, the underdog had to find a suitable car.

The previous year's Brabham BT24 which Frank was sending to the Tasman Series was all very well but, ideally, Frank needed to lay his hands on a 1969 model, the BT26, for Formula One. Since the Brabham team was entering its own cars for Jack Brabham and Jacky Ickx, it was unlikely that Brabham would want to give himself even more competition by providing Frank with an identical car. Apart from anything else, such a move would not go down well with Goodyear, Brabham's contracted tyre supplier, particularly if a Williams Brabham took Dunlop to the victory circle. On balance, Frank thought, it was best to keep his F1 plans to himself for the time being.

Keeping his well tuned ear to the ground, Williams discovered that Brabham had sold a BT26 to an enthusiast and part-time racer from the north of England, presumably in the belief that this man, Charles Bridges, would not be going Grand Prix racing. Frank managed to persuade Bridges to part with the car for £3,500. Jack Brabham, by all accounts, was less than impressed when he found out. And with due cause, since the Courage/Williams BT26 alliance was about to cause the works team a fair amount of irritation on the track.

The first hint had come during the opening section of the Tasman Series when Courage proved to be a thorn in the sides of the Lotus and Ferrari teams in New Zealand. He had won at Teretonga Park in Invercargill, Frank then returning to England to continue his F1 negotiations while the Tasman circus moved on to Australia. The subsequent race reports arriving at Bath Road did not make encouraging reading as

Frank's boy, more often than not, appeared to be spending his time flying off the road. It was the last thing Williams needed to hear as he tried to persuade trade sponsors that Piers Courage was a champion in the making. Everyone, not least Frank, kept the faith. The team was ready to go Grand Prix racing. Well, almost.

The first Grand Prix was held in South Africa, not long after the final round of the Tasman Series. It was asking too much of Williams to make that trip. Today, teams must commit themselves to the full season; in 1969, you did what you could, a more haphazard arrangement which helped the teams pick and choose according to their progress in the championship, but one which did little for the organisers as they attempted to promote their races without being fully confident that every team would turn up.

Williams postponed his team's debut until the Race of Champions. This event was yet another aspect of a more relaxed era. The Race of Champions at Brands Hatch, and the International Trophy which followed it a few weeks later at Silverstone, was a non-championship race. Such meetings do not exist today because of the necessary commitment to the world championship. Events which do not count for championship points are considered a waste of time; the teams would rather go testing and learn more about their cars without the hassle which comes from attending a minor race meeting. In 1969, however, these races were the equivalent of testing. And good fun, too.

Pre-race publicity for the Brands Hatch race made much of the fact that Jackie Stewart, the winner of the South African Grand Prix, had been entered by Ken Tyrrell in a Matra-Ford. Lotus, McLaren, BRM and Brabham were also represented, the most conspicuous absentee being Ferrari. Admission on race day was £1, with a seat in a covered grandstand costing an additional thirty shillings (£1.50). For the dyed in the wool enthusiasts, braving the brisk March weather, a further thirty shillings for a paddock transfer was worth the price just to admire the immaculate dark blue Brabham as it was rolled out of Frank's truck. And that would be just about as much as the fans would get to see of the car, a succession of teething problems relegating Courage to the back of the grid and then forcing pit stops in the race as the mechanics attended to the gear linkage and, finally, a fuel leak which would bring early retirement.

While the Race of Champions had proved very little, the International Trophy on 30 March would serve warning of the potential of the Williams/Courage combination. Piers gave the works Brabhams a hard time and finished an excellent fifth despite losing fourth gear and struggling with scorched feet thanks to inadequate protection from the radiator mounted at the front of the car. As Frank prepared his team for their first Grand Prix in Spain, bookmakers were quoting Courage as a 25–1 outsider for the championship. Stewart was the favourite and nothing during the remaining nine Grands Prix would change that as the Scotsman claimed his first world title. But by the end of the season Courage's odds as future champion had shortened considerably. He may have managed to complete just four of the races but on two memorable occasions he had finished second, once at Monaco and then at Watkins Glen in the United States Grand Prix.

Frank could not believe his luck. Monaco had been the team's second Grand Prix and here was Courage stepping up to the royal box to shake hands with Prince Rainier. Piers had driven faultlessly on a circuit which punishes the slightest mistake; more than that, the car had run without a hitch and soaked up the punishment dished out by the bumps, gutters and adverse cambers of the principality's streets. Watkins Glen, the final and richest race of the season, had been even more satisfying, a powerful performance allowing Courage to beat Jack Brabham into third place. The former world champion was not best pleased at being defeated by one of his own cars although, once the race was over, there were no hard feelings. The question of whether or not Williams should be allowed to get his hands on the next Brabham F1 car for 1970 did not arise; Frank had already laid his plans for the forthcoming season.

Williams and Courage had continued to run a car in Formula Two, a commitment which meant they were racing almost every weekend throughout the summer of 1969. Piers won at Enna in Sicily but, more significant to his long-term future, he had competed in that race against a de Tomaso, a neat little car built by an innovative company in Italy. Alessandro de Tomaso, a dynamic Argentinian, was intent on manufacturing exotic road cars which would challenge the likes of Ferrari, and his ambitious plans included a presence in Formula One. When he met Frank Williams at the Italian Grand Prix in September, de Tomaso proposed a collaboration between the two which, with the power of hindsight, was very much in de Tomaso's favour. But, at the time, Frank was tempted by the offer of a chassis which was likely to be innovative and, more importantly, would cost nothing in return for Williams supplying the engines, the driver and the organisation. Frank was also influenced by the potential of de Tomaso's facilities near Modena. The Argentinian, in turn, was impressed when Courage, driving the de Tomaso Formula Two car, claimed pole position and ran strongly in a race at Vallelunga in Italy. The deal was done: Williams would enter a de Tomaso powered by the Ford V8 in the 1970 World Championship and Piers Courage, who had declined an offer from Ferrari, would drive it.

The Ferrari package – worth £30,000, a considerable sum at the time – included sports car racing as well as Formula One. Williams would pay Piers £3,000 but much of the shortfall would be made up by a sports car contract with Alfa Romeo which would bring Courage £23,000. Above all else, however, Piers wanted to stay with Frank. They had made such an exciting and productive start to their Formula One association and the two friends were keen to continue it and show the world just what they could do against the might of big teams.

There was little to keep them amused when the de Tomaso Formula One car proved to be overweight and would not handle. A revision to the suspension was helpful, and throughout this period of learning Courage was maturing both in his ability as a driver and in his understanding of the technical side of a racing car. He had earned the complete confidence of his rivals, Jackie Stewart commenting that Piers had abandoned his unpredictable habits of the past. He was, according to the reigning world champion, disciplined, safe and, above all, very fast. Not that Courage was getting much chance to prove it as the de Tomaso ran into a succession of mechanical problems. By the fifth round of the championship in Holland, he had failed to score any points.

The Dutch Grand Prix was a popular event. The Zand-voort circuit, just outside the seaside town of Haarlem, was fast and challenging, the surrounding sand dunes providing perfect viewing places for spectators, many of whom had made the short hop across from Britain. For those not particularly interested in the racing, Amsterdam, a thirty-minute train ride away, provided plenty of distractions.

Williams and Courage were focused on improving the de Tomaso and, at the very least, finishing a Grand Prix for once. The signs were good during practice when Piers claimed ninth place on the grid and then broke free from a mid-field scrap during the race to move into seventh place on lap twelve. A championship point or two seemed a possibility if the car kept going for the remaining sixty-eight laps. This was the first time the de Tomaso had run reasonably well in the front half of the Grand Prix field. Until then, progress had been interrupted by a crash, a failure to qualify and mechanical trouble. Motor racing looked like being fun again. On lap twenty-three, a column of dense black smoke signalled the end of a dream.

Rushing through the fast sweeps on the back section of the circuit, the de Tomaso had run wide at 140 mph, crashed into a bank, hit a fence post and overturned. Protection for the fuel tank was nothing like as sophisticated as it is today. With more than twenty gallons on board, the de Tomaso was quickly ablaze with the driver trapped inside. The fire-fighting equipment was impotent as the magnesium alloy, highly inflammable and widely used in the construction of the chassis, increased the intensity of the inferno. The only blessing was that Courage was likely to have been killed instantly when the impact with the post ripped off the front suspension and catapulted the wheel into the cockpit, removing his crash helmet in the process.

The sickening effect of Courage's death was multiplied by the fact that he was so popular and that this had been the second fatality in nineteen days, Bruce McLaren having lost his life while testing at Goodwood on 2 June. In 1968, four top drivers had been killed. The risk factor was painfully evident and it was clear that the flip side of the sport could be easily induced. Yet the loss of Piers Courage numbed the paddock at Zandvoort. It was too much to take on board. Patrick McNally, Grand Prix correspondent for *Autosport*, later to become involved in the commercial side of Formula One as well as gaining prominence as a close friend of the Duchess of York, wrote:

Success never changed Piers. I dined recently with him and Jonathan Williams and the conversation between these two was exactly the same as it might have been four years before in a London bistro. His background made some people feel he was a cut above them, but he never showed the slightest snobbish tendency and was just as much at home eating in a pub with the boys as he was dining at the Savoy.

When we heard of plans to run Formula 1 [with Frank Williams], there were a good many cynics who reckoned that this had to be a failure. But this was far from the case, for his rapport with Frank made for miracles.

Jackie Stewart kept a diary during 1970. It makes desperately sad reading in the present era of safety standards which go far beyond anything envisaged three decades ago. As a leading driver, Jackie found himself thrust to the forefront in the bleak aftermath of a serious accident. Zandvoort was a case in point. Stewart's diary entry for the following day – Monday, 22 June – tells of the trauma suffered by everyone involved, particularly Frank Williams:

There had to be an accident report and the police wanted me to help them. Frank Williams, Louis Stanley [head of the BRM team and a leading light in Formula One at the time] and I drove out to the circuit to reconstruct the accident. The crash had set off a complete bank of grass and it was still smouldering in places. There was a horrible, tragic smell in the area and it was absolutely quiet. Only the wind coming off the sea, rustling the dune grass, and the three of us there on that empty road.

In Stewart's opinion, a bump in the road had upset the balance of the car and sent it on its perilous course.

The intensity of the fire was overwhelming, so much so that the crews didn't have enough foam to extinguish it and finally had to cover the entire car with a tarpaulin and then bury it in sand, just to cover it, with Piers still inside. It wasn't until well after the race that they finally got him out, and even then, when they took the tarpaulin off to get to him, air got in and the fire started again. Both the chassis and the engine were melted.

Later the police wanted to know what we planned to do with the wreck. I thought about a scrapyard but then realised people might take bits of it for souvenirs and that sort of thing, so I knew this was out of the question. Frank just said, 'Get rid of it . . . I don't ever want to see it again . . . get it away.'

Stewart arranged to have the wreckage taken to an incinerator. Two days later, he attended a memorial service for Bruce McLaren at St Paul's Cathedral in London, and the day after that the motor racing fraternity moved to a small country church in Essex to bury Piers. 'The organist wasn't very good and the choir was composed of ladies from the village, yet it couldn't be any other way,' wrote Stewart. 'For Piers, the son of English aristocracy, it had to be in a place where dignity would prevail without public grandeur.'

Frank was utterly devastated. 'Everybody you've ever heard of in motor racing turned out,' recalled Williams in an interview in 1990. Speaking to Alan Henry of the *Guardian*, Frank said: 'Nobody ducked the funeral. And there were plenty of red eyes from the hard guys, I can tell you. It was a very moving event. I was heartbroken. I worshipped the guy. He was totally adorable.'

For Frank and the happy band from Pinner Road, an era had ended. It was strictly business from here on.

CHAPTER THREE

On the point of collapse

Though utterly devastated by the loss of Piers, the thought of giving up motor racing never entered Frank's head. Why should it? He knew about nothing else. He might walk away, determined never to look at a racing car again, but the first rasp of a finely tuned engine would pull him back with such an irresistible force, his feet would barely touch the ground.

Frank Williams (Racing Cars) Ltd was absent from the entry list at the French Grand Prix which, coming two weeks after Zandvoort, was too much for the team to cope with. But, a fortnight after that Williams entered a car for Brian Redman at his home Grand Prix at Brands Hatch. The British driver never made the race thanks to a broken stub axle during practice. Two weeks later at Hockenheim, he failed to qualify. Redman, a competent and thoroughly professional driver, was fast enough but the events in Britain and Germany summed up a team effort which had lost its impetus.

Redman made way for Tim Schenken, Frank deciding to risk giving the young Australian driver his chance in Formula One after impressive performances in the junior categories. In fact, it was Schenken who was taking the gamble. The twenty-six-year-old appeared to be on a hiding to nothing when he qualified near the back of the grid and failed to finish any of the four races entered thanks to mechanical trouble of one sort or another. Yet his mature approach, and the chance to prove himself by being quick in the wet during practice for his first Grand Prix in Austria, brought Schenken a drive with the works Brabham team for the following season. Despite Schenken's lack of results, Frank had opened the F1 door – and with typical enthusiasm. Schenken commented:

Looking back, I recall Frank as being someone who was incredibly enthusiastic. He was totally dedicated to succeeding but he had a complete lack of technical knowledge; he had none whatsoever! As a result, he was totally reliant on his mechanics at the time – and there were only two of them. When I moved on to Brabham the following year, it was a complete contrast because the guy who designed the cars, Ron Tauranac, was extremely competent technically. Frank's skills were finding the money and putting the programme on the road. I don't think anything could have stopped Frank's determination to succeed. Not even the loss of Piers Courage. In fact, I suspect he might have been spurred on by that in a strange sort of way. Certainly, he never talked about giving up.

The season ended when the organisers of the final race in Mexico City chose to pay the travel expenses for just eighteen cars. Not surprisingly, the de Tomaso-Ford was not among them. Equally, it was easy to predict that Alessandro de Tomaso's enthusiasm for the project would go into rapid decline when faced with one of the sport's terrible realities at Zandvoort the previous June. The sole surviving red car was eventually returned to Italy where it sat, minus its engine, in a corner of the de Tomaso factory, a forlorn reminder of the difficulties associated with Grand Prix racing.

Frank was left with two engines, a transporter, a handful of equipment, considerable debt and, miraculously, unlimited enthusiasm. In fact, a surfeit of zeal would lead him deeper into the mire as the new season progressed. Ever the optimist, Williams would bite off far more than he could chew.

The first priority was to find an off-the-shelf chassis. Step forward March Engineering, a slick-tongued operation designed for the seventies and the advent of hopeful drivers with more money than talent and, in some cases, common sense. Previously, the wealth a driver possessed had largely been his own. With it, he would either enter a car or run a team. But the advent of sponsorship meant drivers could secure financial backing and be welcomed with open arms by team owners who, increasingly, could see motor racing as a means of making money, a notion which was a comparative novelty in a world where sport had always come before commerce.

The ground rules were changing and March Engineering had been quick to spot the opportunities which would arise. Founded in 1969 by four racing men (one of whom, Max Mosley, would become president of motor sport's governing body, the FIA, a couple of decades later), March built and sold racing cars for the prominent formulae, including Grand Prix racing. It was daring initiative, one which was tailor-made for the likes of Frank Williams as he contemplated entries for both Formula Two and Formula One. But who would do the driving? Was there another Piers Courage on the horizon?

Frank tended to view racing drivers through rose-tinted glasses. The quick guys were heroes as far as Frank was concerned. If they showed a dazzling mixture of speed and bravery then Frank tended to ignore the fact that they might fly off the road from time to time. Flashes of flair would disguise the absence of consistency and race craft necessary to complete the chemistry possessed by the few candidates destined to become world champions. Henri Pescarolo, as courageous as any, did not fall into the latter category. But he was Frank's man for 1971. 'He's been good in Formula Two, and extremely brave at night, in the rain, at Le Mans,' was how Frank explained it. No one doubted that. But Frank barely mentioned that Pescarolo had laid his hands on enough financial support from Motul Oil to fund a Formula Two team of two cars for 'Pesca' and the Englishman, Derek Bell. It was only a short step from there to persuade the French lubricant company to top up the kitty and include Formula One as well. Orders were placed with March Engineering for cars for both categories. Pescarolo won the opening race of the European F2 Championship at Mallory Park in England. It was downhill from that point on.

The irony was that the Mallory Park result had prompted Carlos Pace, a young and very promising Brazilian driver, to ask Frank if he would run a third F2 car with support from a Portuguese-Brazilian bank. It was too good to refuse. It was also the straw which broke the camel's back. Frank's small team, stretched beyond the limit, finally tumbled over the ragged edge in September when all three F2 cars failed to qualify for a race in France. By which time the Grand Prix effort had reached the point of collapse.

Pescarolo had won a heat of a non-championship F1 race with a meagre entry at Oulton Park in Cheshire but, elsewhere, Williams struggled with a car which was difficult to work into competitive shape, particularly by a team without technical leadership. Pescarolo claimed fourth place, one lap behind the winner, Jackie Stewart, at the British Grand Prix. He scraped home sixth in Austria. And that was it. The season was largely a succession of mechanical failures as Frank desperately stuck elastoplast on gaping wounds caused by a shortage of money, manpower and know-how.

The finance raised by sponsorship deals for 1971 was being used to pay outstanding bills from the previous year. Both the Formula One and the Formula Two projects were going nowhere. Disillusionment set in everywhere – except in Frank's office. He resolved to forget about Formula Two, concentrate solely on Grand Prix racing and take steps to ensure he built his own car rather than relying on something 'off the shelf'. It was the right way to go. He argued that things could not get any worse in 1972. But they did.

Williams got off on the right foot when Politoys offered £40,000 towards a project which would be named after the Italian model car company. This gave Frank the start he needed even though he did not have the facilities to build his own car. Arrangements were made to hire the services of Len Bailey, a design engineer, and Maurice Gomm, a respected sheet metal worker operating from Woking in Surrey. It was the first small step on the very long road towards Williams being recognised as a world leader in the manufacture of racing cars.

His first product would be called a Politoys-Cosworth, Frank resorting to the Ford-Cosworth engine used by the majority of F1 teams. In order to keep pace with such comparative grandeur, it would be necessary to vacate the cramped premises at Bath Road, Cippenham. On 2 February 1972, Frank Williams (Racing Cars) Ltd moved into a 5,000 square foot industrial unit in Bennet Road, Reading. It would amount to the only positive step that year.

When it took longer than expected to produce the Politoys, Frank reluctantly became a customer of March Engineering once more. Unable to afford the £15,000 necessary for a 1972 model (less the engine and gearbox),

Williams did a deal to have one of the latest cars built around a chassis left over from the previous year. The new car would be entrusted to Pescarolo thanks to a continuation of the Motul sponsorship link which was worth £40,000. Williams still owned the original March from 1971 and he used it to enter Carlos Pace for his debut season in F1 – on the understanding that the Brazilian would bring at least £10,000 for the privilege. Additional funds (between £10,000 and £15,000) came from the continuing support of Ted Williams and T. W. Ward.

Prize money? Williams should be so lucky. Appearance money? There was no rigid framework for payments by the various race organisers. Worthwhile amounts were generally limited to the top teams although that was about to change with the arrival of Bernard Ecclestone and the restructuring of the Formula One Constructors' Association. In the meantime, Frank's budget of just over £100,000 had to cover the design and manufacture of a car, the purchase of engines and gearboxes, general running costs and the expense incurred travelling to twelve Grands Prix. The same figure would not pay for a couple of gearboxes on a Williams-Renault in 1997.

Pescarolo made a moderate start to the season but Pace soon began to show his potential as he finished sixth in Spain and scored two more points in Belgium. The Politoys took six months to complete and made its debut at the British Grand Prix at Brands Hatch, where Pescarolo promptly crashed heavily during the opening laps. Having written off the brand-new car, the Frenchman really got into his stride and set about destroying the March in a series of accidents during the next three races.

As the repair bills mounted, it was clear that Pescarolo's tenure was destined not to go beyond 1972. But, having brought Pace into Formula One on a two-year agreement,

Williams was keen to make the most of his gamble and build on the relationship. The Brazilian had other ideas about the gentlemen's agreement and took himself off to the Surtees team for 1973. It was another lesson learned. Twenty years later, Williams would prove to be much more forceful when framing contracts and exercising his options. In the meantime, he was left with wrecked cars, no drivers and even more debts.

There was no question about continuing with his own car. The Formula One Constructors' Association (FOCA) was beginning to make its presence felt, Ecclestone negotiating with race organisers on behalf of the teams. In return for an agreed fee from the promoters, Ecclestone would guarantee to provide a set number of cars. And, for races outside Europe, these teams would enjoy subsidised travel and freight facilities provided by FOCA. However, to qualify for membership of the association, the team concerned would be required to manufacture its own cars. For Williams, there-fore, purchasing the likes of a March would be out of the question. He had to resurrect the Politoys.

In fact, Pescarolo's badly damaged car was repairable. Just about. A few more were built for 1973 and the name was changed from Politoys to Iso-Marlboro in deference to promised financial support from Iso-Rivolta, the manufac-turer of Italian sports cars, and Marlboro cigarettes. Politoys scaled down their financial involvement to around £10,000 in return for a sticker on the car alongside the Ward logo from the ever loyal Ted Williams. Additional money was pledged by Nanni Galli as the Italian driver sought finally to establish his name in Formula One after unsuccessful attempts to do so with various teams during the previous two years. If all the support came to fruition, Williams would have more than £100,000. It was about half of what he really needed to put his team on a par with leading lights such as McLaren and Lotus. In the event, he would have to make do with even less than the promised figure. Frank should not have been surprised but, once again, his boundless optimism was carrying him through.

The concept of an association with an exotic sports car manufacturer had its merits for a small company such as Williams, but Iso-Rivolta was about to drift into the slow lane before heading towards bankruptcy in 1974. The payments, when they came, were never to the agreed amount. Worse still, Galli's money failed to materialise and he was out of the team, and out of Formula One for good, after just five races.

The mainstay of Frank's driving force turned out to be Howden Ganley, a New Zealander nominated by Marlboro. Philip Morris, the company which owned the Marlboro brand name, was at the start of what would turn out to be a powerful and lengthy sponsorship association with motor racing, and Formula One in particular. However, the initial foray had been shaky, to say the least. Money poured by Marlboro into BRM, a British team in rapid decline from its position of pomp and glory, had failed to produce consistent results. The link with Williams, orchestrated by Pat Duffeler of Philip Morris, was seen as a second string to the bow. This new liaison would not bring success either. But it would keep Frank Williams afloat as his financial package sprang leaks left, right and centre. Marlboro would provide one of the most crucial life lines in the history of the team.

The negotiating of various deals in Europe meant Frank was a regular visitor to London's Heathrow airport. Viv Orriss, who worked in the British Airways Executive Lounge, remembers Passenger Williams better than almost any other:

Everyone adored him. We would get a call from the girl at check-in: 'Frank's on his way,' she would say, and that would have girls dashing to check their hair and make-up. I worked in the lounge for four years and, generally, you don't remember one passenger from the next. But the two I remember clearly are Frank and David Niven. They were undoubtedly the most charming passengers at the time.

Frank always treated you like an old friend. He always remembered what you had been talking about the last time he came through. I was learning to fly at the time and he was fascinated by flying. If it was quiet and I was on my own, we would sit and chat.

There were no upgrades in those days because there was only First Class and Economy, and the divide between the two was huge. But we helped Frank with his flights, even when we weren't supposed to. He would say: 'I'm booked on the ten o'clock but I really need to be on the nine o'clock. Unfortunately it's full.' He wouldn't make a fuss or anything like that. But he was so nice about it and he always managed to get his way. You would realise that after you had been downstairs to the check-in and somehow found a seat for him on the early flight!

He would always look you straight in the eye. But it was his smile which made you melt. It was devastating. Everyone loved him – and one of the girls was absolutely besotted by him. He just had such a wonderful way with people.

Frank needed all of his persuasive powers and enthusiasm during 1973. Additional expense was incurred when the regulations called for all cars to be fitted with crash structures as a means of giving the driver and fuel tanks additional protection in the event of a side impact. It meant the building of completely new cars. Williams needed that like a hole in the head.

Frank employed an engineer, John Clarke, to do the job. The result was a neat and workmanlike car which had an unfortunate and costly shortcoming: the oil system designed to service the Ford-Cosworth V8 proved inefficient and led to engine failure on more than one occasion. When everything worked satisfactorily, Ganley would bring the car home without drama. His best result was sixth place in the Canadian Grand Prix, scarcely a highlight in a year when consistency was hardly the watchword as Marlboro replaced Galli with a succession of drivers. One of them, Gijs van Lennep, scored a point by finishing sixth in his home Grand Prix in Holland. That gave Frank Williams a grand total of two points at the end of his first year as a constructor. He would never register such a low score again as a bone fide manufacturer. But he would come close.

Marlboro's continuing financial support also meant the nomination of Arturo Merzario as the replacement for Ganley. The contrast between the two drivers could not have been more complete: Ganley looked as though he had stepped from an All Blacks three-quarter line; Merzario, a wiry, chain-smoking Italian, appeared to need lead in his boots in case a puff of wind should blow him away. Whereas Ganley was placid and reliable, Merzario was excitable and unpredictable. He proved it straight away by over-revving not one, but two engines during practice for the first race of the 1974 season in Argentina. Once was just about forgivable, but twice was sheer exhibitionism – not to mention expensive as he reduced the internals of the Ford-Cosworth to junk on each occasion.

It was a symptom of Merzario's past. He had driven for Ferrari, where the twelve-cylinder engines revved more freely than the Ford V8, and where the budget was scarcely a consideration, replacement engines being fitted as though they were light bulbs. And yet, despite this destructive element in the cockpit of his car, Williams thought Arturo was the business. In Frank's opinion, the little man was trying. 'Art' was giving the car some stick. He was going *racing*. That evaluation said a great deal about Frank's preferences when it came to drivers, and his love of the very basics of his trade. You had to be a racer to make any impression on the boss, even when he scarcely had two pennies to rub together.

The team's budget continued to take a terrible hammering but Frank put that to the back of his mind when, incredibly, Merzario qualified third for the South African Grand Prix. Williams was absolutely thrilled. This justified all the hardship and the struggle. Arturo finished sixth and scored a point but, thereafter, the team began a slow decline to more familiar territory in the middle and rear quarter of the grid. Typically, Merzario bounded back at his home Grand Prix by charging through the field to finish fourth at Monza. That was it for 1974: four points and a mountain of debt.

Marlboro had indicated through official channels that the sponsorship would cease in 1975 and, of course, by now the Iso-Rivolta deal was at an end. For the first time, Frank's car would be called a Williams. That was all very well, but having your name on a car meant nothing if funds were not available to pay for an engine. Pat Duffeler shuffled around his Marlboro money and managed to find £15,000 for Williams. That paid for one new engine. Ward bought another. And so it went on.

Merzario was signed for a second season, the mishmash of rent-a-drivers used in 1974 making way for a permanent seat for Jacques Laffite, as the reigning European Formula Two champion took over the second car. Laffite, a jolly Frenchman only marginally bigger than Merzario, possessed plenty of ability and, just as attractive, backing from a Swiss businessman named Ambrozium. Once again, Frank Williams began the season with a surfeit of optimism and, once again, the results were not forthcoming. With one notable exception.

Merzario's enthusiasm declined in inverse proportion to Laffite's increase in maturity and promise. But, as the season progressed, Laffite's potential was hamstrung by a run of engine failures, most of which stemmed from the team's inexperience with oil systems. In 1975, the Tyrrell team, having won the championship three times, was a leading contender and Ken Tyrrell took pity on Williams by giving Frank's engineer valuable technical advice which, if nothing else, would make the Williams-Fords reliable. It was a timely intervention. By mid-season, Williams had just one engine left and no money to buy a replacement. When the single entry for Laffite (Merzario having quit the team six weeks before) retired with a broken gearbox from the British Grand Prix in July, Williams was in dire straits.

The next race, due to be held on the ferociously demanding fourteen-mile Nurburgring in Germany, threatened to take the car and the team apart. Laffite qualified in the middle of the grid, made a circumspect start, but then gradually moved forward as those in front either broke down, had accidents or picked up punctures on the sharp stones flicked onto the edges of the track. At the end of the 198-mile race, Laffite was a minute and a half behind the winner, Carlos Reutemann. But he was in second place, more than a mile ahead of Niki Lauda's Ferrari. It had been an excellent performance, a perfect mix of speed and caution.

Frank was overjoyed. This was manna from heaven. In one hit, he had earned £5,500 in prize money and scored enough points to guarantee his right to FOCA travel subsidies which would be worth £150,000 in 1976. But he was not out of the woods yet. Far from it. The chances were that he might not reach the end of the current season, never mind racing into 1976. The £5,500 would scarcely make an impression on the pile of unpaid bills. In fact, it would make no impression at all. The first priority was to pay for bits and pieces for the car. Never mind about the outstanding debts. This had always been Frank's priority. To the exclusion of everything else. Absolutely everything.

Twelve months before, in August 1974, Frank had married Virginia Sawyer-Hoare. Ginny knew what she was letting herself in for. She had fallen hopelessly in love with Frank in 1967 when her fiancé, Charles Sawyer-Hoare, paid a visit to Bath Road, where Frank was looking after Charles's Formula Three car. Attracted by Frank's zest for life, and hooked by his flirtatious wink and winning smile, Ginny was in turmoil as her marriage, a lavish affair befitting a couple of generous means, went ahead. She did the best she could to make it work. But it was a hopeless cause for as long as F.O.G. Williams was around. Infatuated by him, Ginny bowed to the inevitable; she and Charles eventually parted company.

Now began the slow but steady game of winning the trust of a man who was effectively married to motor racing and who had no intention of jeopardising that relationship for a woman, no matter how attractive he found her. Ginny's love and tenacity paid off by degrees; she did his washing, ironed his shirts, cooked dinner on the rare occasions when he put in an appearance. The profit from the sale of Ginny's maisonette in Rawlings Street, behind Harrods, was passed on as a means of helping to pay a few of Frank's outstanding bills in 1972.

The move from Cippenham to larger premises in Bennet Road had meant the loss of Frank's flat. Not that he had anything in it, of course, all his worldly goods such as radio, stereo and bits and pieces of furniture having long since been sold to help fund the racing project. Frank had been sleeping in the home of his friend Charles Crichton-Stuart, but when Charlie and his wife decided to move Williams realised that, like Ginny, he too was about to become homeless. Ginny was quick to seize the moment when Frank suggested that perhaps they should find somewhere to share.

After a tenuous start – Frank, in a fit of uncertainty over being tied down, walked out of a cottage they had rented from a friend in Old Windsor – the move to a furnished detached property in the village of Mortimer, five miles from Reading, proved to have a more stabilising effect. Or, at least, as much as Ginny knew she could reasonably expect from someone with such a single-minded approach to making his business successful.

It was common to find that the telephone had been cut off due to the bill being unpaid. This applied to both the house in Mortimer and the industrial unit in Bennet Road. While Ginny, who had attended finishing school in Monte Carlo and had been brought up never to mention money, found the inconvenience mildly irritating to say the least, Frank took it in his stride. There was no choice. He could not contemplate paying on receipt of the first invoice. The patience of suppliers was stretched to the limit, and sometimes beyond. It was not unusual to have visits from the bailiffs as desks and chairs were removed to pay for an outstanding bill. When the telephone was periodically cut off, business was conducted from a public call box outside the Reading Speedway located at the rutted end of Bennet Road.

Inside the sport, Frank's predicament was more readily understood. Walter Hayes, the director of public affairs for Ford Europe, played a leading role in motor sport by massaging his company's support, not just in the manufacture of engines through Cosworth Engineering, but through the provision of peripheral items such as loan vehicles.

I used to lend Anglia vans to Frank from time to time, and he would sell them. That was how people like Williams raised money to survive. It was the sport's currency at the time. 'We need money to go motor racing,' they would say, 'and so we get it any way we can.' Now, if you had brought in someone from outside the sport and they had seen what was happening, they would have said: 'But you can't let him do that with your property. It's illegal!' But we didn't see it that way.

Patience was a great virtue for anyone associated with Williams, but most long-suffering of all were Frank's mechanics. Dennis Rushen, later to run a team in Formula Ford 2000 and one of the first to spot the nascent talent of Ayrton Senna, cut his teeth in the business by wielding spanners for Frank.

There were very few of us. Fewer mechanics than you'd have on a Formula Ford team today. Compared to the likes of Ferrari and Lotus, we had nothing. But it didn't matter because you didn't need an image as such in those days. Not like now when, if you don't have three trucks, paint the garage floor and run a hospitality unit, you can't compete. It wasn't like that then. There was a camaraderie which you don't see nowadays.

Everybody would help Frank. We would borrow things all the time – never to be returned. But it wasn't a problem. Frank was very popular. It was the underdog syndrome, but everyone could see that he just tried a lot harder than anyone else.

My memory is of the team having no money. We had to do all sorts of things that you wouldn't get away with now. Little Arturo [Merzario] was so small that we simply put blocks of wood on the pedals! Can you imagine doing that today?

I used to go in the truck with a chap called Simon to the races. We had to drive this great big long rigid thing – it would probably be illegal now. It was a Leyland of some sort, painted red, and I remember at one race having to borrow £50 from Bernie [Ecclestone] in order to pay for enough diesel to get the thing home.

We couldn't afford new tyres most of the time. So I would have to go down to the Goodyear compound and root around among Ferrari's cast-offs, trying to choose a matching set after Regazzoni and Lauda had finished with them.

Despite the hardships, we all liked Frank. I think the thing which kept us there was his enthusiasm. He had a way about him. At the end of every week, we'd ask for our wages. 'Ah,' he'd say. 'It's on the way from Switzerland.' It was always coming from Switzerland, never anywhere else. We used to go for weeks without any money. It always arrived eventually but it was obvious that he was having to struggle. He had this belief that everything would sort itself out but I think we worried a lot more than Frank did. And yet we'd hang on, even though there were times when the mechanics became a bit restless.

Frank would inevitably win them over. He always seemed to know what to say at precisely the right moment. The mechanics came to expect it.

The one thing Ginny had not anticipated was a proposal of marriage, even though she was expecting their first child. Typically, Frank mentioned it, almost in passing, as he set off for the Austrian Grand Prix in August 1974. And, typically, Ginny acted immediately. When Frank returned from another mediocre weekend of racing, he found an appointment had been made at the Reading registry office on the following Tuesday, 20 August. Frank did not have a personal bank account and Ginny had no money. Dave Brodie, a close friend of Frank, lent Ginny the £8 necessary for the licence. The £30 which had been set aside for rent was used to buy a wedding ring.

The ceremony was due to take place at two p.m. Ginny arranged a lunch beforehand with Brodie and his wife. At one p.m., Frank rang to say he was delayed at the factory and could not make the lunch. He eventually left Bennet

Road ten minutes before the appointed hour, said his vows clearly and distinctly in front of the registrar, Ginny and the Brodies, and was back at work by two-thirty. Job done. Now, how are we going to pay for the engine rebuilds necessary for the next race in Italy? The only person unsurprised by all this was Mrs Virginia Williams.

Jonathan Piers Williams was born on 22 February 1975. A few weeks before, his parents had been served with an eviction order. The landlord, unhappy about the frequent late payment of rent, had not been impressed when he discovered the presence of a black labrador, and then learned about Ginny's pregnancy. The terms of the agreement forbade dogs and children. Frank and Ginny had six weeks to find a new home.

Dispirited initially by being thrown abruptly out of house and home, Ginny followed Frank's relaxed attitude. He had more pressing matters to take care of and left Ginny to get on with looking for a replacement. She began the search in no less a place than *Country Life* magazine, where she discovered a laundry house on the estate of the Colman family, of mustard fame. The peppercorn rent of a few pounds a week was hugely attractive, less so the stipulation that renovations worth £8,000 had to be carried out. They did not have £80 between them, yet Frank and Ginny presented themselves for interview. Frank, once again acting on instinct, chose the right moment to flash his winning smile and inform Sir Michael and Lady Colman that he had no money – but hoped to have some soon.

To Ginny's amazement and delight, they were chosen from a long list of applicants. Somehow, they would make it work, even though they had no furniture beyond a couple of sofas, a bed and two small glass tables. The inventory was unlikely to be increased for as long as there were components to be bought for the racing team. The kitchen was in urgent need of repair and, during the spasmodic visits by the builder as and when he received payment, the absence of a washing machine meant Ginny had to pay regular visits to a launderette. She even had to borrow a cot for Jonathan and, for at least a year, there was not a single carpet in the house. Frank, of course, scarcely noticed the bare boards as he brought his worries home with him each night. As their first wedding anniversary came and went, the financial situation seemed even worse than before, if such a thing was possible.

The joy associated with Laffite's second place in Germany had been short-lived. The Frenchman had retired from the next two races and a succession of rent-a-drivers in the second car had fared little better. At least the team could look forward to the final race of the season at Watkins Glen in the United States. Situated in the Finger Lake district of New York state, 'The Glen' looked stunning as the autumnal tints added to the relaxed end-of-term feeling. The prize money was generous. Williams continued to live in hope.

The cash flow – in the wrong direction – began during practice when the second driver, Lella Lombardi, failed to notice that a valve spring had broken in the engine of her car. The team could hear it as she passed the pits, the harsh sound ripping into Frank as he thumbed the leaves of his metaphorical cheque-book. This was in the days before pits-to-car radio. As the Italian pressed on, Williams feared the worst. Sure enough, the valve dropped into the engine and simply ripped it apart. The rebuild would cost over £9,000 and there was not a replacement engine to allow Lombardi to race.

There was worse to come. On race morning, Laffite was cleaning his helmet visor when he asked his wife, Bernadette, to apply Optrex drops to his eyes. It was a routine procedure before a race and no one noticed when Bernadette mistakenly picked up the bottle of visor cleaning fluid. Seconds later,

Jacques was in agony. He was rushed off to hospital where, fortunately, it was discovered that his eyesight had not been impaired. But there was no question of Laffite starting the race. There was the thought that Lella could start in Jacques's car but, to everyone's frustration, she failed to fit the cockpit. It was not that Lombardi was too big, merely that the sparrow-like Laffite was incredibly slim. Either way, it meant Williams had travelled all that way only to have neither car start the race.

Frank returned home and donned his trainers and track suit. Ever since moving to the rural setting surrounding the house at Mortimer, Frank's penchant for the occasional run had become more than a hobby. He had reached the stage where he would not be happy unless he had covered at least five miles after work each evening. As with everything in Frank's life, he took his running seriously and became extremely fit. It also gave him time to think. And there was much to mull over as autumn gave way to winter in 1975.

In the spring of that year, Frank had been on the phone to Gianpaolo Dallara, the man who had designed the ill-fated de Tomaso F1 car. They chatted about this and that, Frank using his fluent Italian to explain that his financial situation seemed even worse than usual. Dallara mentioned Walter Wolf, an Austro-Canadian who had made millions through the oil equipment business. Wolf loved fast cars and motor racing. He had been in Italy investigating the possibility of running a Lamborghini or some such exotic machine at Le Mans. Dallara noted that the cost of the proposed operation did not seem to be a problem.

Frank was on the case immediately. He tracked Wolf down by telephone and found he needed no introduction. Williams asked Wolf if he would like to be his guest at the International Trophy meeting at Silverstone. The invitation was accepted.

The race may have been a non-championship event for
Formula One cars but there was no let-up in the misery for
Williams. During a cold and frequently wet two days,
Merzario suffered two engine failures and was unable to start.
Wolf arrived in the midst of this disarray, introduced himself
to Williams and was immediately enthralled by the buzz of
excitement in the pit lane. Rather than be put off by Frank's
problems, Wolf offered to help sort them out by paying for
the engine rebuilds. He attended several races that season,
his timely advances of cash keeping the team from
insolvency.

Wolf was no fool. He may have been captivated by all he
saw but he was a tough negotiator. While appreciating
Frank's sincerity, zeal and passion, he could see there was
little sense in throwing good money after bad. Towards the
end of the 1975 season, Wolf had suggested that he should
become a shareholder in the company. Williams did not
want any part of that. But Wolf was persistent. He offered
to settle the team's debts (estimated to be £140,000) in
return for a 60 per cent interest in Frank Williams (Racing
Cars) Ltd. Again, Frank said no.

Wolf was determined to get into Formula One by some
means. At the end of 1975, the Hesketh team – which had
introduced James Hunt to Formula One – went into liqui-
dation and Wolf was offered the stock, which included what
appeared to be a promising new car, for £450,000. Wolf told
Frank he was considering the deal and wanted Williams to
be a part of it. Frank was in no doubt that Walter was
serious about his intention to go motor racing in a proper
manner.

Frank discussed this latest development with Ginny. She
shared his reluctance to give up everything they had worked
for. Besides, Marlboro was offering Williams £100,000 to
give a drive to Jacky Ickx in 1976. That was a tidy sum for

a former Ferrari driver and Grand Prix winner. And there were the FOCA benefits to consider as well. Even so, Wolf's offer was tempting: no more bad debts; no more rent-a-drivers; a new car and the money to operate it on a proper basis.

One night, towards the end of November, Frank went for a long run. He returned to the laundry house and phoned Walter Wolf immediately. It was to be a crucial turning point. But not in the direction Frank had hoped.

CHAPTER FOUR

Can this be true?

Frank Williams could well have his best ever Grand Prix season next year, especially if his recent announcement is anything to go by. A telephone call last week from the 33-year-old effervescent Formula One entrant confirmed that he'd acquired the Hesketh 308C Grand Prix project and the car's designer, Dr Harvey Postlethwaite. If that was not enough, Williams also confirmed a three-year agreement with wealthy Austrian businessman, Walter Wolf, to finance his team and also hoped to finalise plans with Jacky Ickx to head his Grand Prix attack.

The emphasis of the lead story in *Autosport* on Thursday, 11 December 1975, may have been inaccurate – it was Wolf calling the shots, not Williams – but the basic facts were correct. In essence, Frank Williams (Racing Cars) Ltd was no more. The team would be known as Walter Wolf Racing, the plan being to have Frank run it and enjoy the benefit of adequate funding. The long-term reality would be quite different.

The initial side-effects proved very attractive. For the first time in his life, Frank received a salary. His £25,000 annual fee would go into his first current bank account, which had been opened not long before. Ginny was in a position to purchase luxuries such as a table, thus ending the practice of balancing meals on their knees. Meanwhile, Bennet Road was bustling with activity as the former Hesketh team moved lock, stock and barrel from their closed-down premises in Northamptonshire. The pity was, they also brought the Hesketh 308C.

The original Hesketh, the 308 with which James Hunt had won his first Grand Prix, had been a reasonably straightforward car which had been taken to its limits thanks mainly to the skill of the driver. The 308C was more complex and not even Hunt could overcome its idiosyncrasies when he first drove the car halfway through the 1975 season. He referred to the 308C as 'giving me all kinds of funny messages. It feels queasy', a warning which should have been taken more seriously since the new team would be heartily sick of the car by the time 1976 was over.

Hunt had been snapped up by the McLaren team (with whom he would win the world championship that year), his place taken by Jacky Ickx on the strength of the Belgian's reputation, not to mention the £100,000 from Marlboro. Ickx, brilliant on his day, had passed his best. Certainly, he was not motivated enough to battle with a car which suffered through a lack of rigidity in the chassis and suspension. Continual modifications during the season brought the additional handicap of excess weight, and trouble was looming when Ickx failed to qualify the 308C (renamed Wolf-Williams) for the British Grand Prix. What made it worse was the fact that Walter Wolf had brought a number of influential guests to Brands Hatch to see his car race. And he was even less impressed by the discovery that Frank's now legendary absence of financial control was allowing the team to run £100,000 over budget. Ickx was replaced by Merzario. It made no difference; the little Italian failed to finish a single race.

Frank, rather naively, had thought Walter Wolf would

make allowances and give the new team time to find its feet. It took Dave Brodie, more worldly-wise in these matters, to spell it out to his friend that successful businessmen such as Wolf expect success immediately when they invest a considerable sum of money. When the season ended, Wolf took steps to hire Peter Warr, then team manager with Lotus. Frank's salary was doubled and he was given the role of sponsorship seeker and personal assistant, the latter a euphemism for general dogsbody.

Williams went along with it. He spent a couple of months working in the office of a major advertising agency, learning the rudimentary skills of marketing. In between, he was fetching and carrying in the grand manner as he moved Wolf's expensive road cars around Europe at the behest of his boss. Despite Frank's love of motor cars, his new role acted like an arrow through the heart of such a genuine free spirit, an entrepreneur who had done things his way for more than a decade. The final straw came in January 1977.

Harvey Postlethwaite had wisely decided to design a relatively simple car and Wolf had hired Jody Scheckter, a future champion, to drive it. The team went off to the first race in Argentina – and left Frank behind. It amounted to incarceration for a man with racing in his blood. The agony was complete when Scheckter actually won the race. The easy inferences in the press suggested that the revamped organisation had been the catalyst for this remarkable turn-around. The subtext was that they were better off without Frank. Williams went to the next race in Brazil but that merely compounded the feeling of emptiness. He was no longer directly involved in the actual racing. There was nothing for it but to start all over again. This time, however, there would be one crucial difference: he would have the services, and ultimately the close friendship, of someone with a deep and straightforward understanding of what makes a racing car work.

Shortly before agreeing the deal with Wolf at the end of 1975, Williams had hired Patrick Head, a young designer who had learned the ropes at Lola, the company from Huntingdon which produced racing cars for a variety of formulae around the world. The new arrangement, which saw Harvey Postlethwaite moving into Bennet Road, put Williams in a difficult position because he did not want to lose his new recruit. Head, rather than walk out in a huff, chose to stay, on the reasonable assumption that he would learn something from a designer already involved in Formula One. It would turn out to be a key decision. Head, in fact, would learn from the dreadful 308C how *not* to go about designing and building a Grand Prix car.

Having spent the year with Wolf, Head faced another decision, one which would turn out to be the most important of his career. Patrick was attending a test session with Wolf in South Africa when he received a call from Frank. Williams said he was starting afresh and had a budget to do perhaps ten races. Would he be interested? Head said he would think about it. In effect, Frank wanted Patrick to leave the comparative security of a team on the up and join a new venture masterminded by someone whose track record was, well, less than impressive. Patrick felt that the time was right to, as he put it, 'do my own thing'. He was also swayed somewhat by the personalities involved.

Head, the son of Colonel Michael Head, a military attaché in Sweden in the late 1940s, was a feet on the ground, meat and two veg sort of chap who didn't think much of Walter Wolf's rather brash approach epitomised by leather jackets and expensive jewellery. Colonel Head had competed in club races in a Jaguar sports car and Patrick learned to enjoy motor racing for motor racing's sake; he appreciated having things done in a gentlemanly and proper manner. He was a racer, very much in the manner of the lean and hungry team owner extending the offer of employment. For all Frank's foibles, Patrick knew where the future lay. Or, at least, the short-term future because Patrick, a child of the sixties, had enjoyed a rather bohemian lifestyle in London for a period. The decision to join Frank's latest effort was seen as a suitable job for the moment. By no means did Head regard this as a long-term venture with the world championship at its height.

When the new venture was announced, critics scoffed. They said it was to be expected of Williams, who appeared not to know any better. But as for Head, he was committing motor racing suicide. Both men were to prove that rumours of their imminent demise were greatly exaggerated.

One of the first tasks was to select a name for the company. Wolf owned the title Frank Williams (Racing Cars) Ltd. The simple choice of 'Williams Racing', 'Frank Williams Racing' or some such combination was scuppered by the discovery that several bookmakers were so named. In the end, they settled for 'Williams Grand Prix Engineering', a bit of a mouthful but a typically straightforward description of the company's business, as and when it got going.

Frank had the bit between his teeth and no amount of persuasion would divert him. Wolf had offered Williams a large amount of money to join him in the oil business and stay out of racing; there was about as much chance of that as there was of night failing to follow day. Even though Frank stood at the foot of another massive mountain, there was no doubt in his mind that he could climb it.

Whereas in the past everything had been a struggle from start to finish, the new operation exuded a positive air which, whether by accident or design, opened doors when least expected. During the winter of 1976/7, Frank learned that a personable Belgian driver, Patrick Neve, was looking for a Formula One ride and, to help him on his way, he had £100,000 from the Belle Vue brewery. This suited Williams perfectly. His next concern was to find a car and somewhere to keep it.

By selling out to Wolf, Williams had automatically lost his membership of FOCA. There was no chance of rejoining because he would not be competing in every round of the championship. On top of that, building his own car would be out of the question. Once again, he turned to March Engineering and bought a Formula One car, supposedly based on the previous year's design, at a knock-down price of £14,000, of course. Ford-Cosworth engines were picked up from an Italian privateer, from Bernie Ecclestone (who owned Brabham as well as masterminding FOCA) and from the American Penske team, which had abandoned a brief foray into Formula One. The latter engine was in a sorry state thanks to a major mechanical failure which had punched a hole in the side of the block. At the bargain price of £1,500, the V8 was worth having, Williams sending it to Cosworth Engineering to be rebuilt, more or less from scratch. It was a sign of Frank's continuing good fortune and new-found luck when the engine came back as good as new, but with Cosworth appearing to have omitted the cost of a new block, worth at least £2,000 alone, from the final bill. Frank said nothing, but the apparent miscalculation bothered him. Years later, after becoming one of Cosworth's most important customers, he would reveal the engine company's inadvertent but valuable contribution to the Williams cause.

Ginny, meanwhile, had been leading the search for premises, the decision finally being made in favour of a 5,000 square foot former carpet warehouse on a small industrial estate in Oxfordshire. With their first race looming in Spain on 8 May, the little team was desperate to get going. In fact, they were to move in prematurely. 'I can't remember what happened exactly,' says Head, 'but for some reason we didn't have a key, so we forced an entry. We just couldn't wait to get started. The place was absolutely filthy inside, so we had to sort that out even though, at that stage, we had nothing to put in it. We really were starting from scratch.'

One of the team's first employees was Bob Torrie, a former Lotus mechanic who has remained with Williams ever since:

I knew all about Frank because I had seen him at the circuits while I was with Lotus. He was ambitious and you could tell he was going places. The first place we went to was Station Road, Didcot, and I have to admit I had my doubts as soon as we got inside. Yes, we did go in before we should have done but I think we managed it by spinning the estate agent some story so that we could get the key.

It really was in a dreadful state. It looked enormous; 5,000 square feet and nothing to put in it. We had absolutely nothing. Then a grotty little lathe arrived, and then a small drill. That's all we had for quite a few weeks. One of my first jobs was to paint the dark green walls white and my first technical question to Patrick Head was 'One coat or two?'. I could see that Frank was ambitious but I never imagined for a moment that Williams Grand Prix Engineering would turn into what it is today.

Unit 10, Station Road, would see the transformation of Frank's dream to reality. It was the stuff of television adverts trumpeting the merits of assistance from your friendly local bank.

Williams, in fact, had developed an aversion to bank officials. Over the years he had received more than his fair share of correspondence from financial institutions, and none of it had been very friendly. He was caught completely off his guard when the manager from the Didcot branch of Barclays Bank arrived unannounced to see if he could help. John Makepeace had just been transferred from the north-east and he was making it his business to seek out new clients. Once he had breached Frank's initial barrier of suspicion, Makepeace quickly assessed that Williams Grand Prix Engineering was worth the risk. To Frank's amazement, he suddenly discovered that his company had a £30,000 overdraft facility.

Williams remained a credit risk elsewhere, a legacy of cheques which had tended to bounce rather than travel smoothly through the fiscal system. Frank received invaluable assistance from Dave Brodie, his old friend not only becoming a director of the company for a short while but also offering himself, and his considerable reputation as the owner of a successful metal plating business, as a guarantor and business reference. Brodie had contacts in all walks of business life and one of them put Frank in touch with a finance company which would offer favourable terms for the purchase of a Ford truck capable of carrying the car. Finance was also arranged for the top-quality machine tools Head required if the job was to be done properly. Once again, the indefatigable Ted Williams came to the aid of the party by providing a brand-new capstan lathe as well as the services of Ward's joinery crew when it came to making work benches and partitions for the factory.

The WGPE workforce was six-strong, one or two having moved from Wolf before Walter, alarmed by the sudden exodus, raised his pay scales in order to prevent further defections. The secretarial work was carried out by Alison Morris, the wife of a British Leyland executive and a tower of strength to Frank and Ginny during the dark days at Bennet Road. Bailiffs held no fear for Alison, but there seemed the very real chance that their presence would not be required at Station Road, Didcot. Even though there was more money than before, finance continued to be tight. But that hardly seemed to matter. Events were continuing to move at an exciting pace, none more so than a new development which would have far-reaching consequences.

Tony Harris, a friend of Frank, worked in a London advertising agency which handled the account for Saudia, the airline of the Kingdom of Saudi Arabia. Harris, alert to the airline's need to project its image in the western world and aware of Frank's willingness to cooperate in any promising scheme, introduced Williams to Mohammed Al Fawzan, the airline's sales manager in Jeddah. Al Fawzan was interested enough to visit a Formula Two race with Frank at Silverstone. He liked what he saw and quickly grasped the benefits of being associated with Formula One. Williams was given the go-ahead to carry the 'Fly Saudia' emblem on the back wing of the March in return for £30,000.

This was the start of something very big indeed – not that you would have known it by watching Patrick Neve as the new team made its debut at the Spanish Grand Prix on 8 May 1977. To be fair to Neve, the March was not a good car. In fact, it was probably even older than at first thought, the removal of layers of paint on the bodywork revealing sponsorship colours which suggested this particular chassis dated back to 1974. But it was a start, albeit an inauspicious one which was not helped by Frank's truck driver – 'a slightly dippy character' according to Head – backing into the gleaming transporter owned by none other than Walter Wolf.

Head had made minor weight-saving modifications to the March and Neve qualified near the back of the grid in Spain and finished twelfth. He failed to qualify in three of the races that season and his best finish was a rather fortunate seventh at Monza. Throughout this period, the team was working on a marginal budget, travelling on the cheapest bucket shop airline tickets and staying in low-grade hotels. By the time of the final Grand Prix in Canada, Williams was running the race team on his own. Patrick Head was flat-out at Didcot, designing WGPE's first car. Neve hoped to be driving it in 1978 but Frank and Patrick had other ideas. Everyone agreed Neve was a tidy driver and a very pleasant young man – a polite way of saying he was not hungry enough to make the grade, not the sort of aggressive hard-charging driver WGPE needed. The question was, who would they choose? Or, put another way, who would want to drive for Frank Williams? After all, nothing seemed to have changed. A Williams-entered car, backed by very little money, had just spent another season trundling along as an also-ran. No up-and-coming driver in his right mind would want to be tied in with that.

In subsequent years, Frank would earn a reputation for talent spotting and choosing the right driver at the right time. His payroll would include names such as Rosberg, Piquet, Mansell, Prost and Senna. In reality, he would often stumble upon the ideal choice, almost by accident. This would be a case in point.

Aiming high, Frank had spoken to Ronnie Peterson, one of the fastest and most spectacular drivers of the moment. The Swedish driver was between teams and eventually chose March. There was contact with Jochen Mass, Hans Stuck, Riccardo Patrese and other middle-ranking candidates, some of whom did not even bother to return Frank's calls. Strangely, none of the foregoing – not even Peterson – had won a Grand Prix in 1977 and yet, near the bottom of his list, Frank had placed the name Alan Jones, who had finished first in Austria.

It had been an unexpected result. The Australian had

been driving for Shadow and neither party had won a Grand Prix until that day at the Osterreichring, a fast track sweeping through the foothills of the Tyrol. Rain had made the circuit very slippery indeed but Jones, running in tenth place, began to pull off daring overtaking moves with a car which was handling perfectly under the conditions. When James Hunt's McLaren retired from the lead with an engine failure with eleven laps to go, Jones found himself at the front of the field. He couldn't believe it. Neither could most of the pit lane. Circumstances had fallen in his favour but, as Frank Williams noted, the tough, broad-shouldered antipodean had made the most of them. Almost as an afterthought at the end of the season, Jones was invited to visit Station Road.

He struck up an immediate rapport with Patrick Head, two no-nonsense racers with one thing in mind: winning Grands Prix and, ultimately, the championship. Jones could sense that Frank Williams was finally heading in the right direction. He was even more impressed when he saw the result of Head's labours at the drawing-board. The Williams FW06 was a straightforward but neat little car. When Frank said he could pay Jones £40,000 to drive it, the deal was done.

Members of the motor sport press were invited to Station Road to witness the unveiling of the FW06 in December 1977. All the regulars turned up, including representatives from Reuters Television. It was immediately apparent to those who knew him that Frank was more hyper than usual. Dressed in a two-piece suit with a broad striped tie, Williams bade everyone a generous welcome and talked about the car. It was white, with a green flash and Saudia logos front to back. A press kit, put together for Frank by Andrew Marriott of CSS Promotions and Alan Henry, a motor sport journalist, consisted of ten typed pages, photocopied and placed inside slide binders bought from WH Smith. Page one paid due homage to Saudia, the team's major sponsor. Page two listed the secondary sponsors, whose logos had been placed along the sides of the car: Fruit of the Loom, introduced to Williams by his former driver, Nanni Galli, who had since become a distributor for the American clothing company; Personal, a steering wheel manufacturer with whom Williams had been involved since 1969; ABMTM, the Association of British Machine Tool Makers, introduced to Williams through his connection with Ward in 1968; and trade sponsors Goodyear and Champion. Five in all. When Williams unveiled his 1997 contender, the press kit ran to 32 pages and listed 23 sponsors. 'It was novel for Frank to have a press kit,' recalled Henry. 'It was even more novel to be paid for doing it. I remember a man travelled down from Didcot to London, giving me £50 in cash and taking away the typed pages.' Andrew Marriott added:

I gathered material for the press release in association with Patrick. I remember noting that the oil tank was a very neat and novel arrangement located between the engine and the gearbox. Aerodynamics were the coming thing at the time and there was some surprise that Patrick had not been influenced by that. In fact, FW06 was typical of Patrick. It was very neat and straightforward. Just what the team needed at that stage. It looked good and everyone present was aware that, at long last, maybe Frank was going places. Certainly, we were aware that this was the start of a new era.

As coffee was served in the workshop, the beat of a helicopter's rotor stirred Williams into demonic action. Straightening his tie, he threw open the back door of the factory and watched the helicopter land on a football pitch at the back of the industrial estate. On board was a party of four from Saudia, including Al Fawzan and the airline's director-general, Sheikh Kamal Sindhi. Buttoning his jacket, Williams prepared to walk towards the temporary landing pad. There was no question in the minds of those watching that this was a major moment for Francis Williams. Perhaps realising that his guests could recite horror stories which would have the Saudis homeward bound sooner than expected, Frank paused and then turned towards the knot of press men. 'Don't let me down lads!' he said, and then flashed the winning smile. If those present had been asked to write references on the spot, Williams would have been embarrassed by the depth of warmth and affection on that bright but chilly December morning.

The car was pushed into the back yard, alongside the small lorry which would carry it to the European races. Alan Jones, dressed in white driving overalls gleaming in the sunshine, stood behind the rear wing and posed for photographs with the Saudis, Frank positioned slightly in the background but beaming all the while and looking on like a proud father. No one knew whether or not the car would be competitive, but there was an unmistakable feeling that Williams, Head and Jones would carry it on their backs if necessary.

Helping them do it would be a staff of twenty-one, Williams having expanded considerably from the original workforce of six. A recent recruit was Neil Oatley, a quietly spoken young engineer not long out of college:

I had been working for a general engineering company in Chesterfield. I had a passion for racing and, ever since leaving college, I had been looking at every opportunity to get in. There was an advert in *Autosport* for a junior draughtsman at Williams, and I applied.

I was under no illusions. I knew Williams was pretty low-key;

Above: Frank the Racer. Aboard his Formula 3 Brabham in 1966. *(GP Photo/Nygaard)*

Right: In the thick of it. Williams (No. 2) dices for the lead at Djursland-Ring in Denmark in 1966. *(GP Photo/Nygaard)*

Left: Humble beginning. Frank cleans up the suspension on his F2 Brabham in the Bath Road workshop. *(Action-Plus)*

Left: Frank and Piers Courage discuss progress in the rudimentary pits at the Nürburgring during practice for the 1969 German Grand Prix. *(Sporting Pictures)*

Right, opposite page: Courage and his ill-fated De Tomaso. *(Sporting Pictures)*

Left: Courage hurls the immaculate Brabham through the streets of Monte Carlo on his way to a remarkable second place in 1969. *(DPPI/Action-Plus)*

Below: Piers Courage. Frank never quite got over his loss. *(DPPI/Action-Plus)*

The Williams-entered cars were at their worst during the impecunious early seventies. Frank talks to the Danish driver, Tom Belso. The method of securing the aeroscreen leaves a lot to be desired. *(GP Photo/Nygaard)*

Jacques Laffite heads towards an excellent and desperately-needed second place for Frank at the Nürburgring in 1975. *(Sports Pictures (UK) Ltd)*

Hammering home. Clay Regazzoni powers his Williams towards the first F1 victory for Frank at Silverstone in 1979. (DPPI/Action-Plus)

Above: Perfect combination: Alan Jones and Frank in 1979. *(Sporting Pictures)*

Right: Jones waits patiently in the cockpit of FW07 during practice for the 1979 German Grand Prix. *(DPPI/Action-Plus)*

Above: First title. Jackie Stewart gives Alan Jones his first interview as 1980 World Champion on the rostrum in Montreal. *(DPPI/Action-Plus)*

Left: One for Frank. The boss celebrates victory after a saloon car race for team managers at Brands Hatch. *(Sporting Pictures)*

Reutemann leads Jones in the 1980 Spanish GP. Pironi's Ligier follows. *(Sporting Pictures)*

Keeping track. Frank mans the pit wall at Zolder in 1981. *(Sporting Pictures)*

Charlie and Keke. Crichton-Stuart and Rosberg check lap times on the computer during the Finn's second season with the team in 1983. *(Sporting Pictures)*

Above: Keke Rosberg's persistence and quick reactions gave Williams a rare victory at Dallas with the troublesome Honda-powered FW09 in 1984. *(DPPI/Action-Plus)*

Below: Two weeks after his accident, F1 team owners and personnel send a message to Frank from Nelson Piquet's front-row Williams at the first race of the 1986 season in Brazil. *(DPPI/Action-Plus)*

Can this be true?

I could see they were scratching around at the back of the field with an old March but, whatever the cost, I wanted to get into racing. It meant a huge pay cut but, if this didn't work, I thought I was young enough to get out and make a normal career. It was worth a gamble.

I was interviewed by both Frank and Patrick. It had boiled down to two applicants and I think, to be honest, Patrick wanted the other guy. But it was immediately apparent that Frank had a mercurial personality and a tremendous enthusiasm for racing. He asked me a few questions about what had happened at previous Grands Prix and, because it was my passion at the time, I knew all the answers. I've never asked him since, but I think that swung it. Frank preferred me – and he won out.

I arrived in September. Very little of the new car had been drawn; certainly, nothing was made. And yet the car was ready for the launch in early December and then a test prior to Christmas. You would struggle to do that these days.

Oatley is well qualified to make the comparison. He has since gone on to head the design team at McLaren, one of the leaders in the technology race which became rampant in Formula One during the 1990s.

It was very different in 1977/8. Nowadays, almost everything bar the engine is made in-house. Then, you bought a gearbox from Hewland, the radiators were the same as those used on a VW Golf, and the engine installation was very simple. There weren't that many pieces to draw. I remember we took the car for its first run, not long after the launch, at Brands Hatch and it was bitterly cold. It gave us no idea of how competitive we might be. But it certainly looked like a nice neat car.

It would turn out to be surprisingly fast, although Frank was not there to see FW06 make its race debut. The relentless search for additional sponsorship kept him away from the first race in Argentina, where the inevitable teething problems saw Jones retire when a vapour-lock in the system starved the engine of fuel. In Buenos Aires, Jones had qualified in the middle of the grid, which was about as far forward as the team could reasonably expect to be.

The next race was in Brazil. Frank flew into Rio de Janeiro, where he received a considerable shock. On the second day of practice, Jones was eighth fastest, ahead of notables such as world champion Niki Lauda in a Brabham and, significantly for Frank, the Wolf of Jody Scheckter. If Williams was surprised, then so were Goodyear, now engaged in a fierce tyre war with Michelin. Far from having to make do with the cast-offs of others or, at best, the standard Goodyear tyres earmarked for the also-rans, Frank found himself being offered the softer and faster rubber normally reserved for the likes of Lotus (the winner in Argentina) and McLaren. This was a major breakthrough, a signal that his team was being taken very seriously indeed.

Frank could scarcely cope with the rapid elevation to the hierarchy. In an interview with Doug Nye for his book *Racers*, Williams said: 'I was almost speechless. It was a completely new world for me. I had difficulty coping with the enormity of it. Alan was among the quick boys. For years, I had become accustomed just to hanging in there hoping to qualify and now we were showing signs of becoming truly competitive once again.'

In the race, Jones finished eleventh, five laps behind the winning Ferrari of Carlos Reutemann. That looked like the Williams of old, but the reality was quite different. A wheel bearing problem had induced difficulties with the brakes and handling, Jones having to stop three times to change tyres (this was in the days before refuelling and scheduled pit stops) but, throughout the race, Jones had shown the steely determination which would become his hallmark. He was the fastest Goodyear runner.

Frank had the nagging feeling that this might not last. During practice for the next race in South Africa, Jones crashed and damaged the car. Fortunately, by this stage the team had built a second car (which Jones was actually driving at the time) but engine trouble in the original car (coupled with a severe head cold for Jones) kept the combination in eighteenth place on the grid. So much for the moment of glory in Brazil.

Not quite. Frank was astonished when Jones, forgetting his personal discomfort, sliced through the field during the race and worked his way into fourth place. Indeed, he might have had a go at taking third but for the debilitating effects of the heat. Even so, this was a major milestone for Williams Grand Prix Engineering. The new team had scored their first championship points. Williams travelled to California for the fourth round of the series with genuine expectation rather than the usual dose of over-optimistic hope. They were not to be disappointed. Or, at least, not in the short term.

The United States Grand Prix West was run over the streets of Long Beach, a spectacular combination which punished machinery and taxed the drivers' accuracy and reflexes. Jones really got his teeth into the circuit and qualified eighth, alongside James Hunt and ahead, once again, of Scheckter's Wolf. And that was just the start of it. Once the race got under way, Head and Williams began to realise the true worth of their driver. Proving that South Africa had not been a fluke, Jones attacked. At the end of the first lap, he was sixth. By lap ten, he was fifth. There had been an element of good fortune thanks to the retirement of John Watson's Brabham from second place, but Jones's passing of the Lotus of Mario Andretti, destined to become world champion that year, was the product of pure aggression. When Niki Lauda retired and Gilles Villeneuve crashed out of the lead, Jones found himself in second place – and closing on the leader, Reutemann.

Frank Williams simply could not believe what he was seeing. This was confirmation that he had a driver who was truly world class, a 'racer' of the kind Frank truly appreciated. A Williams car was holding second place. On merit. It was nothing short of miraculous.

Then the full-width nose wing on the FW06 began to collapse. Slowly at first, the outer edges gradually drooping towards the track. When the engine began to misfire, Jones could not help but drop back to an eventual seventh place. Patrick Head was furious with himself. This was not a miscalculation. During pre-season tests, he had discovered precisely where the strengthening ribs inside the wing needed to be. The concept had come from the March raced the previous year and this particular wing, from the March, had been brought along as a spare. It should never have been put on FW06 without first revising the strengthening ribs to suit. But it was. One of many lessons to be learned as the team found its feet.

There were no championship points from Long Beach and yet Jones and the Williams-Ford had more than made their mark, not least by establishing a new lap record during the race. With Monaco – another street race – next on the agenda, there was every chance that Jones could pick up where he left off. That would suit Frank very well as his sponsorship negotiations continued at a similar pace.

When Frank accepted £30,000 from Saudia in 1977, the money was useful, but nothing to get excited about. More important would be the vote of confidence from the state-owned airline. This was the key which Williams hoped would eventually unlock the door to the oil-rich kingdom and give access to untapped sources of sponsorship. Saudia had increased its support to £100,000 for 1978. That brought additional credibility to the Williams effort in a part of the world which knew next to nothing about Grand Prix racing. If Formula One was good enough for Saudia, then Frank would be operating from a position of strength when putting his proposals to other major companies in Saudi Arabia. The problem would be getting in to see them in the first place.

Cue Charles Crichton-Stuart. Frank's old mate had left the motor racing scene for a period. Having flown with the RAF, he had been operating as a private pilot for businessmen such as Sir Hugh Fraser, the boss of Harrods. When plans to fly for Lord (Alexander) Hesketh fell through, Crichton-Stuart turned to selling cars. Expensive ones, of course. A period with H. R. Owen in Kensington brought him into contact with Prince Sultan bin Salman. Charlie sold him a Ferrari. When the twenty-two-year-old Prince moved out of the Dorchester Hotel and on to the United States in late 1977 to study at Denver University, Charlie also began to sell him the idea of motor racing sponsorship. He paid a flying visit with Frank to Colorado. Their proposal was good enough to persuade Prince Sultan to bring it to the attention of his family in Riyadh.

In January 1978, Frank flew to Saudi Arabia where Prince Sultan introduced him to his cousin, Prince Muhammed bin Fahd, the second eldest son of King Fahd. After a brief audience with the Prince, Frank came away with nothing more than a promise of assistance. The reception had been positive but, since Williams was not entirely sure of how business deals operated in this part of the world, it was difficult to know what would happen next. The impetus for the second phase came from an unexpected direction.

Prince Muhammed operated an international trading

company by the name of Albilad. The company's interests in Britain were looked after by Jonathan Aitken, at that time the Conservative MP for Thanet. Not long after the visit to Riyadh, Williams was asked to call on Aitken and provide background to the team. This was duly done, Williams being no further on in his quest to elicit a firm commitment. And yet, throughout, there was the feeling that anything could happen.

Williams heard nothing until he received a call saying that Prince Muhammed was in the country and a visit from Frank might be appropriate. Needing no second bidding, Frank not only went to London, he took his racing car with him and unloaded it in Park Lane. Right outside the front door of the Dorchester Hotel. In the rush hour. When Prince Muhammed emerged to see FW06 with the Albilad name on it, the deal was as good as done. If the Saudia sponsorship had provided the key, recognition from Prince Muhammed would turn the lock.

Which brings us to Monaco, the fifth round of the 1978 championship. Practice had not been without its problems, Jones qualifying in ninth place. Not long after the start, a haze of blue smoke indicated that all was not well with the Williams. A stud had come adrift from the oil tank and it was obvious to the team that the engine would not last. Under normal circumstances, Frank would have pulled Jones into the pits and saved the team the cost of an expensive engine rebuild. But, on this occasion, Williams let him continue, the Australian hanging on to Villeneuve's Ferrari and the leading bunch of cars. Frank was only too aware that the race was being watched on television by a group of influential Saudis in a hotel suite in Paris and, even closer to the action, Prince Muhammed was track-side in Monte Carlo. Far better, Frank reasoned, to have his car in the thick of the action for the best part of an hour and retire dramatically rather than have it parked in pristine condition in the pits after a handful of laps. Sure enough, the oil ran out before half distance, although Jones did help by switching off the engine before the internals were destroyed completely. In one respect, the damage may have been done. In another, good was to come from the plan to put on a show.

Prince Muhammed had been accompanied by Mansour Ojjeh, a young Franco-Saudi whose family owned Techniques d'Avant Garde (TAG). Founded by Akram Ojjeh, Mansour's father, TAG dealt in all manner of businesses, ranging from arms deals (mainly on behalf of the Saudi Ministry of Defence) to marketing the Canadair Challenger executive jet. Charlie Crichton-Stuart acted as liaison between the team and its Saudi guests, a post he would assume on a full-time basis with WGPE at the end of the year. Mansour Ojjeh could see the benefits of an association between his advanced technology company and Formula One. He followed the progress of Saudia-Williams with more than a passing interest.

On paper, the subsequent results were not particularly impressive: tenth, eighth, retired, fifth place in France, then four retirements in a row, followed by thirteenth place at Monza. The reality was quite different, Jones consistently running in the first six and frequently in the top three. Indeed, he might have won the British Grand Prix were it not for the mixture of bad luck and mechanical failures which affect any team finding its feet. In Britain, for instance, a driveshaft had broken when Jones was lying second (behind Scheckter's Wolf, which was also destined for retirement). It was discovered that the driveshaft had come from the first batch delivered by a new supplier. The supplier had not carried out the crack tests asked for by Patrick Head because time was short and the supplier did not think it that important. His lesson learned, Head implemented a series of double checks to ensure such a failure would not occur again. It was another part of the learning process concerning the implementation of quality control. Then there was bad luck, such as at Monza when a valve of a type rejected some time before by Goodyear somehow found its way onto a tyre fitted to Jones's car and caused a pit stop for a replacement while he was lying fifth. Tyre changing had not reached the super-fast art it is today. Jones rejoined at the back of the field and set the fifth fastest lap on his way to a distant thirteenth place, another sign of his refusal to give up.

If the team was impressed with that, they were to be quietly in awe of his response when potentially serious problems struck at the next race in the United States. It was to be a weekend when Frank Williams and, in particular, Patrick Head would go through every emotion in the Grand Prix lexicon. The first practice session at Watkins Glen had not been running long when Head experienced the sickening feeling which comes with knowing your driver has crashed. A number of questions run through a designer's mind. Is the driver okay? Did he make a mistake? Or did something break? And, if so, was it my fault? Everything was answered at once when an ashen-faced Jones returned to the pits on foot and, without saying a word, tossed a broken bolt in Head's direction. The sinking feeling in the pit of his stomach increased ten-fold when Patrick realised that this was not a manufacturing problem. The bolt, designed to hold one of the wheels in place, had sheared because it was not man enough for the job. Head had no one to blame but himself.

Not that he was the sort of person to look for excuses. Any thought of self-pity was banished by the need to find an answer. And quickly. If one bolt was inadequate, then the same would apply to the other three on the car. *And* the four in place on the spare car, which Jones was ready to climb into and continue his practice as if nothing had happened. Williams accepted Head's judgement completely when he said Jones had to forget about practice for the rest of the day. Patrick did not allow himself to think about having to tell them to forget about the rest of the weekend if he could not find a solution.

The team located a heat treatment company and Crichton-Stuart used his persuasive powers on the owner, who was neither interested in working all night nor becoming involved with racing cars, an area he knew nothing about and a risky one when it came to the product liability laws which dominated commercial life in the United States. Lengthy tests and calculations were carried out in this dusty, dirty and unbearably hot workshop. By dawn the following morning, the job had been done to Head's satisfaction.

The four bolts were rushed back to the circuit and fitted in time for final practice. Jones arrived, didn't ask any questions, climbed into the car – and put it onto third place on the grid. It was a steely performance from a man who, through no fault of his own, had suffered a massive accident in the sister car fewer than twenty-four hours before. Better than that, he would finish a brilliant second in the race. The car performed perfectly. Nineteen years later, Jones continued to play down the incident even though the shunt could have had serious consequences:

Well, yes, it could have been a bloody big one. It was through a real quick left-hander and, at the time, Watkins Glen did not have a particularly good record when it came to crash barriers. It could have been a particularly nasty shunt. But I got away with it.

When I came in the next day, Patrick assured me that the problem had been dealt with. And once Patrick said that then, bang! That was it. I had absolute blind faith in Patrick's ability –

and still do. I just dismissed it immediately. I mean, if a racing driver is going to dwell on that, then he may as well dwell on every other bloody thing that the designer has done.

The Watkins Glen incident had been a stiff test for the team and a measure of their driver as they struggled along making the most of the little they had. Neil Oatley recalled the working conditions of the time:

I went to a few races in the middle of the season and it was pretty much a hand-to-mouth existence. We had just two cars but we only had two tiny trucks. I can't remember where Frank had got one of them from, but when we went to load the car for the first time on the rising ramps, as soon as we started to crank the car up the struts supporting the ramp began to bend.

Each car had its own truck; they were too small to carry two cars. The second truck broke down on the way to Austria and some of the parts needed for the first car were on the second truck. The night before practice began, we didn't have exhausts for the car and we tried to borrow from other teams in the hope that the tail pipes would be in the right position. The truck eventually arrived during the night and we just about had the car ready for practice. That was fairly typical of the operation at the time.

We were short of money and I remember paper bags, filled with cash, arriving from some of the Arab sponsors. Frank's reputation was such that we couldn't have credit, so almost everything bought from outside had to be cash. We could only buy enough gear ratios to get us through the next race. Vans had to go back and forth to the suppliers as and when we had the cash. It was actually a more expensive way of doing things but we had to live from one week to the next. But at least things were better than they had been. We used to hear stories about the mechanics dropping their tools and running to the bank after receiving their cheques. It was never that bad in 1978. Things had improved!

Williams finished the season with eleven points. That was impressive enough but everyone realised the potential was there to double that score at the very least. Frank could scarcely believe that his team was a force to be reckoned with. No more would he be considered an also-ran, a back-of-the-grid make-weight.

With that had come the responsibility of giving a driver of Jones's potential the tools to do the job. The bolt failure at Watkins Glen had been a sobering experience, particularly for Head. It would help establish the standards of engineering excellence and integrity which would become a hallmark of the team. By now, of course, Patrick was convinced he would be staying on board. The move to Williams had been the right one:

I think working with Alan in 1978, with a car which I had more or less designed exclusively, I went through the period of thinking, 'Well, this is all a bit of fun and maybe I'll go and do something else next year,' to thinking, 'Actually, this is quite good and, if we put our heads down, we could maybe achieve something and perhaps win a Grand Prix.' In 1977, we had been just jousting at giants. But in 1978, we were actually starting to annoy a few people . . .

CHAPTER FIVE

The first is the best

Frank could barely keep up with the pace of events as the first race of the 1979 season beckoned. Williams had won back their FOCA membership and, since FOCA had a preference for two-car teams, it made economic sense for Williams Grand Prix Engineering to follow the party line. The cost of designing and building the first car would not be repeated with subsequent chassis and yet having two cars in the field would increase the chances of success as well as giving the sponsors more exposure.

Frank was commuting regularly between England and Saudi Arabia as he chased up contacts presented by his association with Saudia and Albilad. Prince Muhammed gently leaned on associates at Dallah Avco, an airport maintenance company which, in truth, would not gain a lot from a link with Formula One. Similarly, Bin Laden, a road builder, and Baroom, a steel and cement merchant, were hardly expecting a massive increase in turnover just because their names were being carried on a racing car in Belgium or Spain. But, if it was good enough for Prince Muhammed then, on his say, it was good enough for them. It was image rather than commerce.

The problem was, it took time for the decisions to be made and the details to be agreed upon. The business culture in Saudi was different to anything Frank had come across before. And he thought he had seen everything. He was running himself ragged as he worked in the searing heat and humidity of Saudi Arabia, but the end result – sponsorship heading towards seven figures – was worth the effort. It was a massive sum by Frank's previous standards. And it was being consumed faster than he had imagined possible. The team's budget was in excess of £500,000 and much of it was being directed towards a completely new car.

The design rethink had been instigated by Colin Chapman, the genius behind Lotus Cars. Mario Andretti had won the 1978 World Championship in a car which had introduced 'ground effect', a revolutionary concept which allowed the car to corner much faster than anything which had gone before. Chapman had discovered that, by enclosing inverted wings on either side of the car, the effect would be the reverse of an aircraft wing. Instead of causing the car to rise, it would be pulled towards the track, thus increasing the grip of the tyres under braking, while cornering, and during acceleration on the way out. Patrick Head, along with every designer in Formula One, recognised that he had to follow a similar theme. It would involve the use of a wind tunnel, something a Formula One team in the nineties cannot afford to be without. But, when the design of FW07 began in mid-1978, Head had no idea what he was going to learn. Indeed, he hardly knew where to find a wind tunnel.

Lotus had been using a quarter-scale tunnel at Imperial College in London. When Head managed to book time at the same facility, he was pleasantly surprised by the success of what he had in mind for the new car. And he was even more startled when a comparison, using a model of the existing car, FW06, showed just how inefficient it had been. Yet, despite venturing into an exciting new area which presented all manner of possibilities, Head chose to remain conservative in his specification rather than adopt a pioneering spirit at this crucial stage in the development of WGPE. It was to be a typically sensible decision. Chapman, perhaps carried away by the success of his 1978 car, had taken the ground effect theory a stage further. It was to be a step too far, the 1979 Lotus proving almost undriveable, thus demonstrating how much of a black art the design of Formula One cars could be.

Head's pragmatism was also governed by lingering memories of that mechanical failure at Watkins Glen. Every calculation was double-checked and confirmed. This took time, particularly as the design staff remained small by comparison with the likes of Lotus and Tyrrell. Williams had been joined by Ross Brawn and Frank Dernie, an aerodynamicist. Brawn, a bespectacled engineer, had worked briefly with Williams at the time of the Wolf take-over before leaving to spend 1977 travelling Europe with the March Formula Three team. Brawn was just as hungry as Williams and Head to succeed, but had you told him he would one day mastermind Michael Schumacher's double world championship with Benetton before becoming technical director at Ferrari, he would have said there was more chance of Williams becoming the dominant force in world motor racing for the best part of a decade.

I had arrived at Bennet Road just after the Walter Wolf take-over. It was quite a big outfit then and I was interviewed by Patrick. I discovered years later that I was his second choice! Maybe that was because I was just out of college but, for whatever reason, the first choice didn't take the job. So, I was in.

I did all sorts of jobs and then, at the end of that year, Frank was ousted and Peter Warr came in. There was nothing wrong with Peter, but he wasn't who I had gone to work for. Peter got up at a meeting and said if anyone didn't feel like supporting the team in the future, they should say so and leave. A short while afterwards, I said I really wanted to try something else. It was all fairly amicable.

I did a spell in Formula Three, which was being a mechanic, doing engineering, truck driving, the whole thing. It was a great experience for a lad who had hardly travelled.

Frank and Patrick asked me to go and work for them. When I arrived at Station Road there weren't that many of us at the time. I did machining, acted as a mechanic, did some drawing. When you only have a limited number of people, you have to be pretty flexible.

Frank had tremendous drive; so did Patrick. But it continued to be tight financially. They were pretty strung out and there were a few times when it looked a bit shaky. Even when they started to do well, Frank would extend himself as far as possible. There were a few times when we had the meter man come round to cut us off, but we managed to persuade him not to.

It was great for me. Those sort of experiences don't exist any more. Join a Formula One team now and you are one of over 100, usually more than 200 people. I was one of eleven. I drew bits, I machined them, I put them on the car. You had to be ready for anything. And, by now, Williams had to build enough cars for two drivers.

Jones had agreed terms as long ago as the previous July. On his trips back and forth to the Middle East, Frank had been giving thought to a suitable number two for 1979. He wanted someone reliable and reasonably quick. He wanted a driver who would bring the car home without running up a considerable repair bill, someone who would get on with Jones and not have ideas above his station. Clay Regazzoni fitted the bill perfectly.

The Swiss had turned in one or two magnificent drives when at the peak of his power with Ferrari. When the Italian team dismissed him at the end of 1976 for no other apparent reason than that he had been around too long, Regazzoni spent a couple of indifferent seasons with Ensign and Shadow, two middle-order teams which had just been overtaken by Williams in 1978. Regazzoni was only too pleased to take up Frank's offer.

If Regazzoni thought otherwise after a couple of months, he kept his opinions to himself. Tenth, fifteenth and ninth in the first three races were hardly results worth writing home about. But Jones had not done much better, finishing ninth in Argentina and retiring in Brazil and South Africa. This was proving to be another lesson for Frank Williams who had thought, in the absence of the new car which had not yet been completed, that the trusty FW06 would still be competitive in the opening races. Not so. It was a sign of how everyone else had been working hard over the winter on their new cars. Williams were being left far behind. It was self-evident that FW07 would need to be good.

The new car appeared for the first time in the pit lane on race morning at Long Beach, too late to run in the US Grand Prix West. FW07 had been completed at Didcot and flown to California in readiness for initial testing at the Ontario Motor Speedway. At least it gave the team a fillip, as did third place in the race for Jones, the old car working at less of a disadvantage on a street circuit which did not favour ground effect. The same would not be true for the next race at the permanent track at Jarama in Spain. Time was marching on. FW07 would need to be on the pace straight away and part of the team's problem lay in the fact that the money due from Saudi Arabia had not been released. Fortunately, the cash flow problem was finally resolved and two FW07s were made ready for the opening of the European sector of the championship.

Neither Jones nor Regazzoni qualified inside the first ten in Spain and neither driver finished due to various technical problems. It was not an auspicious start, and yet the team had been buoyed by certain aspects of Jones's performance. He had set the second-fastest lap of the race before stopping with gearbox trouble and, during the warm-up in the morning, he had been faster than Andretti's Lotus. Andretti was not alone in believing that the Williams must have been running with less than a full load of fuel. Frank Williams knew that it had been brim-full – but made no comment.

There was no disguising the full potential of FW07 at the next race in Belgium. Jones qualified on the second row, Regazzoni on the fourth. When Clay got himself involved in an accident on the second lap, Alan was settling down behind the Ligier-Fords which had been the pace-setters during most of the races thus far in 1979.

Jones was completely at ease. The car felt terrific. He had no trouble at all in taking the lead on lap twenty-four. Another milestone had been reached. This was the first time since Piers Courage in 1969 that a Williams-entered car had led a Grand Prix. More importantly, it was the first time for a car bearing Frank's name. Jones extended his lead by three seconds in as many laps. All being well, he was going to win this race.

On lap forty, with thirty to go, Jones failed to appear. The Williams was parked on the grass verge, an electrical problem having caused the engine to cut out. Jones trudged back to the pits. He should have been reasonably happy. The body language suggested otherwise.

Twenty-four hours later, his frustration had barely subsided. Jones drove his new Mercedes-Benz 6.9 onto the Zeebrugge/Dover ferry, grabbed his leather briefcase from the back seat and marched up to the cafeteria. Not for Jones the luxury of the restaurant. He did not seem to notice the bizarre juxtaposition of a gold Rolex watch above a large hand carrying a tray of fish and chips and a mug of tea. He sat down beside a journalist preparing his Grand Prix follow-up piece for the next day's *Guardian* newspaper. If the writer had been searching for an interesting angle, one was about to fall into his lap. Rather than eulogise about the progress at Williams and the promise of FW07, Jones proceeded to criticise his team in terms which left no doubt about his displeasure. The writer's pen flew across his notebook which of course was precisely what Jones had intended. The headline in the next day's *Guardian* read 'Reliability weak point at Williams'. If that summary seemed rather harsh, Jones was to be proved right at the next race in Monaco. Unfortunately, the Australian would also demonstrate that he was not beyond criticism himself.

It was not unreasonable to expect Jones to qualify, if not on the front row of the grid, then at least on the second, a vital prerequisite at a cramped circuit on which overtaking is almost impossible during the race. The trouble began when the team could not get the Ford-Cosworth engine to run cleanly throughout the first practice session. With the problem sorted out in time for the second practice on the same day, more time was lost when a cracked exhaust bracket had to be wired as a temporary measure. Bearing in mind Jones's comments about the team's poor preparation, he was working himself into a right state as he sat in the cockpit listening to his rivals thrash round the track as they established grid positions. When the repairs were complete, Jones tore out of the pits and crashed halfway round that lap. 'It's the first time I have ever seen him do anything remotely silly,' said Head. It would not be the last time either. Jones qualified in a disappointing ninth place but, during the race, he had worked his way into third by half distance. Then he touched a barrier and damaged the steering and suspension, Williams number 27 joining the growing list of retirements.

Once again, sponsors from Saudi Arabia were on hand to watch 'their' cars. And it was fortunate there were two, for

Regazzoni was doing rather well. In fact, he was rapidly becoming the man of the moment. Having started from sixteenth place on the grid, the experienced Swiss had allowed the race to settle down and some of the more hotheaded members of the competition to eliminate themselves against the waiting kerbs and barriers. Regazzoni chose his moments and gradually moved forward, his teammate's retirement promoting him to fourth place. A pit stop for Jochen Mass moved Regazzoni into the top three, and that became second when Villeneuve's Ferrari broke its transmission. Regazzoni's Williams was now without second gear – a major handicap at a circuit with nothing but slow corners – but that did not prevent Clay from mounting a spectacular charge. Only the Ferrari of Jody Scheckter stood in the way of a Williams victory.

Despite the absence of second gear, and driving with a thrilling blend of neatness and aggression, Regazzoni reduced the lead from thirteen seconds to one second. As the red car and the white car set off on their final lap, they were nose to tail. Regazzoni lunged at the Ferrari as they sped downhill towards Mirabeau Corner. But Scheckter had the move covered. Victory was his. Nevertheless, Regazzoni and Williams had brought the race alive.

There was a dramatic swing in fortune at the next Grand Prix in France when Renault scored their first win amid emotional scenes. Renault had come into Grand Prix racing in 1977 and persevered with a turbocharged engine, a technical route which had been open to every engine manufacturer but rejected on the grounds of cost, complexity and the belief that turbos would be uncompetitive. Jones was fourth and Regazzoni fifth, bit players on a stage which seemed increasingly likely to be dominated by big manufacturers with huge budgets and unparalleled technical resources.

That was Frank's worry as his cars, with their off-the-shelf Ford-Cosworth engines, were loaded onto the transporter bound for Didcot. The next race was the British round of the championship. All Williams could think about was the effect the powerful turbocharged Renaults would have on the wide-open spaces of Silverstone. The Saudia-Williams pair would be lucky if they could finish third and fourth. Events during the next few days would almost banish that thought completely. The Williams-Fords were to prove embarrassingly fast.

At first, the pre-race test session at Silverstone showed that, in terms of lap times, the Williams was there, or thereabouts. Meanwhile Frank Dernie, the team's aerodynamicist, had been perfecting a faring which would smooth the airflow beneath the engine. Such items are commonplace on even the most humble racing car today, but in 1979 this was virgin territory. Dernie's calculations and tests had shown a potential improvement in efficiency. Frank's stopwatch was about to prove the point in the most dramatic fashion.

When the faring was eventually put in place, Jones was rattling off lap times which were six seconds under the three-year-old F1 lap record and two seconds better than anything he had managed during the previous day. It was true that Jones's car had been fitted with an engine which turned out to be particularly strong (each engine varied for no obvious reason) but it was the ease with which he was able to produce the fast times which shook the opposition. Frank, perched in his usual position by the pit wall, stopwatch in each hand, could hardly believe what he was seeing. During an interview for *Racers*, he told Doug Nye:

As I handled the watches that fantastic feeling swept over me again. It was just like the previous year in Brazil, or at Brands Hatch when Alan was suddenly fourth fastest. I just could not believe after all those years of mentally straining and wrestling, thrashing about trying to make things come good, sometimes thinking here we are, this is it – and BANG, straining and struggling once again. And here Alan was going record breaking in almost unprecedented style.

It hardly seemed to matter – or, at least, not to the British press – that Renault were absent from the test session. The turbos, for all their power, would be hard pressed to match the Williams. The Williams team was the centre-piece of every national daily sports page at some point during the Grand Prix weekend. When Jones claimed pole position – another first for Frank – with a breathtaking lap which averaged 145 mph, it would have taken a brave man to bet against Williams achieving his long-cherished dream of winning a Grand Prix. One or two members inside the team, however, were not so sure.

Reliability continued to be a worry, particularly on the numerous straights and fast corners at Silverstone where the engines were worked hard for long periods. Cosworth had been having difficulties with abnormally high oil consumption on their latest batch of engines and Williams were advised to change the engine in the pole position car for a fresh one on the eve of the race. Jones's mechanics, Wayne Eckersley and John Jackson, carried out the routine swap, finishing at 11.30 p.m. on Friday in time for a beer and some well-earned sleep. As a final act, they prepared to run the engine, only to discover that the fuel pump was not working. There was nothing for it but to take the engine out and start all over again. Eckersley, a straight-talking Australian in the manner of his driver, was not best pleased. They finished at 5.30 a.m. and never did get to bed. No matter. Victory would chase away any tiredness.

That appeared to be the case as Jones, with Jabouille's

Renault in pursuit, led the field at the end of the first lap. As Jones began to ease out his lead, Jabouille was making a mental note that the engine in the back of the Williams was one of the most powerful he had come across. The efforts of the Williams mechanics had clearly been worthwhile and not a hint of the feared problem with oil consumption.

For thirty-seven of the scheduled sixty-eight laps, Jones remained in command. Then, as he passed the pits, Frank Williams noticed a white mist swirling from the back of the leading car. 'Something's gone,' he said, with barely a flicker of emotion. 'I'll give him two more laps.' Sure enough, Jones failed to appear on schedule at the end of the thirty-ninth. When he did come into view, he was trickling slowly down the pit lane, the engine coolant having drained away through a crack in the neck of the water pump. The car, with smoke rising from the engine, was quickly surrounded by Williams team members as they pushed it towards their garage, Eckersley unscrewing the engine cover locks as he stumbled alongside. There was no point. Jones was already climbing from the cockpit, bitterly disappointed by yet another mechanical failure. He had not put a foot wrong. He had built up a lead of twenty-five seconds and then taken care of the engine by reducing the revs. Short of freewheeling through the corners, there was nothing more he could do. And now this.

Frank Williams, showing absolutely no emotion, cast a quick glance along the pit lane, had his suspicions confirmed when he saw the hobbled car, and then returned his attention to the track. After all, a Williams was still leading the British Grand Prix!

Almost forgotten in the excitement of the weekend, Regazzoni had been doing his usual competent job as number two. He had qualified on the second row, made a brilliant start (a Regazzoni speciality) to take the lead initially before dropping into a respectful third place on the first lap. When Jabouille disappeared into the pits to change tyres, Regazzoni was perfectly placed to pick up the pieces when his team leader fell by the wayside. And, as if to show his pursuers that he was not to be trifled with, Regazzoni immediately set the fastest lap of the race and extended his new-found lead to fifteen seconds. Once again, only a technical problem would deny Frank Williams his first Grand Prix win.

It was almost too much for Ginny Williams to take. The birth in 1976 of Claire, a sister for Jonathan, had made travelling to the races abroad impractical. But at least Silverstone was not far from home, Frank and Ginny having moved to an old rectory in need of repair in Aston Tirrold, a village near Didcot. As events unfolded, Ginny began to doubt the wisdom of being at the track. This race was tearing at her emotions. After consoling Jones's wife, Beverley, Ginny returned to the pits dreading that the same thing might happen to Regazzoni.

Frank sat by the pit wall, studying his stopwatch and lap chart, his face deadpan. As Williams counted down the laps, Jones, having changed out of his overalls, slipped onto the pit wall, said goodbye and quickly left the circuit with Beverley. Under any other circumstance, Jones would have stayed for a beer and enjoyed the post-race garden party atmosphere unique to Silverstone. But not today. The win had been there for the taking. He expected it. He had earned it. Everyone said so. But he did not wish to bask in self-pity. By the time he was halfway to his house in west London, Regazzoni was about to make history for Francis Owen Garbett Williams.

Five years before, Frank would never have thought it possible. Neither would Ginny. As the countdown continued, the pressure mounted. For the first time, the Williams garage became the focus of television crews and photographers as they homed in to capture the story of the winners. When Regazzoni crossed the line, there were tears among crew members: a mixture of relief, euphoria and exhaustion. The entire pit lane rushed to congratulate Frank. His rivals knew what he had been through, they appreciated exactly what this meant. The man himself was virtually speechless. Neil Oatley was the engineer in charge of Regazzoni's car:

It was a very nice feeling for me. In a relatively short period of time, I had come into motor racing and here I was working on the car which had just won the British Grand Prix. It's difficult to imagine a team starting up these days and winning halfway through its second year as a constructor.

Having said that, it was not as emotional as I thought it would be. Frank is not one to show his emotion, not even on a day like this. Not in public. I think, also, with Alan retiring and then leaving the circuit, that put a little bit of a dampener on things for Frank.

Even though there had been a collective groan from the 110,000 crowd when Jones disappeared, Regazzoni had filled the breach in more ways than one. For reasons which the Swiss driver found difficult to understand, the British spectators had taken him to their hearts. They had enjoyed his cut and thrust driving during his days with Ferrari, admired his sunny approach to his racing, appreciated his sportsmanship. Above all, they were won over by Clay's bandit grin. And that was very much in evidence as he stood on the rostrum and basked in the rapturous applause from the packed grandstand opposite the pits.

As the victory ceremony got under way, onlookers were puzzled when Clay insisted on passing the bottles of champagne to René Arnoux and Jean-Pierre Jarier, who had finished second and third for Renault and Tyrrell. Everyone knew that Clay liked a drink at the appropriate moment, but his refusal to handle alcohol in public was in deference to the team's sponsors, an astute move by Regazzoni on a day when Prince Muhammed was attending his first race.

Frank had arranged for his important guest to fly in by helicopter. It had been a glorious day when the Prince landed on the infield to witness Silverstone at its best. He had watched the race in its entirety and been intrigued by the reaction of the British public as they spilled over the grass safety banks and cheered Regazzoni throughout his lap of honour. Rather than leave immediately as planned, Prince Muhammed stayed in the motor home to talk to the team and enjoy the atmosphere. When it was time to go, he turned down the offer of a car to make the return journey to the helicopter pad, preferring to walk and take in the gentle warmth at the end of a perfect summer's day. Frank Williams could not have wished for more. And yet, quietly, he was still fretting over the water leak which robbed Alan Jones of victory. Meanwhile Regazzoni, on the departure of the Saudi guests, had got out the whisky.

As darkness closed in, Frank and Ginny eventually found themselves alone in the team's motor home. Nothing was said. There was no need. As they sat together on the bench seat, looking out at the deserted circuit which, a few hours earlier, had been a cauldron of passion and excitement, neither of them wanted the day to end. They had been through so much. This made the hardship worthwhile; irrelevant, almost. At midnight, they walked slowly to the car park and headed home. Despite the success which was to come to Williams Grand Prix Engineering, there would never be another day like Saturday 14 July 1979. The first is always the best.

CHAPTER SIX

Double top

The romance of the moment did not last long. Frank's routine remained unaltered the following morning. As usual on a Monday, he dropped Jonathan at school and arrived at Station Road shortly after nine a.m. On his way through the workshop, he spoke to every employee, thanking them for the part they had played. Meanwhile, in the office upstairs, the phone was ringing constantly with calls of congratulations from friends and colleagues. And on Frank's desk sat a telex from Enzo Ferrari. Mr Ferrari's team had won seventy-one Grands Prix but he obviously remembered the importance of the first.

Williams was touched. But that was put in perspective by the thought that Ferrari and the rest would be out to beat Williams in Germany in two weeks' time. Frank double-checked that he would be having his usual post-race briefing later that morning with Patrick Head. He had yet to see the race on television but there would be little opportunity for that now. Time, as ever, was pressing.

Despite Frank's caution and concern about the ability to repeat the Silverstone performance, Jones went on to score his first win for Williams by leading every lap in Germany, Regazzoni giving the team their first of many one-two finishes over the next two decades. Having got the taste,

Jones won again in Austria, Holland and Canada, making it four in total to place the Australian third in the series. Jody Scheckter, the new world champion, had won three races for Ferrari; Villeneuve, the runner-up, had taken just two victories.

The lesson here was that the Ferrari drivers had consistently racked up points throughout the season. Williams had lost too much ground in the beginning with FW06 while waiting for the new car to appear. The point had been noted. As Frank and Patrick had that debriefing on the Monday after Silverstone, plans were already under way with their car for 1980, the aim being to go testing during the winter and have it ready for the first race. Alan Jones had already agreed to drive with Williams for a third season and new contracts with the team's employees were also being finalised.

'What's next, Frank?' He seemed surprised that anyone should ask. 'You've got to keep thinking about the real reason you're in racing,' he said. 'You've got to have a go at winning the championship.' He stopped short of saying that everyone expected it. Not least the new sponsors he was taking on board for 1980. By now, though, some of his supporters were old friends.

On the day after Jones won his first race for Williams in Germany, Mansour Ojjeh flew the entire team to the next race in Austria in the TAG company's specially fitted Boeing 707. Ojjeh was becoming more and more engrossed in Formula One in general, and Williams in particular. It did not take much to persuade him to join his fellow Arabs as a sponsor of the team. This was all very well but, in the age of growing commercialism, it was not the bedrock of future planning. The Saudi involvement had been Frank's lifeline, but it could end just as quickly as it had begun. There had to be an alternative, a back-up which, in an ideal world, would work hand-in-hand with the Saudi sponsorship.

That very thought had occurred to Steve Herrick when the overseas sales director of Leyland Vehicles paid a visit to Long Beach in April 1979. Herrick was on a mission to sell bus chassis to an operator in Los Angeles when he took time off to watch a practice session for the Grand Prix. Apart from being impressed by the drama and international flavour of the occasion, his eye was drawn to the white car with Albilad and Saudia symbols on its flanks. The Arab market-place, awash with petrodollars, was wide open at a time when Leyland Vehicles was going through an ambitious phase of redevelopment. The morning spent in Long Beach gave Herrick food for thought as he flew back to England.

Three months later, Williams won their first Grand Prix in a blaze of publicity. The deal, for half of the 1980 budget which would be in excess of £2m, was concluded by September. The entry would be known as the Albilad-Williams Racing Team with cars referred to as Saudia-Leyland Williams. Leyland Vehicles could not have found a better way of earning recognition in their target area, even though the autocratic way of doing things in the Middle East did not sit easily at first with the commercial marketing methods which were a necessary fact of life in Europe.

Indeed, tact and diplomacy had to be employed at home. When the Leyland deal was announced in the forecourt of a hotel by London's Tower Bridge, a Williams was fired up for the benefit of the business and commercial vehicle media, new to the world of Formula One. When the V8, financed originally by Ford but designed and built by Cosworth Engineering in Northampton, was finally shut down, Frank pointedly referred to the engine as being a 'Cosworth'. Clearly, there could be no mention of Ford after signing a lucrative deal with one of their great rivals. That potential minor discomfort aside, the Leyland transaction was to be the first of many which would draw major names onto the bodywork of a Williams Formula One car in return for sponsorship worth millions and the use of a unique marketing tool on a global basis.

In 1980, the merry-go-round started in Argentina on 13 January and, as planned, the latest car, FW07B, had been ready for action some time before. As the title indicates, this was a modified version of the successful FW07. Head and his team had not been naive enough to think that they could ride into the new season and hope to pick up where they left off. As ever, they had no indication of the advances made elsewhere. After three races, Williams was trailing behind Renault despite the fact that Jones had won in Argentina, more through dogged persistence than anything else on a track which was crumbling in the searing heat. René Arnoux was leading the drivers' championship on eighteen points. Jones had scored thirteen, which was eleven more than his new team-mate.

Williams and Head had decided that the time had come to employ two top drivers. Regazzoni had served his purpose well as a reliable number two who had fitted in admirably with a team finding its feet. But he was not quick enough for their needs now that winning was expected as a matter of course. When Frank scrutinised the list of likely candidates, Carlos Reutemann stood out as the strongest contender. The Argentinian had won races with Ferrari and, after a disappointing season with Lotus, he was keen to re-establish himself, even more so following a disastrous start to 1980 when his Williams failed twice and a distant fifth place in South Africa had been his only finish.

In 1979, Reutemann had put his Lotus on the front row at Long Beach. Twelve months later, he went back to California with the same intention. It was not to be. Reutemann could manage no better than seventh, two places behind Jones. It was not what the team and drivers had hoped for, which was a pity in more ways than one since the Williams team had some influential guests on hand. The last time Prince Fahd had come to a race, Williams had won. The head of Albilad and his friends expected to see 'their' team win again.

On the night before the race, Frank and Charlie took Reutemann to meet the Prince and have dinner with Arab business associates. Sitting in on the evening was the sports editor of *Autocar*, Peter Windsor, who was also a good friend of Reutemann. Six years later, almost to the day, Windsor would be team manager for Williams and would survive the road crash which changed Frank's life. For now, however, Windsor was one of the most incisive and entertaining writers in Formula One. Watching intently from the side-lines that evening, Windsor noted:

Over dinner, the conversation is led by the Prince. He talks about American politics, British politics, the economy and racing. Frank is completely at ease, and you sense that there is indeed more than just a bond of business between the two. Frank is honest and determined – and that, for Fahd, is enough.

Finally back at the [Fahd's] apartment, where things are quieter, you notice the pictures on the walls. There is an official portrait of Fahd's uncle, the King; there is a copy of the front cover of *Time*, which features the King; and there are many small snapshot photos of Fahd with Frank and Fahd with the Williams car in 1978. We all sit down and Fahd says that he would like to officially welcome Carlos into the team and wish Frank the best of luck for Sunday. As a token of his feelings for Williams, he would like them to accept these small gifts. He gives Frank and Charlie a box each. Inside is a Rolex watch.

Windsor's race report, dispatched by telex to the *Autocar* offices in London the following evening, did not make happy reading for the growing band of supporters of Williams Grand Prix Engineering. Jones had been eliminated when Patrick Depailler, driving an Alfa Romeo, had shut out the Williams as the Australian made a legitimate move to snatch second place. Ironically, it was at exactly the same place where, several laps earlier, Reutemann had been forced into a spin by Depailler's team-mate. A driveshaft had snapped as Reutemann tried to make his angry departure from the scene. No points for Williams on the day a new name emerged as a threat for the 1980 World Championship: the race at Long Beach had been led from start to finish by the Brabham-Ford of Nelson Piquet. Jones was to hear much more of the Brazilian as the season unfolded.

Piquet failed to score points after spinning out of the next race in Belgium, Jones moving ahead by one point in the championship thanks to finishing second. The roles were to be reversed two weeks later when Piquet claimed four points in Monaco and Jones scored none after retiring from second place with a broken differential. Reutemann's luck changed for the good in Monte Carlo as he drove a beautifully measured race, waited for his moment and scored his first win for Frank. That was exactly what he had been paid to do on a day when Jones had fallen by the wayside. The win put Williams back on top of the constructors' championship, where they would stay for the remaining ten races, gradually easing into an unassailable lead. For Jones, the situation was not so clear-cut thanks to the advances of Nelson Piquet.

At the next race in Spain, however, Jones would have been forgiven for thinking that good fortune was on his side and nothing would stop him from taking the title. He went to the starting grid with an engine which was already showing signs of overheating. Applying caution, he dropped to fifth place in order to avoid the furious activity at the front. To growing amazement, Jones watched Reutemann's lead vanish as the second-place Ligier of Laffite crashed into the Williams due to a misunderstanding while lapping a back-marker (who, ironically, was driving a 1979 Williams bought from the team). Piquet inherited the lead but retired soon afterwards with mechanical trouble, elevating Jones to second place as he did his best to unsettle the leading Ligier of Didier Pironi. Jones could scarcely believe his luck when, twenty-three laps later, a front wheel fell off the Frenchman's car. With almost a minute in hand over the Arrows of Jochen Mass, Jones was able to nurse his car to maximum points.

Well, not quite. The Spanish race had become a pawn in a struggle for power between FISA, the sport's governing body, and FOCA, which had been gradually gathering strength and influence. Without going into the laborious detail, suffice to say that FISA had outlawed the Spanish race and declared that points scored would not count towards the championship. It was frustrating for Jones because, instead of now leading the points table on twenty-eight points, six ahead of Piquet, he was still in third place on nineteen, two fewer than Arnoux and three behind the leader, Piquet. No matter; Jones, given half a chance, would simply grind their faces into the dirt.

There is perhaps no more satisfying win for Williams and Jones than their victory at the next race in France. Ligier were the favourites to win at home when Laffite and Pironi took first and third places on the grid, with the Renault of Arnoux in between. Jones was fourth fastest, Reutemann fifth. At best, Frank hoped to have his cars finish third and fourth.

Throughout practice, while the local media focused on the blue Ligiers, the Williams team quietly got on with their preparations, assessing every possibility by trying various tyre compounds and wheel sizes, both while running with a full load of fuel and when half empty. The drivers could share the load because, thankfully, they liked similar set-ups to their cars. It meant that, while one was checking out tyre wear by running endless laps, the other could be working on the chassis set-up. It was a lesson in carefully managed tactical planning, something which Frank relished as he sat in his folding chair, placed high on a green packing case by the pit wall. The two drivers, their respective engineers, plus Patrick and Frank, then spent hours in their small motor home examining and discussing the information they had assembled. Meanwhile, the Ligier pit resembled a circus act as their prime sponsor, Gitanes cigarettes, organised a film shoot in the middle of an increasingly xenophobic atmosphere of expectation. The Williams crew, in the garage next door, looked on and said nothing.

The race ran to the French plan as the Ligiers and Arnoux shot into the lead, Jones biding his time. It was a gloriously hot midsummer's day in the south of France and, as the laps ticked by, the ferocious pace of the Ligiers began to play havoc with their front tyres, particularly through Courbe de Signes, the 170 mph corner at the end of the long back straight. Williams's homework was about to pay off: the tyres on Jones's car were perfect. With Arnoux having succumbed to Jones early on, the Australian bided his time, picking off one Ligier, then the other. By lap thirty-five of the fifty-four-lap race, Jones was in the lead. And there was nothing the Ligier drivers could do about it.

Given the ongoing dispute between FOCA, with its British teams, and the French-based FISA, this victory was sweet indeed. As Jones crossed the line, he slowed down to receive a large Union Jack from his chief mechanic, Ian Anderson, Jones then raising a finger briefly at the dignitaries looking dismally on before completing a victory lap with the red, white and blue flag flapping above his head. Not only had he defeated the French at home, his championship lead was now legal, with or without the points from Spain, Piquet having finished a distant fourth, with Arnoux fifth, ahead of a lacklustre Reutemann.

Understandably miffed, the French teams prepared to return the compliment at the next race, which happened to be on British soil. Once again they would fail, in almost identical circumstances. The Ligiers occupied the front row of the grid at Brands Hatch, with Jones and Reutemann lined up behind them. Since the British press had found little to shout about since James Hunt's heyday at the same circuit four years earlier, the Anglo-French needle match was fuelling jingoistic copy on the sports pages. As a result, there was no question about where the allegiance of the capacity crowd lay as the cars formed on the grid. The Grand Prix annual, *Autocourse*, takes up the story:

Jones had expected the Ligiers to take off at a fairly brisk pace but their incredible speed simply left him standing. Besides, he had enough to worry about for Piquet was pushing the Williams hard. Reutemann had fallen back to a lonely fifth.

Pironi [in the lead] had been going as hard as he was worth. When he slowed suddenly, it was obvious he was not simply easing his pace. Small cracks had begun to appear in his front wheel rims. The first hint the Ligier driver had was on lap 17 when his front-left tyre began to deflate. By lap 19, he was in the pits. Any thoughts of a quick return were thrown away by a chaotic stop which involved changing all four tyres and recovering from a stalled engine. Laffite was now in command, some nine seconds ahead of Jones who, in turn, had opened up a breathing space over Piquet.

That seemed to be the way of it until Laffite suffered a deflating rear tyre. But, instead of stopping at the pits, he attempted to carry on for one more lap. It was more than the tyre could take, the subsequent blow-out on the back stretch of the circuit sending the Ligier crashing out of the race, fortunately without injury to the driver. As Jones completed that lap and entered the natural amphitheatre around the start-finish area, he was left in no doubt that he had taken the lead:

I came into Clearways [the last corner before the pits] and I knew I was in the lead for sure. The fans were on their feet, waving programmes, beer cans, anything they could. They cheered me all the way round the circuit. It was an extraordinary feeling, particularly as the British Grand Prix was the one I had wanted to win most. I had lived in Britain for quite some time; it was where I had made my name in motor racing. It was my 'adopted' Grand Prix.

It was fortunate that the Ligiers had retired because, on this day, Jones had no answer to them thanks to a front tyre which had begun to blister. Typically, the point had not been lost on Frank. Despite winning, he was not satisfied. Speaking to Peter Windsor, Williams summed up the day in his typically intense manner:

When I walked out on the grid today, I said to myself that I had only been mediocre this weekend. There were so many people about, so many people to see, to talk to, so many functions and so on that I didn't do some of the things I should have done. Next year [at the British Grand Prix] we will be tougher on ourselves. This year we were lucky. Alan blistered a tyre and he won the race once the Ligiers had stopped. Next time we'll do it better.

Nonetheless, the win more than made up for Jones's disappointment at Silverstone twelve months before. Since then, Frank Williams had scored another nine victories; Jones had won eight of them. But, as he maintained a six-point lead over Piquet, it was crucial that there should be more victories in the remaining six races. On present form, there seemed no reason why Jones could not at least beat the Brabham driver although, with fast circuits in Germany and Austria next on the schedule, the more powerful Renaults were expected to come into their own.

That proved to be the case in Germany when the French cars led, and then retired on successive laps with valve spring failure. That let Jones into the lead, only for the Williams driver to lose it when he picked up a puncture thirteen laps later. A pit stop dropped him to third. But at least he was ahead of Piquet, the Brabham finishing fourth. The championship table showed Jones on forty-one points, Piquet second on thirty-four.

In Austria, Jones extended his lead to eleven points when he finished second (behind Jabouille's Renault) and Piquet struggled home fifth. With the fast, sweeping turns of Zandvoort, ideal territory for the Williams, next on the schedule, Jones was confident of victory. The championship was looking good. The Renaults caused a surprise by filling the front row of the grid but, when Jones simply drove round the outside of them at the first corner and pulled out a two-second lead by the end of the first lap, it was like stealing candy from a baby.

Even though Frank would never mention it, the loss of Piers Courage exactly ten years before must have been on his thoughts each time he walked through the gates that weekend. The paddock was surrounded by race track, the outward leg running behind the pits before swinging inwards briefly to a hairpin, and then away, over the crest of a sand dune and on towards the back section that had claimed Courage's life.

Any thoughts of that terrible day would have been far from Frank's mind at the end of the first lap as the white and green car swept past the pits with its two-second lead.

The race, and possibly the championship, appeared to be settled already.

Jones braked hard for the hairpin at the end of the straight, before a short burst of acceleration took him behind the paddock and into the next hairpin. He negotiated that without a problem but, as he floored the throttle and drifted the Williams towards the edge of the track, he glanced in his mirror (in search of the Renaults) a fraction too long and allowed the car to slide across the broad concrete kerb. And over it. The right-hand wheels dropped off the edge and, in the process, destroyed the side-skirt running the length of the side-pod. This skirt (illegal today) was essential to seal the passage of air passing beneath the side-pod and under the surface of the inverted wing, thus creating the so-called ground effect which helped pull the car onto the track. An ineffective side-skirt was as crippling as a punctured tyre. Jones had no alternative but to stop for a new one. It took three laps for the mechanics, working flat-out on a very fiddly job, to fit the replacement skirt. The championship story was rewritten there and then.

Jones stormed back and drove his heart out. He finished eleventh, three laps behind the winner – none other than Nelson Piquet. Jones's championship lead had been slashed to two points with three races to run.

Jones completed his slowing down lap and pulled up at the Williams pit. This time there were no mechanics descending on his car, no Frank Williams or Patrick Head poised to plug their headsets into the car. Everyone knew the driver needed to be left alone. Frank was aware that any comment or criticism would be superfluous. Jones flicked his belts aside and wriggled from the cockpit before pulling off his gloves and walking briskly away. As he went, he cast a backwards glance at the right-hand side-skirt. There was no need to ask what he was thinking. How could he have made such a stupid mistake? And, just to rub it in, the Brazilian national anthem rang out from the podium a hundred metres further down the pit lane.

That race was a complete disaster for me [Jones reflected later]. I had been a bit twitchy because everyone was going around saying 'Hello champ!' and stuff like that. I kept telling them not to say anything; it was too early. I said anything could happen. It did. I had quite a nasty accident during practice when my throttle stuck open. And then I threw away nine bloody points in the race. I couldn't believe it.

If Jones was feeling twitchy in Holland, then he began to show outward signs of anxiety two weeks later at Imola in Italy. He spun more than once during practice, his demeanour not helped by an engine failure and the fact that he had qualified sixth fastest. Reutemann, who had disappointed the team by failing to step into the breach in Holland by denying Piquet, had gone into one of his brilliant phases in Italy, setting the third-fastest time behind the all-powerful Renaults. But, more worrying for Jones, was that Piquet was fifth fastest and in tune with the Brabham on this tricky circuit, one which Jones, just to round everything off, did not particularly like.

Typically, though, he put all his trials and tribulations behind him on race day. The Renaults fell by the wayside, leaving Piquet and Jones to do battle at the front, but brake trouble on the Williams meant Jones had to accept second place. Reutemann, who had fallen to the back of the field with an overheating clutch, had charged back to third place and, in the process, helped to clinch the constructors' championship for Williams Grand Prix Engineering. Such a momentous event for Frank and Patrick was completely overshadowed by the excitement generated by the drivers' championship. Piquet now led by one point, and the change in mood was noticeable.

Previously, Piquet had been working on the basis that he had nothing to lose. It suited his relaxed manner. Immediately after the race at Imola, despite having won, there was almost no emotion. Piquet wore a preoccupied look. The hunter had become the hunted. And Jones knew it. Beer in hand, the Australian was wallowing in his rival's discomfort. Whereas Piquet did not want to discuss the championship, Jones was more than happy to talk. 'Yeah,' he grinned. 'It's great. Now Piquet's going to have to answer all the bloody stupid questions about what it's like to win the championship. The pressure's on him, for sure.'

Frank Williams had similar feelings but was unwilling to express them in the direct manner of his driver. As Jones unwound in the paddock, the team boss was already en route to the airport. Despite losing the lead in the championship, he somehow felt relaxed. He was accustomed to being the underdog; defending the lead of the championship had been infinitely more uncomfortable. There were two races left. Williams knew all he had to do was give it everything, just as he had all his life. That suited him very well.

No detail was left unchecked at Station Road as the team prepared to fly to North America for the races in Montreal and Watkins Glen. The points system was complicated by the fact that drivers could only count their best five scores in each half of the season. This favoured Jones slightly but the simplest solution was to say that if Jones won in Montreal, he could do no more and would only need to gather a few more points in Watkins Glen, regardless of where Piquet finished in the final race. For now, however, the final qualifying session in Montreal would be crucial. The report in *Autocourse* takes up the story:

With so much hanging on this race, the final hour on Saturday was incredibly tense. Piquet was strapped in and waiting at the end of the pit lane long before the appointed hour. Jones polished his visor one more time and zipped up his unfamiliar dark green overalls [he usually wore white] before climbing into the Williams. Alan had recorded the fastest lap on Friday – 1m 30.710s – and he set the ball rolling with a handy time in the 29-second bracket. Nelson, however, didn't care about that. He was into the 28s – and some.

World War III could have started; Montreal could have been a smouldering heap but the Grand Prix circus would scarcely have noticed. Attention was riveted on the tiny Longines screens dotted around the pit lane. The list of times would simmer slightly before disappearing to allow the tracer to dart back and forward and map out the next instalment. And what a cracker that turned out to be. PIQUET: 1m 27.831s. That had barely registered before the list had vanished and the tracer was into the realms of the unbelievable. PIQUET: 1m 27.328s. On his eighth lap!

After 30 minutes, there were more gasps. Not Piquet this time but (Bruno) Giacomelli, into second place [in an Alfa Romeo which had not been particularly competitive hitherto] with 1m 28.575s. Pironi (Ligier) was not far behind and Jones was back in fourth place. Fifteen minutes later and Jones had slipped to sixth. Piquet was now regularly cutting laps in 1m 27s. That was too much. Jones tightened his metaphorical belt a notch or two and put his head down. Everyone squinted at the simmering screens. The chequered flag came out. The tracer began its work. JONES: 1m 28.164s on the 30th of 31 laps. Piquet and Jones: side by side on row one. Phew!

Quite. Williams was staggered by Piquet's speed. What they did not know – but suspected – was that a special engine, high on power but short on endurance, had been installed in the Brabham. Ironically, it would be the cause of Piquet's downfall twenty-four hours later. Jones was exactly where he wanted to be. Again, the pressure was on Piquet.

And Jones was about to turn the screw one more time before the race had even started.

The Montreal circuit had been constructed on a man-made island in the middle of the St Lawrence. The island had been used originally as part of Expo '67, and then as a base for the rowing events in the 1976 Olympic Games. It was the ideal place to stage a motor race, close to the city and yet remote enough for the noise not to be a problem. But, in 1980, only the third year the race had been run at this venue, the facilities for the teams were less than ideal. The pit buildings were nothing more than a collection of portacabins. The garages were half a mile away, down at the far end of the rowing lake, the teams working in former boat houses which had never been designed for the task. Cars and equipment had to be towed back and forth, the drivers hitching rides on golf trolleys or motor boats. Except that, on race day, Jones decided to walk.

There was a gladiatorial quality about his body language as he emerged, fully kitted, from the Williams motor home. He was wearing his olive-green overalls, gloves, crash helmet and a deep scowl. He marched the half-mile, speaking to no one. His belligerent gait suggested he was not to be trifled with. It was an extraordinary sight, one which would have petrified the wiry Piquet, had he seen it. The psychological battle for the championship was as good as won.

The first corner, a few hundred yards from the start line, swung right, then left, then right again. It was lined by concrete walls on both sides. The cars would be accelerating all the way through but, in order not to lose momentum, it was necessary to take the racing line; in other words, use all of the road. Easy enough to do when racing alone, a tall order as the pack is unleashed with cars side by side. And, of course, the world only had eyes for the two on the front row of the grid.

Piquet was on the right, Jones on the left. Jones made the better start and was on the racing line for the right-hander. Believing – or not, depending on who you talked to – he was far enough ahead of Piquet, Jones began to move right, towards the apex. The left-front wheel of the Brabham made contact amidships with the Williams. The Brabham began to spin, hitting the wall as it did so and causing chaos behind as drivers tried to take avoiding action within the limited space available. The race was stopped. Damage to the Williams was slight, but Piquet's car was beyond immediate repair. He prepared to take the restart in the spare Brabham, the one he had used to claim pole position, the one with the special engine. Incredibly, the team had not made contingency plans for an incident such as this and the engine was still in place.

When the green light came on for a second time, the contenders made it through the first corner without incident. Jones led with Pironi – who would later be adjudged to have jumped the start – second and Piquet third. Piquet meant business. By the third lap he was in the lead and pulling away. But not for long. On lap twenty-four, the Brabham was parked by the side of the track, its engine a smoking wreck.

Frank Williams, in his usual position by the pit wall, did a quick calculation. If Jones held onto his lead, he would be champion. But Pironi was chasing hard and second place for Jones would not be enough to wrap up the title this afternoon. With Pironi breathing down his neck, Jones could not believe his eyes when a Williams pit signal told him that the Frenchman had been penalised one minute for the jumped start.

Frank had been given the news by his team manager, Jeff Hazel. Refusing to accept it, Williams told Hazel to get confirmation in writing. The officials would not oblige but, when it became clear that the Ligier team had been informed officially, that was good enough. The sign was duly hung out for Jones.

Like Williams, Jones refused to believe it. Next time round, there it was again. Jones signalled for confirmation. On the following lap, there was the pit signal, with Frank himself hanging over the pit wall nodding for all he was worth. Jones let Pironi through and finished second on the road – but as the winner of the Canadian Grand Prix and the 1980 World Championship.

It was the usual story from Frank. He was quietly thrilled to bits but, while accepting the warm congratulations flooding in his direction, he attempted to contain the excitement by talking about the next race in seven days' time. His view was that everyone would expect Williams to relax after winning both championships. He was utterly determined to show the world that this was not the way of Williams Grand Prix Engineering. The team was not about to go downhill.

Jones and Reutemann finished first and second in the United States Grand Prix. It was the perfect way to conclude a superb year. Now Frank was worried about being unable to do it all over again in 1981.

CHAPTER SEVEN

The end of an era

Neil Oatley, an engineer with Williams Grand Prix Engineering throughout the championship-winning 1980 season, reflected on the changes wrought by success on his boss's life:

You could see that Frank was getting even more intense as we became more competitive. We were being viewed as one of the top two teams and the pressure to stay there was great. Obviously, as you are rising up, there is pressure – but it's different. When you get there, you have to maintain your position, and Frank was very aware of that. But he was very good at keeping the momentum going.

He was always good at dealing with people in the factory. We were gradually expanding, taking over other units in Station Road. Frank would take time to ensure that everyone knew what was going on. He was always looking round the factory, trying to make sure that everyone's morale was up and going in the right direction.

He was a keen runner and, as time went on and the pressure began to increase, he was doing more and more. It was as if he had to run a bit faster and further than he did the week before. It was becoming an obsession. I lived quite near him at Aston Tirrold and, quite often, he would run the four miles or so from the factory to his house in the evening and I would take his car home. Then I would collect him and bring him to work the next morning. But, after a while, that distance wasn't long enough. He needed to stretch himself even further.

Oatley's role as part-time chauffeur in the white Jaguar XJ-S had ended during 1980 when Frank and Ginny moved from the repaired rectory to Battle House, an elegant nineteenth-century six-bedroom two-acre property in Goring-on-Thames complete with rolling lawns, vegetable patch and tennis court. It was the first perk associated with their success, the first house they had moved into which did not need major renovation or pile on worries about how the complete redecoration Ginny had decided on in this instance might be paid for.

Williams, of course, had no time to make use of any of the trappings. Work continued to dominate everything. He had no use for a video; he did not even possess a hi-fi. His Adidas running shoes meant far more. Frank would take his running kit with him to each race. When the bulk of the work was done at around eight p.m., he would don his track suit and complete two laps of the circuit. His pace was impressive, each mile covered in around six minutes. As with everything else that mattered in his life – in other words, motor racing, with his family a distant second – he did it to the maximum. While out running each evening, his mind would be churning over the day's events and thinking ahead. As champion constructor, he was busier than ever.

Sponsors were beating a path to Williams, rather than the other way round. Even so, it was a case of choosing carefully and, to that end, Sheridan Thynne, an associate from the London crowd Frank had been hanging on to in the sixties, was taken on board to employ his smooth skills while working with present and prospective backers. This was just as well because Frank had become deeply involved with political matters which were threatening to split the sport in two.

The power game between FISA and FOCA had reached such a state that it seemed for a while the small teams (broadly speaking, the 'British') might run a separate series to the rest (namely, the major manufacturers such as Renault, Ferrari and Alfa Romeo). As a compromise was sought, another bombshell burst over Williams when Goodyear, to whom Frank had been loyal throughout, suddenly withdrew from racing, leaving Williams and others at the mercy of Michelin, who would naturally put the interests of their regular customers – Renault and Ferrari – first. Frank admitted to being more depressed than he could ever remember.

In a trial of strength, the FOCA teams raced in South Africa but the race, won by Reutemann's Williams, was not recognised by FISA as part of the championship. That would start at Long Beach and, if the FOCA teams wanted to participate, their cars would have to run without side-skirts and with flat bottoms, thus ruling out the use of ground effect, one of the major bones of contention between the FOCA teams – who wanted to keep it – and FISA – who wanted to ban ground effect in order to slow the cars. Despite fears of a drubbing because the likes of Ferrari and Renault had been testing all winter without skirts, Jones and Reutemann finished first and second in California with the latest car, the Williams FW07C. Then the teams moved to Rio de Janeiro, where Frank suddenly found he had another problem to contend with.

Jones had received approaches to drive for Ferrari and Alfa Romeo in 1981, the Italian teams catching the Australian's keen eye as they waved handfuls of lire. Jones did not wish to leave Williams, a team with whom he felt entirely comfortable, and the promise that he would remain number one driver, with Reutemann in support, sealed the decision to stay for another season. Everything was fine until the closing stages of the Brazilian Grand Prix.

The arrangement was that, if Reutemann was leading Jones by fewer than seven seconds, then he should let his team-mate through. Reutemann had agreed to this for a second season because, in 1980, only once had he been close to stepping aside. He felt he could live with the clause; all things being equal, he could beat Jones fair and square, win the championship for himself and stay within the terms of the contract. Reutemann had tried to win at Long Beach but he had failed to open a large enough advantage during the race. He took the lead again in Brazil, this time in treacherously wet conditions. Driving immaculately, he pulled away. But not far enough. When the time came to move aside, Reutemann stayed put. He failed to respond to pit signals showing 'JONES-REUT'. Jones, suddenly realising that he could expect no help, was incensed. He did his best to close the gap with a car which was not handling particularly well, but Reutemann was inspired and took his win. Frank didn't need to be told that he faced a minor internal crisis.

Jones stalked into the garage and slammed shut the door. The team did their best to pacify him but he was incandescent. Reutemann, meanwhile, merely shrugged and said he hadn't realised Jones was that close. Williams deducted Reutemann's share of the prize money and nothing more was said by either side. But Jones knew where he stood. The relationship with Reutemann had been formal and workmanlike at the best of times. Now it was ice cold. They continued to exchange information, both drivers bright enough to appreciate it was to their mutual benefit, but Jones could barely contain his dislike of the South American.

That animosity was fuelled when Jones, in an effort to

show who was boss, crashed while leading the Belgian Grand Prix, his frustration made worse when Reutemann assumed a lead he would not lose. Reutemann, thanks to establishing a record by finishing in the points for sixteen races in succession, had built up a healthy lead in the championship. He had scored an average of 6.8 points in the first five races of 1981, an impressive achievement which said as much for the immaculate preparation by the Williams team as it did for consistency at the wheel. Then his luck ran out at Monaco when the transmission broke.

With one South American out of the way, Jones focused on another as he closed in on Piquet's leading Brabham. The two rivals had clashed in Belgium when, according to Piquet, Jones had shoved the Brabham off the track. Piquet, rather unwisely, had made disparaging remarks about Jones and he had cause to regret them as the white Williams loomed in his mirrors. As Jones darted every which way, Piquet became more and more ragged. In his desperation to overtake a back-marker, Piquet made a fundamental error of judgement and slid straight into a crash barrier. History does not record what Jones said as he sailed past the stricken Brabham and into the lead. Neither does it record his reaction when his engine began to misfire with a handful of laps to go. A pit stop to take on more fuel did not cure the problem and Jones was powerless as the Ferrari of Gilles Villeneuve snatched the lead with four laps to go.

Williams failed to win the next three races as well. Nevertheless, due to a spread of success among his rivals and a further run of point-scoring by the Argentinian, Reutemann left the British Grand Prix with a lead of seventeen points over Piquet. Jones was third, a further two points in arrears.

Any hopes that Jones may have had about retaining his title were dashed at Hockenheim in Germany when he lost the lead due to a return of the mysterious misfire which had cost him the Monaco Grand Prix. It required little imagination to appreciate what sort of mood he would be in. Traffic problems outside Hockenheim meant that team personnel, hoping to make a quick exit, were advised to line up their road cars in the paddock and leave under police escort. Jones's Mercedes-Benz was waiting in line. Charles Crichton-Stuart opened the boot in readiness as the Australian stalked into view. When still several yards away, Jones flung his expensive briefcase into the boot. Upset? There was no need to ask. As a final point – or nine points to be precise – the race had been won by Piquet. Reutemann had retired with engine trouble. His championship lead had been cut in half.

It was down to zero by the time the teams reached Monza in September, Piquet holding the lead jointly with the Williams driver on forty-five points. There was no one else in the competition by this stage. That may or may not have had a bearing on an important decision which Jones had reached during the preceding few days. When the world champion got to Monza, he went straight to Frank and told him he was going to retire. At the end of the season.

Frank was not altogether pleased with his number one driver. Not only had they opened discussions about 1982, there had been no hint of this about-turn. It was late in the season and most of the leading drivers were already accounted for in terms of the following year. And, while he was taking all of this on board, Frank noticed that two fingers on Jones's right hand were heavily bandaged. A few days before, Jones had been involved in an altercation with the driver of a van after they had disputed the same piece of London's Chiswick High Road. Jones might have won the encounter had not one or two of the driver's heavily built mates emerged unexpectedly from the back of the van. Jones said he was lucky to get away with a broken little finger (the fourth strapped to it as a splint). Frank didn't see it that way since this was the hand Jones needed to change gear. Typically, Jones cut off two fingers from his driving glove, poked the bandaged limbs through, and carried on as if nothing had happened. He finished a brilliant second. Reutemann was third, Piquet sixth. By the time they were ready to set off for the final round in Las Vegas, Reutemann led Piquet by a single point.

The feeling was that Reutemann and Williams had the capacity to clinch the title. And yet, with Reutemann, you never knew. When at the height of his campaign at Silverstone, Reutemann had actually bet Alan Henry, the Grand Prix editor of *Motoring News*, that he would not win the championship. It was an extraordinary thing to do, but it summed up this moody, enigmatic man perfectly. If he was on form in Las Vegas, no one would be able to touch him. If not . . . Frank and his team waited with bated breath to discover their driver's frame of mind when he reached Nevada.

They found that Reutemann had got there first. He had arrived early in order to wind down and acclimatise himself. He was relaxed and confident, a point he was to prove with a truly mesmeric qualifying lap which put the Williams on pole position. Piquet struggled into fourth place. If Reutemann could keep this up, Williams would have their second world champion in succession.

The outgoing title holder was second fastest. This would be Jones's last race and he didn't seem to care that much about his team-mate's bid for the championship. In fact, he began to chuckle twenty minutes before the start as everyone gathered on the grid and Reutemann, oblivious to the stifling heat, was the only driver to remain in his car and ignore the briefing from the clerk of the course. He had set pole position time on the first day of practice. That, according to Carlos, had been the last good thing to happen. On the second day, he had collided with Piquet and the damage was such that Reutemann had to use the back-up Williams for the rest of the weekend. Somehow this car did not feel right. He had improved it but then, as he drove to the grid, the handling felt all wrong. For a perfectionist such as Carlos, this amounted to a mammoth disaster. Even as he sat on the grid, Reutemann had the mechanics checking tyre pressures and spring rates. He was, in effect, talking himself out of the championship. The point was not lost on Jones as he stood behind his car and noted dryly: 'I see Carlos is fussing again.' Jones knew the race would be no contest. And so it proved.

The Australian powered into a lead he would never lose. Reutemann appeared to go in the opposite direction as he dropped back, offering no resistance, particularly when Piquet overtook the Williams. Piquet was ill at ease on this temporary track lined by concrete walls which zig-zagged their way through a car park behind Caesar's Palace Hotel. By the time seventy-five laps had been completed, Piquet had vomited in his helmet and was on the point of collapse as he steered his Brabham on automatic pilot, fifth place giving him the two points needed to clinch the championship. Reutemann, having suffered the ignominy of being lapped by his team-mate, came home a dispirited eighth.

He had not been happy with his car from the outset, even though nothing was ever found to be seriously wrong. With Piquet in such a disastrous physical state during the closing stages of the race, it would not have taken much of an effort to push the Brabham driver out of the points. Yet, for all the good he did, Reutemann may as well have stayed at home. Peter Windsor, writing in *Autocar*, claimed that 'the Williams team contrived to be one-two in qualifying yet, in the race, produced cars of such widely differing performances that it was as if Reutemann was driving for another team'.

119

Williams disagreed with that view. Jones's response was unprintable, but that was to be expected. What made Reutemann's drive that day seem so disappointing was the knowledge that, when everything was right, he could perform with such dazzling brilliance. And, of course, he had been made to look foolish by his team-mate.

It had been a consummate display by Jones. He could not have chosen to retire on a better note, victory in the Caesar's Palace Grand Prix bringing the total number of wins for Williams to fifteen. Jones had left his impression on the day and, although Frank and Patrick did not realise it, he had left an indelible mark on the team. Jones had set a standard which very few drivers would emulate – at least, not in the eyes of the Williams bosses. In Grand Prix terms, Alan had grown up with the team. He had played a major part in achieving the level of respect which Williams now enjoyed. More than that, he spoke the same language as the team. He was a no-nonsense racer. He did not need mollycoddling; his ego did not require a gentle massage when the going got rough. That suited Frank and Patrick perfectly. The triumvirate worked exceptionally well, as Jones recalled:

I can honestly say that I can never remember having a stand-up row with Frank. There was one occasion – I think it was in Spain – when I spun my wheels leaving the pits and dragged a jack with me. I can't remember what that was all about but we did have a bit of a verbal to-do afterwards. And that was it. We had our say and the whole thing was forgotten immediately. We had our little blues now and again – as anyone does in any working relationship – but none of them were really serious.

I know this sounds like a mutual admiration society, but, to be perfectly honest, Frank is the best bloke I've ever driven for. I used to say that at the time and I still believe it. Frank worked on the basis that if he was paying you that sort of money and he didn't believe what you were saying, or he didn't have any faith in your ability, then he was the bloody idiot for paying you the money in the first place. The trust between us was absolute. If I said to Frank that I thought the engine was down on power, or something like that, he would always give me the benefit of the doubt because I was the guy with my bum in the car.

We had a really special rapport and I certainly had a fantastic working relationship with Patrick. It got to the stage where we could almost communicate without talking. Patrick would say he was going to try something on the car and I would say, 'Yeah, that feels better,' and we'd just get on with it. Nine times out of ten, his ideas would work. Our understanding was such that we even changed things on the grid. We reached the point where we didn't have to verbal very much because we knew what we needed to get to the source of the problem. We could find a fix in a very short space of time.

I suppose you could say that the three of us grew up with the team. It was just one of those relationships. We all had the same goal: we wanted to win. Sounds simple, but I look at some teams and they seem to be pulling in opposite directions. I think the important thing was that we had an enormous amount of respect for each other. And we enjoyed ourselves.

The trouble was, Frank and Patrick now thought that all good drivers operated in the same way. It was a point of view which would cause untold difficulties as Williams began to achieve the status of a Super Team. When Alan Jones said farewell over several beers that night in Las Vegas, a wonderful era had ended for Williams Grand Prix Engineering. Things would never be quite the same again.

CHAPTER EIGHT

Stumbling across another champion

Williams may have lost the drivers' championship in 1981 but the second constructors' title in succession led to formal recognition which meant just as much to Frank. His team became the first to be honoured with the Queen's Award for Export Achievement. The award was handed over by Sir Ashley Ponsonby, Lord Lieutenant of Oxfordshire. It was typical of Frank, however, that he should choose two of his longest-serving members of staff to represent the team and attend the subsequent reception at Buckingham Palace.

Frank selected Bob Torrie and Bernie Jones since they had made up almost 50 per cent of the workforce when WGPE came into being in 1977. Jones had served his apprenticeship in the aircraft industry before answering the advertisement looking for someone to make the chassis of the first Williams Grand Prix car. The subsequent demise of the aluminium chassis in favour of carbon composite did not do Jones out of a job, his unique skills employed today on suspension and other components. Even now, Jones fondly remembers the day he met the Queen:

Wonderful. It was a brilliant day; I'll never forget it. But it was typical of Frank to think of us in the first place. And you could see he was really thrilled by the award and getting to meet the Queen.

He's just brilliant to work for. The company has grown out of sight, but Frank still likes to know what's going on. He always has time for a word.

The expansion in 1980 and 1981 had included the installation of the team's own wind tunnel, the employment of a team manager (Jeff Hazel) and various secretarial and clerical staff to look after the paperwork and logistics created by a team attending sixteen races around the world with test sessions in between. That left Frank free to take care of more pressing matters, such as finding a replacement for Alan Jones. And, in another tentative decision similar to the one which had brought Williams and the Australian together, Frank would choose a driver whose capacity and thirst for winning was far greater than anyone could have imagined.

Kiejo 'Keke' Rosberg had not scored a single championship point in 1981. He had failed to qualify for races almost as many times as he had managed to finish them. To all intents and purposes, the diminutive Finnish driver with the thick moustache had been given his chance and was no longer flavour of the month in the paddock. In the fickle world of Formula One, it didn't seem to matter that his chance had not amounted to much.

When James Hunt retired without warning midway through 1979, Rosberg was chosen as his replacement. On the one hand, this meant a permanent seat in Formula One; on the other, it was with Walter Wolf Racing. The Wolf team had achieved very little since the encouraging fresh start with Scheckter in 1977. Wolf's enthusiasm was on the wane and, just as Rosberg was settling in, the oil man was deciding to sell out. The Wolf team merged with the struggling Fittipaldi outfit at the end of 1979 and Rosberg accepted a two-year contract. During that period, he would finish just twice in the top six. His career was as good as over. Small wonder he jumped at the chance when asked by Williams to attend a driver trial at the Paul Ricard circuit in the south of France in the autumn of 1981.

Frank had been in contact with John Watson and Niki Lauda, two established drivers of proven quality, but a deal could not be finalised with either. Williams had got to a stage where, quite rightly, he was only interested in top-rank drivers. The annoying thing was that there were none available: Gilles Villeneuve was staying with Ferrari; Didier Pironi had agreed to move from Ligier to Ferrari; Nelson Piquet would remain with Brabham; Jacques Laffite had re-signed with Ligier. There was no option but to trawl the second division.

The trial at Paul Ricard was treated as something to be got through. Frank, in fact, did not attend on the day that Rosberg drove the car, leaving Charlie Crichton-Stuart and Frank Dernie in charge. They didn't quite know where to begin when reporting back to Frank. On the one hand, Rosberg chain-smoked, something the super-fit Williams abhorred. He had sat up to one a.m. drinking with Crichton-Stuart. The following morning, he turned up at the track, knocked back a couple of coffees, jumped in the car and was quick straight away.

It wasn't quite as straightforward as it sounds [recalled Rosberg]. We drank Beaujolais Nouveau in the evening and then, at eight o'clock the next morning, they put qualifying tyres on the car and, without warming it up, they said get in and see what you can do! Frank [Williams] sometimes made strange decisions and this was one of them. I came from nowhere, did this test, and he signed me up straight away.

It was immediately obvious that Rosberg had an abundance of natural ability which, if channelled correctly, could produce results. He may not have been as technically complete as Jones, but he was from the same mould. It was clear that Rosberg was as good as the team would get. Rosberg did not need to be asked twice to sign on as number two to Carlos Reutemann. And therein lay another problem which was looming on the horizon. In fact, Frank should have seen it coming.

Not long after his disastrous finish to the 1981 season, Reutemann had announced that he, too, was retiring. Then, typically, he changed his mind. When he competed in the first two races of the new season, the Argentinian felt that the spark was no longer within him. He announced his retirement once more. This time for good. The decision may have been prompted by the thought of having to fend off the cocky Rosberg. Maybe he genuinely did feel that he had had enough. Or perhaps it was no coincidence that, not long after, Argentina invaded the Falkland Islands and sparked a conflict which would have made it untenable for Reutemann to lead a British team in the international sports arena. Either way, it left Frank with the job of scanning a driver market even thinner than before. Mario Andretti, the 1978 world champion, acted as a stand-in at the third round of the championship at Long Beach, Williams eventually choosing the Irishman Derek Daly as Reutemann's replacement for the rest of the season.

In many respects, the Williams team was starting from scratch. Daly's experience in Formula One had been limited to back-of-the-grid teams before he earned a drive with Tyrrell (then at the beginning of a long, slow decline) in 1980. He finished fourth on two occasions that year but his season will be best remembered for a first-corner accident at Monaco where he misjudged his braking, slammed into the car in front, became airborne and landed on his Tyrrell teammate. Neither driver was injured but the spectacular accident went some way to relegating Daly to a second-rate team for 1981. The Williams drive in 1982 would be his last chance.

The same applied to Rosberg but, while he may have been faster than Daly, his inability to pinpoint the technical problems with the new car, FW08, led to much frustration for Patrick Head after such a successful period dealing with Jones's precise understanding of what the designer and engineers needed to know. In fact, driver technical liaison was handed over to Frank Dernie while Head busied himself on the development of a Metro rally car for Rover, Williams having accepted the commission because of their links with the parent company, Leyland.

It was also, truth be told, a means of exploring another avenue of development in case the future of Formula One was wrecked for good by the ongoing dispute between FISA and FOCA. That war raged into 1982 and resulted in the majority of British teams (Williams included) boycotting the San Marino Grand Prix at Imola. By then, Rosberg was trailing in the drivers' championship, ten points behind the leader, Alain Prost. It had been an unsettled start for Williams, one which would establish the pattern for the remainder of an extraordinary season.

Formula One was experiencing the beginnings of a technical transition as turbocharged engines were recognised as being the thing to have. Brabham had switched to the BMW turbo; Renault, the pioneers of turbocharging in Formula One, were leading the way; and the Ferrari turbo was beginning to show its potential. Williams, McLaren and Lotus were investigating the turbocharged route but, in the meantime, they had to continue with the Ford-Cosworth. And, of the three, the Williams team was doing it best.

Frank had invested £200,000 alone in developing the V8 to give another 20 bhp more than their Ford-Cosworth rivals. And what the Ford lacked in power when compared with the turbos, Williams made up for with fine-tuning of the chassis and a search for reliability which would allow Rosberg to finish more races than anyone else. Under normal circumstances, that would not have been enough; Rosberg would also have needed the occasional victory thrown in to maintain a points advantage. But, in this exceptional season, unpredictability was just as much an important element as reliability.

Ferrari had by far the best chassis and engine but threw away their chances by allowing Villeneuve and Pironi to fight like cat and dog on the track. Villeneuve, having been duped by Pironi when the Frenchman broke a private agreement at the previous race, was attempting to beat his team-mate during qualifying for the Belgian Grand Prix when a misunderstanding with a slower car sent the Ferrari cartwheeling down the track. Villeneuve died instantly from a broken neck. Pironi looked to be on course to win the championship when, seven races later, he crashed heavily in Germany. The severe ankle injuries would put him out of racing for good.

Brabham and Renault, meanwhile, were suffering from unreliability, Lotus could only muster a competitive car occasionally, and McLaren were either showing competitive form or failing to finish. There was no middle ground in the style of Williams. By the time the fourteenth of the sixteen-race series came round at Dijon in France, there had been ten different winners, three of whom had reached the top of the podium for the first time. Rosberg's name was not among them and yet he was second in the championship, six points behind the injured Pironi.

When the Finn qualified eighth on the grid at Dijon, there was not the despair there might have been in previous years. Given the open nature of this season, a carefully planned strategy could reap dividends during the course of an eighty-lap race. Neil Oatley, who was acting as a race car engineer that weekend, remembered Frank's influence on the decision-making process:

Frank tended not to get involved in the technical side of things at the factory; that was left to Patrick. But, at the races, he had a passion for tyres. This was at the height of a war between Goodyear, who had returned to F1, and Michelin. We were running Goodyear and there was a huge selection of different compounds to choose from. Frank loved that. He had a tremendous feel for it and the tyre choice was generally left to Frank after consultation with Patrick and the drivers. Purely technical decisions were almost entirely Patrick's but, when it came to tyres, Frank really got involved.

At Dijon, we discussed the tyre situation at length. Because of the nature of the circuit, Frank decided on three different compounds spread around the car. Then, just about five minutes before the car was due to go to the starting grid, he decided to go for a harder compound than originally chosen for the left-rear tyre. A lot of people had tyre trouble that afternoon but that harder tyre probably helped us win the race.

Victory at Dijon, the first of the season for Williams, would change everything. By the time the teams returned to Las Vegas for the final encounter, Rosberg was leading his closest rival, John Watson, by nine points. All Rosberg had to do was finish sixth or higher and the championship would be his, regardless of Watson's result. (Lauda also had an outside chance, depending on the outcome of an appeal against his disqualification from the Belgian Grand Prix, but, in the end, his challenge would come to nothing.)

With the odds stacked heavily in favour of Rosberg, you would think Frank Williams might have allowed himself a moment's relaxation. Not a bit of it. His face remained taut with emotion throughout the two days of practice. He refused to discuss the possible outcome of the race, preferring instead to plan his team's attack with military precision. Rosberg had qualified sixth on the grid, three places ahead of Watson. Frank reasoned that Rosberg, through no fault of his own, was likely to become involved in someone else's accident within the tight confines of a track lined by temporary concrete walls. To this end, the team had endlessly practised changing wings and suspension components. In the event of a collision, they could have their driver back in the race and heading for the single point needed to secure the championship. Frank and Patrick played close attention to the transmission components which would receive heavy punishment on this track. Similarly, seventy-five laps in the searing heat would take its toll on the driver. A supply of drinking water – then something of a novelty on a racing car – would be placed on board and plumbed through an electric pump which, on the flick of a switch, would squirt the liquid refreshment through a tube and into Rosberg's mouth.

Frank thought of everything. The progress of the race would be monitored by the Longines computer and displayed on a monitor positioned in the Williams pit. Frank usually kept a lap chart by hand as a back-up in case of computer failure but, on this occasion, he wanted to maintain a general overview of events on the track and in his pit area. I was asked if I would like to watch the race from the Williams pit and keep the lap chart. It was not a problem since lap-charting was part of my usual routine while preparing race reports. In fact, I welcomed it since the Williams pit was normally out of bounds to the media.

Frank and Patrick kept friendly relationships with the press but the pressure of business meant they could appear less than welcoming at times. This was a case in point. There was a championship to be won, there was no time for small talk. The team hashed and dished the possibilities and prepared themselves for every contingency. Nothing was being left to chance. On race morning, as I walked by the motor home, Frank called me inside. 'Will you be all right?' he asked, anxiously. When I replied in the affirmative and showed him my prepared lap chart, he handed me a sheet of paper. 'I find this useful,' he said. 'You'll need it for scribbling down the numbers when they come past in a tight bunch at the end of the first lap. Then you can transfer them neatly to your lap chart before they come round for a second time.' Keeping the piece of paper I had already assigned for that task in my back pocket, I said thanks and reassured Frank everything would be okay. He nodded, and ticked 'Maurice – lap chart' off a long list. On such fine details are championships won.

The chart showed Rosberg holding seventh place for the first twenty laps. Two retirements in the top six then moved the Williams driver into fifth place, good enough for two points and the championship. But Watson, driving superbly, was in second place and Frank's expression, a mixture of intense concentration and barely suppressed anxiety, remained unchanged. All Rosberg had to do was finish, a task which was momentarily put in jeopardy when he pressed the drink switch and was scalded on the lips by water which had reached boiling point. This happened just as he was changing into fifth gear. Rosberg somehow found fifth at around 160 mph, kept the car on the road and managed to stem the flow of scorching liquid.

With just two laps to go, Frank moved across the pit and quietly instructed Charlie Crichton-Stuart to tell Alan Challis, the chief mechanic, to 'get the flags ready'. Ever since Regazzoni's first win at Silverstone three years before, it had become part of the team tradition to wave the Union Jack and a Saudi flag high in the air each time a Williams won a race. That instruction in Las Vegas was the first time all week that Williams had conceded Rosberg was about to win the title. A couple of minutes later, an ecstatic team welcomed home the 1982 world champion.

A couple of hours and many interviews later, Williams relaxed outside his motor home after the unaccustomed luxury of a swim in the hotel pool. Inside, Rosberg stubbed out another Marlboro (even more of a luxury in Frank's motor home), swallowed a piece of chocolate cake and prepared to make a quick departure with Mansour Ojjeh for San Francisco, where they would celebrate both the championship and Ojjeh's thirtieth birthday. Rosberg commented:

The atmosphere at Williams that afternoon was typical. I had won the championship. The attitude was: 'Okay, well done. The next problem is next week.' It was business. I think Frank and I both thought the same way.

But I don't want to give the wrong impression because it was also a lot of fun. There was a gang of nice people around Frank in 1983: Patrick and Charlie, and Alan Jones was around quite a lot. We used to take the piss out of Frank. We would say something every day, maybe about his running or something else he was being very serious about. It was good fun. But it was businesslike too. No bullshit. When I won the championship, that was it for the day. 'Okay, that's done. Next?' So I didn't stay around too long and went off to San Francisco with Mansour.

Ojjeh had strengthened his connection with Williams, TAG identification having been prominent on the nose and cockpit sides during 1981 and 1982, with the entrant's name listed as the TAG Williams Team. After a successful liaison, Leyland had moved at the end of 1981 but, as a side-effect of the partnership, Steve Herrick had joined the

London-based company CSS Promotions and would work closely with Sheridan Thynne as they explored other sources of finance and commercial partnerships for the team. It was becoming clear that cost-cutting, previously unheard of in Saudi Arabia, would mean a reduction in the flow of money from the oil-rich kingdom. Indeed, by the end of 1983 the sponsorship link which had put Williams Grand Prix Engineering on its feet would be at an end. So, too, would the association with Mansour Ojjeh. But this was not because TAG's money was running out. On the contrary, Ojjeh was about to make a major investment in Formula One.

The search for turbocharged engines had been gathering momentum during 1981 and 1982 as the Ford-Cosworth users reluctantly accepted that were was no alternative if they wished to keep pace with the likes of Ferrari and Renault. Turbocharged engines, unlike the Ford-Cosworth, were not available off the shelf. A partnership would need to be formed with a major motor manufacturer. McLaren had committed themselves to an ambitious project with Porsche. The planned V6 turbo, designed specifically for Formula One, would require financing and McLaren boss Ron Dennis saw Mansour Ojjeh as a likely investor. Dennis's timing was perfect, as Ojjeh recalled in an interview in *F1 Racing* magazine:

With Williams, we were a sponsor. But it was getting more and more expensive and I knew that Ron was trying to finance an engine. He approached me and I put it to my father that we finance it, subcontract to Porsche and own the intellectual rights. It put the TAG name right up there with Ferrari, BMW and Renault and gave us an image.

Frank had examined his options and entered discussions with Honda in early 1981. The lengthy and detailed negotiations were conducted in great secrecy, Williams

Above: Doing it for Frank. Ginny Williams says it all on the victory podium at Brands Hatch in 1986. Alain Prost, who finished third to Mansell and Piquet, looks on.
(Sporting Pictures)

Right: Terrible irony. Clay Regazzoni, the man who gave Frank his first victory in 1979, was himself paralysed in a crash two years later during the Long Beach GP. Clay joins his former boss in the pits in 1987. Iain Cunningham, wearing team uniform, looks after Frank.
(Sporting Pictures)

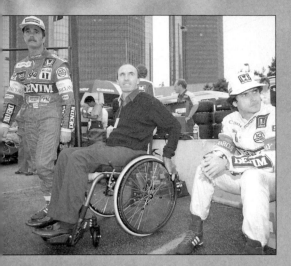

Frank had his work cut out to keep
the peace between Nigel Mansell and
Nelson Piquet (right) during 1987.
(Agence Vandystadt)

Nigel Mansell's best race with the Judd-
powered Williams in 1988 brought him
second place to Ayrton Senna's McLaren
at Silverstone. *(DPPI/Action-Plus)*

Main photo: Splashing to a rare victory. Thierry Boutsen drove an exquisite race in the rain with the first Renault-powered Williams in Canada in 1989. *(DPPI/Action-Plus)*

Right: Frank sits in on a debrief in Japan 1991. Seated round the table (left to right): Adrian Newey, Patrick Head, Nigel Mansell, engineers David Brown and John Russell and, with his back to the camera, Riccardo Patrese. *(Pascal Rondeau)*

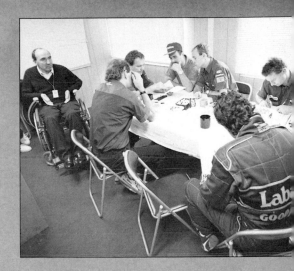

Punctured hopes. Damon Hill is robbed of his first victory yet again,
this time at Hockenheim in 1993. *(Mike Hewitt/Allsport)*

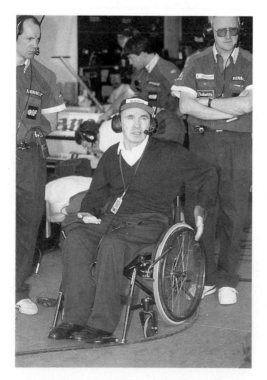

Above: Enduring partnership.
Williams and Head at Monza in 1993.
(Pascal Rondeau/Allsport)

Left: Adrian Newey, Frank and Sheridan
Thynne mind the shop at Kyalami during
practice for the 1992 South African
Grand Prix. *(Peter Tarry/Action-Plus)*

Another champion takes his leave. Frank sits with Alain Prost as the Frenchman announces his retirement at Estoril in 1993. *(Pascal Rondeau/Allsport)*

Above: On board at last. Ayrton Senna gives his initial impressions of the latest Williams during his first test for the team in Portugal. *(DPPI/Action-Plus)*

Left: Peter Windsor: Observed the Williams team from both sides of the fence. *(LAT)*

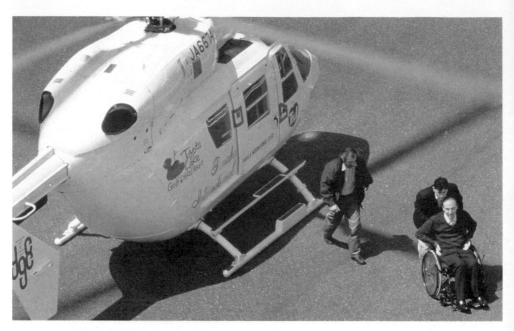

Above: Arriving by helicopter at the Aida track in Japan 1994.
(Pascal Rondeau/Allsport)

Below: Frank senses problems with the Williams as Senna gives his views at Aida, the second race of the 1994 season. *(Pascal Rondeau/Allsport)*

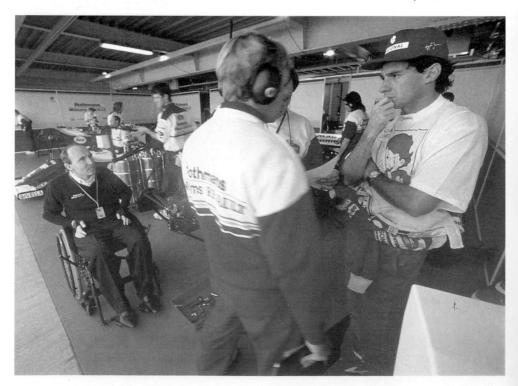

The end of a dream, beginning of a nightmare. Ayrton Senna's wrecked car is hauled off the circuit at Imola. *(Amton Want/Allsport)*

Yeeessss! Hill takes the title for Williams at the end of an emotional race at Suzuka in 1996. *(Pascal Rondeau/Allsport)*

New start. Jacques Villeneuve and Hill's replacement, Heinz-Harald Frentzen, prepare to go to the grid for the first race of the 1997 season in Australia. *(Michael Cooper/Allsport)*

Above: Heinz-Harald Frentzen on his way to a brilliant pole position at Monaco in 1997. *(Michael Cooper/Allsport)*

Below: Appealing to Frank. Jacques Villeneuve on the limit during practice for the 1997 British Grand Prix at Silverstone. The French-Canadian would go on to win the championship at his second attempt. *(Michael Cooper/Allsport)*

playing down the rumours which were gathering within the motoring press. He was finally caught out by his love of flying and aircraft.

Frank kept a meticulous logbook, listing the flights he made and noting the type and registration of each and every aircraft. He was fascinated by aviation and could give a detailed account of the political machinations behind the reason for one airline using General Electric engines rather than, say, Rolls-Royce. Naturally, he knew the shortcomings and plus points of each engine. Alan Henry, the *Motoring News* correspondent who was also an aviation buff, fell into discussion with Williams about airlines and asked to see the logbook. Frank discovered Henry's ulterior motive when the scribe noted out loud that there seemed to be an exceptionally high number of flights between London and Tokyo. 'You bastard, A.H.!' grinned Williams as he recognised a reflection of his own doctrine as Henry's business came before pleasure.

The negotiations with Honda lasted until February 1983, a contract finally being signed just as the Williams team prepared for their last season with the trusty Ford-Cosworth V8. Rosberg would remain on the driving force but Daly's contract was not renewed. The Irishman had been a conservative choice in the first place and his tenure was destined to be short when he failed to produce anything better than a couple of fifth places. More often than not, he was flying off the road. The only surprise is that, in the light of Frank's barely concealed displeasure with under-performing Williams drivers in the years to come, Daly – who now runs a racing school in Las Vegas and commentates for an American cable network – did not feel under pressure:

I saw the pressure [Heinz-Harald] Frentzen was under at the start of 1997. It was nothing like that for me. But it was an entirely different situation. Instead of being a driver who was Frank's personal choice, the best man for the job, I was there as the fill-in driver after Reutemann had left. I didn't make the best of it but I don't remember Frank looking sideways at me, even when I was having a bad race. I don't remember the pressure coming down on me as heavily as I have seen it since with other Williams drivers.

I was there under unusual circumstances. The team's effort was behind Keke, which I accepted. I was there to do what I could. Looking back, it was the best-organised team I have ever been with. By far. The thing I appreciated most was that, even though I was no more than a back-up driver, it was Frank who dealt with me at all times. When he decided they were not going to keep me in 1983, it was Frank who called me rather than have someone else do it. He had been a bit evasive up to that point but driving for Frank had been my golden opportunity, which I blew for personal reasons – I was going through a divorce and had other complications at the time. If I had been in Frank's position, I would have done exactly the same thing. I have never felt the slightest bit of resentment, even though that was the end of my career in Formula One.

I came over to the States to drive Indycars after that. The funny thing is, I have retained a good relationship with Frank after all these years. I'll call him up and he'll say: 'Derek, I'm too busy. I'll be here at six-fifteen. Can you call me back?' I'll call back and he'll chat for as long as I like. I don't know why, but I find that unusual because I was never a race-winning driver and his stature has gone far beyond what it was then.

He's still as intense as he ever was. But when I was racing for him, you could see the sense of humour come out. Frank wouldn't sit down for a bit of a chat and a laugh. But you could make him roar – I mean, really laugh heartily – and then he would switch off straight away and get back to business. But it was a good atmosphere.

That atmosphere was enhanced by the decision to invite Jacques Laffite to return to Williams. Since leaving at the end of 1975, the Frenchman had won six Grands Prix while driving for Ligier. But that was about all that could be said. He would turn out to be no more than a fun-loving journeyman driver, not the sort Williams needed if the championship momentum was to be continued.

Their cause may not have been helped by having to continue with the non-turbo Ford-Cosworth but, if anyone could wring the car's neck, it was Keke Rosberg. Whereas Laffite would finish in the points on just six occasions in 1983, Rosberg used his sublime skill in tricky conditions to give Williams their only win of the season. And he chose to do it at Monaco, the most charismatic race on the calendar. Rosberg turned the power deficit to his advantage by choosing to start on slick tyres on a track made treacherous by a light shower. While the rest of the field struggled to contain unwieldy amounts of turbo horsepower on the damp surface, Rosberg simply drove into the distance.

That would be the high point of the year for Williams, Rosberg finishing fifth in the drivers' championship, Laffite eleventh and the team a distant fourth in the constructors' championship. Just as significant as Rosberg's win, however, was the appearance of the first Honda-powered Williams at the last race of the season in South Africa, where Rosberg finished an encouraging fifth. It was, in some ways, a false dawn. It would take longer than hoped to make the Williams-Honda package a competitive proposition. In fact, both sides were barely scratching the surface of what would eventually become an extremely successful partnership.

Chassis construction had entered a new era when McLaren introduced the use of carbon fibre in 1981. Williams would be one of the last of the leading teams to switch from aluminium alloy honeycomb, Patrick Head understandably cautious about using carbon fibre in the absence of detailed knowledge of its behaviour under every circumstance likely to occur in motor racing. The first Honda-powered car, FW09, would be the last Williams to use the traditional aluminium chassis.

As for the engine, Williams quickly discovered that much work needed to be done if the Honda was to be even remotely competitive. The V6 turbo was based on an engine previously used in Formula Two, whereas the TAG Turbo (Porsche) had been designed from scratch to fit the precise requirements laid down by John Barnard, designer of the carbon-fibre-chassis McLaren. The Honda power tended to be delivered in one lump, within an extremely narrow rev-range, making the car very difficult to drive. Moreover, it was eventually discovered that the engine block and chassis mounts were flexing which, in simple terms, gave the effect of driving on deflating rear tyres.

Everything felt soft [recalled Rosberg]. The engine was soft, the car was soft and the power was like an on-off switch. When the power came in, it was terrible. When we went to Austria, I just couldn't drive the car. It was impossible. I couldn't keep it on the road. It would twist and jump and do things which were totally unexpected. I had to stop. It was the only time in my career when I had to give up during a race.

Rosberg managed to win the Dallas Grand Prix, but that single victory for Williams in 1984 was due to the driver's resilience on a crumbling track as temperatures nudged one hundred degrees, rather than through any technical advantage delivered by his car. Honda engines were failing left, right and centre, giving the increasingly beleaguered Williams mechanics at least four engine changes during each Grand Prix weekend. Honda were at first reluctant to accept that the ball was in their court, and it was not until two top engineers from Tokyo were present at late-season races to witness the mechanical mayhem at first hand that steps were taken to rectify the problem. By then, 1984 had been written off, Williams eventually finishing sixth in the constructors' championship, Rosberg taking eighth place in the drivers' listing.

In the midst of this technical turmoil, the team had finally left Station Road and moved to a purpose-built factory, close to the massive electricity generating cooling towers on the edge of Didcot. Opened on 16 June 1984 by Michael Heseltine, MP for South Oxfordshire and, at the time, Minister of Defence in the Thatcher government, the new premises were far removed from the haphazard collection of industrial units in Station Road. Neil Oatley recalled:

Certainly, we had outgrown the buildings at Station Road. The drawing office had become very cramped but the place continued to have a good atmosphere; everyone could still squeeze into the canteen at tea break! Things were very different at the new factory on Basil Hill Road. It was obviously a much bigger building. The drawing office was at the opposite end to the part of the workshop where the cars were built. Before, you could look out of the drawing office window and the race cars were down below. With the move, more people joined the team and you didn't always know who they were or what they did. That intimate touch was lost. It became less of a family atmosphere, but that sort of thing was inevitable. The team simply had to expand.

That expansion brought two significant changes. Room was made for Honda to have their own separate workshop, thus allowing the rebuilding of engines on site and the growth of a working relationship which would become closer in every respect. There was also sufficient space to allow the introduction of the technology necessary to build the team's first carbon-fibre chassis, FW10. With Laffite about to be shown the door following yet another lacklustre season, the next question was finding someone to drive the second FW10 alongside Rosberg. Frank immediately thought of a young Brazilian he had met for the first time the previous year.

The Formula Three championship in 1983 had been a season-long battle between Ayrton Senna and Martin Brundle. There was little to choose between them but Senna generally had the upper hand, particularly in the wet when he would disappear in a class of his own. His only shortcoming seemed to be an inability to cope with being beaten, a feature which some would say is an asset in any prospective champion. Whatever the interpretation, it was clear to Frank Williams that Senna was fast enough to warrant a test drive in a Formula One car. A date was fixed in the summer of 1983. Senna drove the Ford-powered Williams at Donington Park and Frank came away with the impression that the twenty-three-year-old was quick and worth watching. But nothing more than that.

Senna also drove Formula One cars for McLaren, Brabham and Toleman. Only Toleman came up with a firm offer for 1984. It suited Senna to learn the F1 ropes with Toleman, a small team in which the pressure to win would not be overbearing for a novice. In fact, he would learn extremely quickly, a dazzling performance in the rain almost bringing victory at Monaco. By the time Frank Williams had got his act together and thought about a second driver for 1985, Senna had already been snatched away from Toleman by Lotus.

As time went by and Senna's absolute brilliance became stunningly clear, Frank would not rest until he had Ayrton in his team. It would take nine years. And then the association would be desperately brief.

In the meantime, scanning the list of available candidates,

Frank dithered over his choice. He prevaricated so much that, at Zandvoort in August 1984, Patrick ran out of patience and told Frank to make up his mind; the team would make it work with whomever Frank chose. Williams went straight out of the motor home and signed Nigel Ernest James Mansell.

Rather like Alan Jones seven years before, Williams believed he was taking on board a driver who would be a good and reliable number two. Twelve months later, Frank would begin to realise that Nigel Mansell was someone very special, and quite different from any Williams driver before or since.

CHAPTER NINE

Here's Nigel

The pit lane in Rio de Janeiro could scarcely suppress a collective grin. Charging into the first corner at the start of his first race for Williams, Nigel Mansell had collided with a Ferrari. There was no need for anyone to rush up to Frank Williams and say: 'Told you so!' He did not need reminding of Mansell's reputation as a spectacular loser.

The press had a field day as they dragged up Mansell's past: more than sixty Grands Prix without a win, several well documented incidents, and a dismissive farewell as the manager of Mansell's former team, Lotus, made it plain that he was glad to see the back of him. Mansell was undoubtedly a very fast driver but his inability to contain himself looked likely to drive Williams to distraction. This was a case in point. Having made an excellent start, Mansell appeared to become over-excited as he saw his chance to take second place, and then made contact with Michele Alboreto's Ferrari. The Williams spun off the track, damage to the car bringing retirement a few laps later.

No one was less surprised than Rosberg, who had not wanted Mansell in the team in the first place. And had said so, in no uncertain terms. Rosberg's retirement from the lead with a blown turbocharger after nine laps should not have helped Frank's feeling of annoyance towards his new recruit.

But he did not criticise. The collision was dismissed as a racing accident, one of those things which happen in the heat of the moment. The incident was never mentioned again.

Mansell was amazed – and deeply grateful. At Lotus, he would have been hauled over the coals – possibly in public – and the ridicule would have continued through to the next race. Such actions merely fed Mansell's sizeable inferiority complex and put an impetuous edge on the need to prove himself which, in turn, would bring about another incident. And more criticism. Whether or not by chance, the Williams team had taken the first small step towards the gradual building of a confidence which would lead to mesmeric performances and a world championship. In the meantime, there was a long way to go.

Mansell appeared to have regressed to his former habits when he crashed again at the next race in Portugal, this time while on his way to the starting grid. How could Frank possibly tolerate such behaviour, particularly as he had new sponsors on board? The team was now enjoying support from Canon, ICI and Mobil, the backing from Saudi Arabia having all but disappeared. What on earth would these business people make of Williams employing a driver whose main role appeared to be the butt of paddock humour?

Fortunately for Mansell, he had an influential ally in Peter Collins, formerly with Lotus but now the Williams team manager. Collins had been instrumental in persuading Colin Chapman of Lotus to give Mansell his Grand Prix debut in 1980. The Australian had stood by his man despite the mounting criticism within the team, particularly after Chapman, who supported Mansell strongly, had died of a heart attack in December 1982. Now, as the damaged Williams limped into the pit lane in Portugal, Collins knew he had to go to work on Mansell before his morale crashed back to rock bottom.

Mansell had been the victim of a wet track and a sudden surge of horsepower. As he tried to clear an engine misfire, he had stabbed the throttle, only to find 900 bhp coming in at once and sending the Williams straight into the crash barrier. As the Williams mechanics carried out hasty repairs, Collins told Mansell to forget about it and concentrate on his proven ability as a driver who was fast in wet conditions. Above all, don't get into a state. Relax. And go motor racing.

Mansell started from the back of the field and worked his way through to fifth place despite having to balance the car on a knife-edge for two hours. Nine drivers spun off that afternoon. Rosberg was among them, not even the Finn's impressive reflexes fast enough to deal with the nervous and potent response of the Honda turbo on a treacherous track. Frank Williams may have been suitably impressed by Mansell's drive but he was also making a mental note of the brilliance displayed by Ayrton Senna as the Brazilian won his first Grand Prix in exceptional style.

The question of making the engine more user-friendly was addressed by the Honda engineers when they introduced a new version of the V6 in time for the fifth round of the championship in Canada. Rosberg and Mansell both reported that the car was easier to drive and Rosberg proved it when, almost twelve months since the team's last victory in Dallas, he pulled off a brilliant win on the streets of Detroit. Mansell had crashed due to brake trouble, but that did not lessen his expectation of doing well in the next round in France.

The Paul Ricard Circuit incorporated the Mistral Straight, one of the longest in Grand Prix racing. During untimed practice on Saturday morning, Mansell had reached 205 mph when, without warning, his left-rear tyre burst and ripped off the rear wing. Ahead lay the run-off area for the next corner. The Williams careered into the rows of catch-fencing designed specifically for this purpose. As the car began to slow down in a swirling cloud of dust, a plastic fence pole whacked Mansell's crash helmet and knocked him unconscious. He was very fortunate to escape with nothing more than heavy concussion.

As Mansell was airlifted to hospital, Rosberg faced a dilemma. Would it be safe to go out in the sister car for final qualifying in an hour's time? In the absence of television pictures, and with Mansell unable to shed any light on the cause of the crash, it was necessary to gather as much information as possible. I had witnessed the incident and told Williams what I had seen. Frank asked if I wouldn't mind talking to Rosberg.

I found him sitting quietly inside the motor home, along with his engineer and an official from Goodyear. I said I had heard a muffled 'boom', then saw the tyre flailing at the back of the car as it came towards me. The entire rear wing, whipped by the flailing rubber, had suddenly flown into the air and then begun, in a strangely slow manner, to flutter towards the track. After that I couldn't be too clear about what exactly had happened. Self-preservation had taken over as I simultaneously watched the flight path of the wing and the progress of the wayward Williams, waiting for it suddenly to begin cavorting as broken racing cars sometimes do. It would have been the work of a moment for the Williams to clear the knee-high crash barrier – which perhaps explained why the public were not permitted to come close to the trackside at this point. It was with huge relief that I saw the wing crash onto the track and the Williams, with Mansell a hapless passenger, shoot straight past. The tyre had obviously failed but I could not even begin to hazard a guess at the reason why.

Rosberg lit a cigarette, nodded and said thanks. Half an

hour later, he went out and put his Williams on pole position. The speed trap showed he had been in excess of 200 mph at the point where his team-mate had hit trouble. At times like that, you realise why racing drivers are different. The point was not lost on Frank Williams.

Unfortunately, Rosberg's bravery was not to be rewarded fully the following day. Piquet's Brabham, running on Pirelli tyres, was perfectly suited to the scorching conditions and Rosberg had to make do with second best. Mansell, meanwhile, was beginning a slow recovery at home on the Isle of Man. It crossed his mind that he might not be fit enough for the next race, the British Grand Prix. Predictably, he duly turned up at Silverstone even though, as he would admit many years later, his recovery was by no means complete.

Rosberg made history that weekend. Confident that he could take pole position, he duly set the fastest time and climbed from his car. A light shower of rain a few minutes later appeared to seal pole position in Rosberg's favour. Then the fresh winds quickly dispersed the clouds and the racing line began to dry. With nine minutes of practice remaining, Piquet and Senna edged closer and closer to Rosberg's time. With five minutes to go, Rosberg flicked his cigarette to the floor, ground the butt with his heel, reached for his helmet and said: 'Okay. Let's do it.' The entire place held its breath as the Williams blasted out of the pits.

On a still-damp track, Rosberg flung the FW10 around Silverstone in record time, the first driver to lap the Northamptonshire track at an average speed of more than 160 mph. It was the fastest lap ever recorded by a Formula One car at any circuit during a race meeting. It was inevitable that the authorities, mindful of the rising speed, should subsequently change the character of Silverstone for good.

Mansell, meanwhile, had claimed the fifth-fastest time

even though he could remember very little about it. Rosberg, who was better placed than most to appreciate Mansell's brave effort, complimented his team-mate and apologised for having misjudged him before the start of the season. Then, straightforward character that he is, Rosberg was not afraid to repeat his opinion to the media.

Both drivers were to retire from the British Grand Prix but it was becoming apparent that they were a force to be reckoned with. When Mansell finished second in Belgium a couple of months later, it seemed that a win was not far away. Provided Nigel could keep his head.

Three weeks later, Mansell and Rosberg were on the second row of the grid for the Grand Prix of Europe at Brands Hatch, one of Mansell's favourite circuits. Senna started from pole in the Lotus-Renault turbo and led for several laps with Rosberg pushing him hard. Rosberg would claim later that Senna had been less than fair in his blocking tactics. An almost desperate lunge inside the Lotus saw Rosberg lose control as Senna refused to give way. The Finn spun, and took the hapless Piquet with him.

The contact between the Brabham and the Williams meant a punctured tyre and a pit stop for Rosberg. He rejoined just as Senna, now hotly pursued by Mansell, completed a lap. Rosberg vented his frustration by taking his time to move out of Senna's way. In the ensuing confusion, Mansell shot into the lead, with an angry Senna in pursuit. Could Mansell take the heat?

For the next sixty-six laps, the man in the red, white and blue helmet did not put a foot wrong. He won his first Grand Prix amid scenes of great emotion as the 120,000 crowd stood as one to salute the Briton's dogged determination. It almost went unnoticed that Alain Prost had claimed the 1985 World Championship by finishing fourth in his McLaren-TAG turbo.

Having finally broken through that psychological barrier, Mansell's career took off. He won the next race in South Africa, and Rosberg then wrapped up the season by winning the Australian Grand Prix, his last race for Williams. Despite the new-found harmony with Mansell, and the fact that Williams was clearly a team on the rise, Rosberg was determined to leave:

The only time I ever had a cross word with Frank was when he told me Mansell was joining the team. I said I didn't want him and I was leaving. Frank said, 'No you're not.' I insisted that I didn't want to stay, but Frank held me to my contract. Unfortunately, that moment affected my thinking about the team because I decided to leave as soon as I could. I paid my dues until the end and then left – but only because I had said I would and without really considering the quality of the team and the promising future if I decided to stay.

That was the only clash I had with Frank, otherwise I had no problems at all. We got on very well but I don't think that Frank is the sort of man who builds great friendships. He doesn't let you come close. It's not because he's the boss. He's not distancing himself because he is in authority; he's at a distance only because he chooses not to let you come close. Looking back, you ask yourself: 'Did we have many dinners with Frank?' Answer: 'No.' 'Did we have many breakfasts with Frank?' Answer: 'No.' He was always there, but he wasn't, if you know what I mean.

Telephone contact was with Frank whereas face-to-face contact tended to be with Patrick, except at the race meetings, when Frank would run the debriefs and so on. But he did have a sense of humour; he was very funny at times and, as I said before, we would always be making jokes at Frank's expense.

He was a caring sort of person, but not as much as he liked to think he was. We used to tell a joke about how Frank would go into the workshop and pat one of the lads on the back. 'How's it going, Pete?' he would ask. Pete would say, 'Not so good, Frank. My wife died this morning.' And Frank would say: 'Okay, never mind. D'you think that front suspension will be ready in time for the test at Paul Ricard next week?' Frank thought in his own mind that he was very caring and yet he seemed to forget to do it. It was a strange thing. He wasn't distant – and yet he was very remote.

A few months later, Frank's perspective on life was to change dramatically. And the Grand Prix world would suddenly discover that they cared for Frank Williams very much indeed.

CHAPTER TEN

Upside down

Frank and Ginny had moved house yet again, onwards and upwards, this time to Boxford House, a small mansion near Newbury. Their family had continued to grow. By early 1986, Jonathan was ensconced in boarding school but Claire had the company of another brother, three-year-old Jaime. As usual, time and money had been spent on renovating the property from top to bottom. The result was as perfect as Ginny and Frank could have wished.

All was well with their world on Saturday, 8 March. Frank had left home at the crack of dawn to pay a flying visit to the Paul Ricard circuit, where his team was carrying out final tests with the latest Williams-Honda in preparation for the new season. He would be back that night, if only because he intended to run in a half marathon in Portsmouth the following day. The test session in the south of France had been successful; the sponsors were in place; Nelson Piquet had been signed to replace Rosberg as Mansell's team-mate; Williams Grand Prix Engineering was raring to go.

Frank was in a buoyant mood. Invigorated by the atmosphere at Paul Ricard and the sound of racing cars in action, he was looking forward to Portsmouth. He called Ginny to say he would be home in time for supper. Then he walked briskly to his Ford Sierra hire car and climbed into the driver's seat. Joining him on the ninety-minute journey to Nice airport would be Peter Windsor, who had given up journalism for a job as PR coordinator with the team. The route was well-known to everyone in Formula One. It was an interesting mixture of B-class roads travelling north-east through frequently hilly countryside before reaching the autoroute and heading east towards Cannes and Nice.

Frank, as ever, was pressing on. They were on time but he could not resist driving quickly. Keeping the sloppy handling of the hire car in check was a challenge. On a couple of occasions, the back of the silver Sierra went into a brief slide which Williams was able easily to correct. About fifteen minutes into the journey, the road emerged from the other side of the hills behind Paul Ricard and opened onto a flat valley. Conditions were perfect: late afternoon on a glorious spring day; very little traffic on the road. The world was at Frank's feet.

The road curved left before leading into a short straight. On the right, trees and a gently rising rocky slope. On the left, several feet below the road, a ploughed field. As Williams swept through the curve, the Ford began to slide once more. Frank automatically took evasive action. But this time the correction on the steering wheel was too fast, too soon. The car swung the other way, then back as Williams tried to get out of trouble. By now the pendulum effect was gathering momentum and the car was out of control. It was a classic mistake, easily made but impossible to rectify once the error had been compounded by over-reaction.

As the car swerved towards the field on the left, Windsor noted the top of a concrete retaining wall which poked above the edge of the road. The car was aiming straight for it. Windsor braced himself as Frank continued to saw at the wheel. The impact with the concrete launched the Sierra briefly into the air. Then it nose-dived into the field before landing upside down. The front left-hand corner of the roof collapsed, trapping Frank underneath. His life would be changed for ever from that moment on.

Windsor, finding himself unharmed, began to disentangle himself from the seat-belt and twist his way through the debris. After struggling in a disorientated state to find the key, Peter switched off the ignition. Frank said he could not move. A smell of petrol was in the air. Windsor's next imperative was to get them both out of the wreckage.

The best means of escape seemed to be the rear window, which was cracked but not broken. As Windsor began to bang on the glass, he saw a pair of feet appear on the outside. A local, having spotted the crashed car, had run to help. Picking up a rock, the man smashed the window. Windsor crawled back towards Williams and, cradling Frank's head on his chest, gently dragged him backwards and out of the car. Windsor and his rescuer pulled Williams thirty yards clear. Peter urgently instructed the man to drive to Paul Ricard and find Nelson Piquet who, Windsor recalled, had a telephone in his car.

Piquet and Mansell were in the paddock when the man arrived with news of the accident. The drivers, plus Frank Dernie, jumped into Piquet's Mercedes-Benz and sped to the scene, arriving at roughly the same time as an ambulance. More than fifty minutes had passed: that would be a critical period in terms of Frank's recovery.

The ambulance, a rickety Citroën 2CV, set off for Toulon with Mansell on board to do what he could for Frank, who had been bleeding profusely. Windsor joined Piquet and Dernie as they followed in the Mercedes, Peter going to work on the telephone by dialling into the motor racing network which he knew would come to Frank's aid. A call was placed to Bernie Ecclestone who, in turn, tracked down the man Frank would want to see most: Professor E. S.

Watkins, the head of neurology at the London Hospital in Whitechapel Road.

Sid Watkins – or 'The Prof' as he was affectionately known – was also the resident surgeon in Formula One, a role which took him to all the races where, hopefully, his services would not be needed. Watkins had been instrumental in improving the medical back-up at the race tracks and part of his role, in addition to liaising with the local medical people, was to wait, fully kitted in flameproof gear, in a fast car, ready to attend the scene of any accident. He was highly respected. Frank would feel in safe hands as soon as The Prof appeared by his bedside.

While Ecclestone tracked down Watkins and placed his Citation jet on standby at Biggin Hill, Windsor was making an infinitely more difficult call to Boxford House. He told Ginny that there had been an accident. Not wishing to raise unnecessary alarm, he said they were taking Frank to hospital and he would report back. Then he phoned Patrick Head and gave a more detailed account. When Patrick called Boxford and said he was coming over, Ginny knew instantly that this had to be much worse than at first feared.

Watkins called Toulon and spoke to the surgeon dealing with Williams. It was agreed that Frank should be removed to the Timone Hospital in Marseilles where there was a good neurosurgical unit. Watkins then boarded the Citation for Marseilles airport, where he was met by Piquet. In his book *Life at the Limit* (Macmillan), Watkins described the scene on arrival at the Timone Hospital at approximately eleven p.m.:

The hospital was pretty quiet when we arrived and Nigel Mansell, Peter Windsor, Nelson and myself had a brief chat about the accident. It appeared that the rented car had rolled down a gully and the roof had caved in on his head. Frank was already in the operating theatre, so I changed my clothes and went in. I introduced myself to the operating neurosurgeon, Dr Vincentelli, who was expecting me and was very welcoming. I had a look at the X-rays and saw what I had feared most – there was complete dislocation at C6-C7 (the sixth cervical vertebra on the seventh) with gross reduction of the diameter of the spinal canal. It seemed highly likely that the spinal cord had been irretrievably damaged and one could only hope for the best.

Sid was present throughout the operation, emerging finally at two a.m. to reassure the anxious Windsor, Mansell and Piquet that everything possible had been done for the moment. It was difficult to forecast the outcome but it was clear at this stage that Williams was paralysed from the shoulders down. However, he was breathing well on his own and the vital signs were steady.

Ginny and Patrick arrived at the hospital the following morning. They were met by Professor Watkins and Dr Vincentelli, who explained the extent of Frank's injuries. The terrible truth began to dawn. Not long after, Ginny was even more shocked when she saw her husband in intensive care, a once fit and bubbly man lying prone, connected to every conceivable kind of tube and barely able to breath. He was a pale and dishevelled shadow of his former self.

Professor Watkins and the drivers flew back to London, Patrick Head returning to Didcot to take overall charge of the team. Ginny and Peter stayed in Marseilles, growing more anxious with each passing hour.

Despite assurances from the hospital staff that no more could be done, it seemed to Ginny that they were taking it literally. It was as if Frank was being left to die. As time went on, Ginny was sure of it. Outraged by the apparent absence of decent care and galvanised by the need to do something, Ginny's feisty nature would effectively save her husband's life. A call to Professor Watkins prompted the immediate dispatch of Paul Yate, an accomplished young anaesthetist at the London Hospital. Yate spent one night with Frank and quickly decided that the risk of a chest infection was so great that Frank should be flown back to the London Hospital for further treatment. The Timone Hospital made no objection and an air ambulance was quickly provided, the British consul, acting on instructions from Prime Minister Thatcher, organising an escort through Marseilles to the airport. The Learjet arrived at Biggin Hill shortly before fog closed in on southern England. By early evening, he was in the intensive care unit (ICU) at the London Hospital.

Watkins takes up the story:

That night we struggled a bit with his chest. I saw Peter Windsor and Mrs Williams that evening and took them over to the hospital pub known as 'The Grave' [The Grave Maurice] for a drink to try and cheer them up a bit.

Next morning it was clear we had to do something for Frank's chest so I got Johnny Weaver, our cardio-thoracic surgeon, to see him. We agreed that a procedure known as a mini-tracheotomy should be performed which, unlike a tracheotomy, preserves the capability of the patient to speak, and can control the chest infection by allowing suction of the secretions from the lungs and bronchi. This worked very well and obviated any need for mechanical ventilation.

Frank was a wonderful and remarkably uncomplaining patient – he was suffering a good deal of pain and tingling in his shoulder and neck, but we could not sedate him too much because of risk to his spontaneous breathing. He remained as polite as I always had found him in the past. I do not believe he ever omitted to say 'Please' or 'Thank You' for anything he needed to be done or had been done for him. He was tough and resolute and never once whinged about what had happened to him.

153

A week later, Frank was removed from the ICU to a side-room on the neuro ward. Messages had poured in from around the world: letters, cards, brief notes, short prayers. Some were from friends and associates but many were from people Frank had never met, fans inspired by his success and sharing his love of motor racing. Above all, everyone was deeply shocked although, among those who knew Frank well, there was little surprise that he had had an accident, only deep concern over its effect. Keke Rosberg commented:

I remember being really shocked. But, to be perfectly honest, once the news began to sink in, I don't think anyone was really surprised. Frank was a hooligan on the roads. Many of us were hooligans in those days and Frank actually did us a great favour. His accident really shook us with a reminder that we are not immortal. We thought we were. We thought we will be here for ever, we're so wonderful.

Everyone knew the corner; we knew the exact place where he had gone off. We had been up and down that road so many times, it was like having the accident happen in your own back yard. There was a big message in that accident for all of us. We were just very happy that Frank was still alive even though the news of his condition didn't sound that good.

There was good news from Rio de Janeiro. On Sunday, 23 March, Nelson Piquet won the Brazilian Grand Prix. Frank could just about understand the message before sinking into another period of deep sleep. Then came more bad news. Not long after Frank's move to the ward, he was rushed back to the ICU. It was the doctors' worst fear: Frank had developed pneumonia. His life was once more in the balance.

The staff fought for the best part of a week in the battle to stop his lungs filling with fluid. The pneumonia subsided but doubts about his recovery remained. On more than one occasion, Ginny was summoned from her hotel room in the belief that he would not last through the night. During the third or fourth week, Ginny saw for herself how Frank's life was constantly on a knife-edge. During an interview a year later, Frank remembered one particular occasion:

I had this tube which was used to suck the crap out of my lungs. One night, I suddenly found I couldn't breathe. The nurse raised the alarm and they came and shoved the suction tube into my lungs. It was a very unpleasant thing to have shoved down your lungs. They could not stop the stuff from coming. I remember thinking my spit tasted of yeast but they couldn't understand it. What had happened was I was on a nasal gastric feed and the tube had come out of my stomach and gone into my lungs. That's where all the food was going. The consultant arrived and he realised straight away.

I could have died then or on any number of occasions. But I had no idea that it had been such a close run thing. I really was not aware.

Ginny was only too aware, even six weeks after the accident when Frank was breathing on his own again. A consultant took her to one side and gently warned that she ought to remain prepared for the fact that Frank might not live.

The medical staff did not bargain for Frank's cussed determination not to be beaten. His supreme fitness before the accident played a large part in the slow recovery which began as the two-month mark approached. But there was no getting away from the fact that Frank would be a quadriplegic for the rest of his life. He would be unable to use his legs and lower arms. Since all voluntary functions had ceased beneath the level of his upper chest, he would be unable to breathe by expanding his ribs. He would never again be able to cough or, significantly in Frank's case, laugh. But he was alive. And he could breathe unaided. There was hope that eventually he would be able to swallow again. In the meantime, the nasal gastric feed would continue.

Frank and Ginny were united in their opposition to the widely held view that he should spend a period of rehabilitation at the special spinal unit at Stoke Mandeville. To the growing unease of the medical staff, plans were laid to convert the dining-room at Boxford House into a miniature ward capable of dealing with Frank's needs. On 28 May he finally returned home, twelve weeks after having left in his usual hurry to catch the flight to Nice.

A lot had happened on the race track since then. Apart from Piquet's victory in Brazil, Mansell had just won his first race of the season at Spa-Francorchamps in Belgium. A few weeks later, he would win again in Canada, a victory which pulled Nigel to within two points of the championship leader, Alain Prost. Mansell's initial fears about the team losing its direction had proved unfounded. As he recalled in an interview on 20 June 1986, Frank's accident had reminded him instantly of the loss of Colin Chapman, which had come just as Nigel was settling into Lotus:

I thought: 'No! Here we go again. I've just won two races for Williams, everything is looking fantastic, and now we have the thunderbolt of Frank's accident.' At Lotus, the change after Colin's death had been pretty dramatic for me personally. It was a disaster.

The main difference at Williams was the integrity of the team. Even though Frank was in hospital, there were four or five key people who carried on doing their jobs. Sheridan [Thynne] was the money-getter, Peter [Windsor] handled public relations, David Stubbs was the team manager, Frank Dernie the aerodynamicist and head of research and development, Alan Challis the chief mechanic and, of course, Patrick Head was the chief designer and overall factotum.

We've got tremendous resources and after Frank's accident everyone got together, reorganised and made sure we were pulling in the right direction. It has been a hell of a success story under the circumstances. And now I hear that Frank is thinking of coming into work for a couple of hours every day. So, the team can only get better and better.

Frank, in fact, had caught the team unawares by making a visit to Didcot a matter of days after returning home. Once again, his decision had gone against conventional wisdom. It took Ginny and two nurses to get him into the front seat of the Jaguar. He looked pale and desperately frail. But that brief visit to his beloved factory did more than any amount of medical administration. His bodily functions may not have been what they were, but his adrenalin was pumping as strongly as before. He could not wait to get back in harness.

During the time I had been in hospital, I was aware of Grands Prix taking place. I had seen them on television and I had several visits, roughly every fortnight, from Patrick and then Sheridan. But the visits never exceeded thirty minutes because I couldn't handle any more than that. I was being kept up to date only in very general terms. When I left hospital, I began to go into the factory for two or three afternoons a week, just a couple of hours each time. It was very uncomfortable physically; I found it very hard work.

The basic problem is, I don't have anything working below my armpits. Everything is concentrated in my neck and shoulders. All I can move is my neck, shoulders and, as a result, my arms. But they are all grossly overworked, so they ache like crazy all the time. I get a lot of stinging in my arms because of nerves that aren't working properly. But the bottom line was that Patrick and Sheridan were running the company in my absence and continued to do so while I gradually worked myself back in.

Meanwhile, there was trouble brewing. Prost continued to lead the championship but a win for Mansell in France moved him into second place. More than that, it put Nigel fifteen points ahead of Piquet – and Nelson was not happy about it. The Brazilian was of the opinion that he had unchallenged number one status within the team. Naturally, Mansell did not agree. 'I'm equal number one,' said Mansell. 'That's what I like about Williams. There's no bullshit in the contracts. They don't have a driver as absolute outright number one, and they don't say you are number two.' Frank, of course, had negotiated the contracts before his accident and he was quite clear on the matter:

I believe Nelson thinks he has been guaranteed a repeat of the situation we had with Carlos [Reutemann] when we controlled – or tried to control – the second driver. What we agreed in this case was that if one driver was leading the championship and needing every bit of support then we would obviously control his team-mate. But he was not given unconditional priority over the second driver. We took the view that they were both running for the championship and would have to fight it out between them.

It was a mature decision but, given the fragile egos and strong personalities involved, it was to prove to be a disastrous one.

Frank got to see the mounting tension for himself when he made his first public appearance by visiting the next race, the British Grand Prix at Brands Hatch. It was perhaps too soon during the period of slow recovery but, since travelling to a Grand Prix abroad was out of the question for the moment, Frank wanted to seize the opportunity. Above all, he wanted to go racing again. He needed an infusion of motor racing atmosphere just as much as an injection of medication.

Bernie Ecclestone arranged for a helicopter to collect Frank, Ginny and a nurse from Boxford House and fly them to the Kent circuit. A car picked them up and edged slowly through the crowd milling around the trackside enclosures. Peering inside, many recognised Frank and gave him enthusiastic words of encouragement. When they finally reached the inside of the circuit, Frank and Ginny were moved by the sight of a large banner opposite the pits. It said: 'Welcome Back Frank – from Brands Hatch'.

In the certain knowledge that media interest would be exceptionally high and there would be no peace for Frank, a press conference was organised. It was an emotional occasion, Frank struggling to articulate his words due to his breathing difficulties. But his sheer determination shone through as he sat in his wheelchair, Mansell and Piquet on either side. The standing ovation which followed gave an indication of the appreciation of this brave act and the esteem in which he was held.

Frank returned for a couple of hours on the second day of practice and saw the driving boot move to the other foot as Mansell became slightly desperate in a vain attempt to oust Piquet from pole position. That had been enough excitement. Frank, much to the relief of his medical support team, decided to watch the race at home on television. It made compelling viewing.

Within five seconds of the start, it seemed the anticipated battle between the Williams drivers was over. As Mansell snatched second gear in an attempt to take the lead, a dull explosion from the back of the Williams announced the failure of a driveshaft. Mansell pulled to one side and got on the radio to announce that his race was over. The rest of the field swept past. Or most of it, anyway.

Unknown to Mansell, there had been a multiple collision at the first corner and the track was blocked. The race would be stopped and started from scratch, allowing Mansell to take the spare car. That was the good news. The bad news concerned Jacques Laffite, whose Ligier had smashed head-on into a crash barrier. The ever-popular Frenchman had been an innocent victim but the severe leg injuries would end his Formula One career.

Despite being granted a reprieve, Mansell was pessimistic. He had driven the spare car briefly during practice and he had not liked it. Moreover, it had been set up for Piquet, whose turn it was this weekend to have use of this back-up chassis. Mansell's start was more circumspect than before. As Piquet raced into the lead, Mansell dropped to third place as he attempted to settle into the unfamiliar car. It did not take long. After two laps, Mansell was second and closing on his team-mate. For the next twenty laps, they ran nose-to-tail in a race of their own. Perhaps unnerved by Mansell's menacing presence, which was encouraged by the naked bias of the 120,000 crowd, Piquet missed a gear. In an instant, Mansell was in the lead. Piquet hung on but it was obvious that Mansell was not going to let his opportunity go. The outcome looked likely to be decided by the single pit stop each driver would have to make for fresh tyres.

Piquet came in first. Everything went according to plan and he was on the move again after 9.04 seconds. Two laps later, Mansell made his stop. Again, near perfection by the Williams crew, this stop taking half a second longer. As Mansell roared up the slope leading onto the track, Piquet was powering onto the pit straight. Mansell's preheated Goodyears gave him a limited amount of grip, but not as

much as Piquet, whose tyres had reached working tempera-
ture. Nelson knew he had to strike very quickly if he was to
have any hope of winning. They were tied together for a lap,
Piquet shaping up to have a go at Mansell as they approached
Druids Hairpin. He was perfectly positioned to outbrake
Nigel into the corner, only to find that a car which had just
left the pits was dutifully staying to one side, right on
Piquet's line. Nelson backed off but his moment had passed.
The battle raged for the remainder of the race, the Williams
drivers trading fastest laps. But Mansell always had the edge.
Victory – and an eleven-point lead over Piquet in the
championship – went to Mansell.

As the cars pulled up at the finish, Nigel tottered from
the Williams in a thoroughly dehydrated state, the spare car
having been without the luxury of an onboard drink bottle.
As Mansell swayed around on the victory podium, Ginny
Williams was persuaded by Patrick Head to represent
Williams and accept the trophy awarded to the winning
constructor.

The emotion was almost too much. As Ginny picked up
the gold cup and held it aloft, the grandstand opposite stood
as one and cheered mightily. Barely fighting back the tears,
Ginny's feisty look said everything. Despite such a cataclys-
mic four months, Williams Grand Prix Engineering had
barely broken its stride. There was the inescapable thought,
however, that Frank would never again be able to enjoy his
usual run around the race track, or rush about the paddock
and then take up his command post by the pit wall. Frank's
absence on race day had been keenly felt. Typically, he had
plans to put that right.

CHAPTER ELEVEN

Slipping through their fingers

Frank chose to go to the Hungarian Grand Prix even though this race was something of an unknown quantity for an able-bodied traveller, never mind one who was seriously impeded by a disability. It was the first time that Grand Prix racing had visited an eastern bloc country in recent times, but any fears about a forbidding welcome melted away in the enthusiastic embrace of Budapest and its people.

Having listened to complaints from a tearful Piquet about what he considered to be over-zealous driving by Mansell at Brands Hatch, Frank was to receive a dose of the mutual antipathy between his drivers when Nigel took his turn to whinge in Hungary. Piquet won the race as he pleased and rubbed in his superiority by lapping Mansell as the disgruntled Englishman made his way into third place. Piquet had tried a new differential in his car. He discovered that the revised transmission produced a considerable advantage – and then somehow forgot to impart this knowledge to the rest of the team. Mansell was furious. Neither driver was required to share every detail but Nigel felt that the technical staff, particularly the engineer working with Piquet, should have worked out what was going on and pooled such information for the good of the team as a whole.

Mansell nevertheless continued to lead the championship

and there was nothing to choose between the drivers as they won a race apiece in Italy and Portugal. At the penultimate round in Mexico, Nigel might have wrapped up the championship had he managed to put his car in first gear on the starting grid. He recovered from such a fundamental mistake and finished fifth. Piquet was fourth. Alain Prost took second place for McLaren and moved into second position on the championship table, six points behind Mansell and one ahead of Piquet. All three had a chance of becoming the 1986 world champion at the final round in Australia. Mansell, however, was the clear favourite.

Williams had already won the constructors' championship with a record number of points scored in a single season. Now it was time to sort out the drivers' title. It was to be one of the most dramatic climaxes in the history of the sport.

The Williams drivers fought over pole, with Mansell winning the prime starting position by three-tenths of a second. Prost was fourth fastest and, in the opinion of many, the championship outsider. Piquet took the lead initially but then Rosberg, driving in his last Grand Prix before retiring, decided to go out on a high note as he moved his McLaren ahead of the Williams. Prost, having made a typically conservative start while weighing up the opposition, moved unobtrusively into third place, ahead of Mansell. Prost then overtook Piquet and, almost immediately, the Brazilian spun, dropping to fourth place behind Mansell.

As things stood at one-third distance, Mansell would win the championship; the four points would be enough to give him the title, regardless of where Prost and Piquet finished. Mansell's chances looked even better when Prost suffered a puncture and made a pit stop for a fresh set of tyres. Ironically, this very move by Prost would indirectly cause Mansell's downfall.

Prost's discarded tyres were checked by the Goodyear

engineers as a matter of routine. They reported that the wear was minimal and, on this evidence, pit stops would not be required for fresh rubber. The news was relayed to Williams. The reality was that the wear may have been as expected on Prost's car but it was turning out to be considerably more on the Williams thanks to a higher power output from the Honda engines and the fact that both Mansell and Piquet were running more wing angle than Prost, thus forcing even more heat into the tyres.

Although no one in the pits was to realise it at the time, the first hint of impending trouble came on lap sixty-three. Rosberg, having led comfortably, suddenly pulled up on the far side of the circuit after hearing strange sounds from the rear of his car. Believing he had transmission trouble, the Finnish driver inspected the back of the McLaren, where he discovered the noise had been caused by rubber from a delaminating rear tyre hitting the bodywork.

Prost, having rejoined in fourth place, had worked his way past Mansell. Some time earlier, Piquet had done the same. The order now was Piquet, Prost and Mansell, with Nigel still on course for the championship. Then came the most spectacular defining moment of any championship in recent times. As Mansell reached in excess of 180 mph on the back straight, his left-rear tyre exploded. Nigel wrestled with the Williams as it bucked and lurched this way and that, sparks showering from the underbody as the rear section dragged along the ground. He somehow brought the car to a halt in the escape road. His first thought was that he was thankful to be alive. The bitter disappointment would come not long after.

Thanks to this dramatic turn of events, Piquet looked set to win the championship, but Patrick Head, alarmed by what he had seen on the television monitor, knew the team had no option but to bring Nelson into the pits for fresh tyres. Piquet responded. Prost was now on course for the title.

Piquet rejoined and set the fastest lap. Prost's on-board computer told him that his furious nothing-to-lose charge had extracted terrible dues on his fuel consumption figures. With one lap to go, the computer said he had no fuel left. Prost, backing off as much as he dared, could only carry on and hope that the computer might be wrong. It was. The Frenchman was simply overjoyed as he crossed the line, four seconds ahead of Piquet. Williams had just seen the championship slip through their fingers. Prost could not believe his luck. 'I'm very sorry for Nigel,' said the Frenchman. 'He deserved to be champion this year. But probably I'm more sad for Frank . . .' It summed up a common sentiment in the Adelaide paddock.

Frank had not made the long trip to Australia. However, there had been the consolation of an offer from BBC Television to watch and comment on the race from their studio. Careful arrangements had been at Boxford House in order that Frank could get enough sleep before being roused at midnight in preparation for the trip to London at two a.m. Steve Rider, who presented the programme from Shepherd's Bush, recalled the occasion in *Grand Prix* magazine:

Frank was in discomfort, medical support was constantly in attendance, but his contribution was revealing and provocative. When Mansell's tyre blew with the title almost in sight, his expression hardly changed, his mood immediately philosophical, analytical. It was a privilege to be alongside him at such a defining moment in the sport.

In fact, Williams was perhaps not as surprised as people might have expected. In an interview a few months later, he told me:

It's a funny thing, but I have been around in this business long enough to know how things can happen. As we drove up to London I was thinking about what everyone had been saying. Nigel had received a terrific amount of coverage and, I don't mean any disrespect here, but the television people were inviting me to London because I think it was generally assumed Nigel was going to win the championship. They had a big picture of Nigel on the wall and I could see some champagne on standby. People everywhere were saying that Nigel should be champion by Monday, that sort of thing.

It was a fair assumption to make but my motor racing vibes said to me that it's never that simple. It's more likely that something will go wrong rather than for everything to run smoothly; championships aren't that easy. So, it did not surprise me that Prost won the championship. That was not being pessimistic, that was being realistic.

It was very tough on Nigel – who I thought handled himself very well – but it was not quite so difficult for me. Sure, I knew Nelson, once he had new tyres, would catch Prost hand-over-fist and there would be a good run to the flag, but I also knew the chances of him winning were slim. So, I had a good fifteen to twenty minutes in the studio to compose myself and think of a few things to say.

Ever since the beginning of his recovery, Frank had had plenty of time to think about everything associated with what he referred to as the different kind of life he was now leading. He was not desperately interested in hurling himself into a major programme of rehabilitation. That would detract too much from his team and his work. Nothing else mattered, even though his values had been shaken up in the immediate aftermath of the accident. Typically, he was blunt about the subject when discussing it almost a year after the accident:

When I was lying in hospital, I tended to think that there was so much more to life. My attitude was, don't worry about being in a chair because that will give me more time to listen to music, and all that. I was thinking about how I could appreciate things I hadn't time for in the past: more time with my family, holidays, nature, the seasons, and so on. But all I think about now is racing! Are we going to win again in 1987!

You ask if my values have changed. I don't think they have. I am still as keen to go racing as I ever was; I still want to win; I still feel the urge to make money. I can't say that I have a more charitable view about life in general simply because I am fortunate to have survived. I feel much the same as before.

But the one thing I am aware of is how terribly lucky I am. I have a lovely wife, a family which supports me and takes care of me. I am also lucky because, when I was in hospital, I was terribly afraid that if I disappeared, this place [the factory] might go down hill. That has not happened at all. Therefore I can consider how lucky I am to have Patrick and Sheridan around the place, and all the other line managers who do their jobs so well.

I'm fortunate because I have a job to come back to. A lot of people in my position lose their jobs. Not only that, but I also appreciate how great it is to have a job that really is a passion that consumes you. They can't get me out of here at seven p.m. They want to go home, and I don't want to go!

As he spoke, Frank was sitting at his vast desk, his arms flailing occasionally as he drove them from his shoulders. The physiotherapy had focused, among other things, on Frank building up sufficient muscle power to prevent his head from flopping about, and gaining enough control of his biceps eventually to raise his hand to his face. But progress had been slow. The medical advisers may have had a plan, but Frank did not. He worked at it, but not with the conviction and devotion directed at his racing team. He knew why his body was now functioning as it did. And that was as far as it went.

They explained everything to me only so that I could understand it. You need to understand it. People say, 'Frank's going to crack,' but it's not like that. All you are concerned about is survival. That instinct is very strong, so you just do the things you know you have to do. If you understand what's going on, it helps you do a better job.

I've had to learn about the many complications that such an injury can cause: bladder, bowels, skin care – and I don't mean dry skin. If you are sitting somewhere too long, you get a sore, because of the poor circulation. It can become a break in the skin and, if that happens, you are in deep trouble. You've got to lie on your side for long periods. If I cut myself, it might take weeks to begin to heal.

As I sit here, I actually feel fairly normal, apart from the fact that my shoulders ache a bit. Also, I wouldn't be as bunged up as I am now if my cough worked. But I can't blow my nose because the muscles won't work.

It's a funny thing. God may have made life difficult by providing a very complicated nervous system which runs through the spinal cord and, if you touch it, then it's finished. It's so sensitive. But He did at least give you several vertebrae which operate the diaphragm and that at least allows me to breathe even though the muscles at the top, which should squeeze the lungs in and out, don't work any more. It could be worse! Everything seems complicated at first and you have to become accustomed to it.

Perhaps more difficult to come to terms with had been the sudden end to the precision timing with which Frank had previously ruled his life. Getting up in the morning had been nothing more than a waste of time. The twenty minutes or so spent washing and dressing may have been action-packed and bristling with economy, but it was an intrusion on the main business of the day, that of planning to win motor races.

As a result of the accident, it now took almost two hours to get ready each morning. The former irritation had become a crushing hindrance. It was the simplest and yet the most devastating side-effect. The straightforward business of getting up and mobile – a function which most people detest – was something which Frank would love to achieve with his former dexterity:

The frustration is almost unbearable. I've compared notes with a couple of other guys and it's the same thing for them. It's the amount of time taken to do everything. It takes up to an hour and forty-five minutes to wake me up, give me a cup of tea and an orange juice, get me out of bed, get me into the bath, get me out of the bath, get me shaved, clean my teeth, go to the loo every second, or so it seems. Then get me dressed and do things like put on a tie; it just seems to take for ever.

But it's not finished there. We've moved me from the dining-room on the ground floor to a room upstairs. That meant putting in a lift. Installing a full-size lift would have been a major disruption and, in any case, there were restriction orders on what we could do inside the house. It was bad enough having this one installed, but it means I have to be taken out of the wheelchair, sat in the seat, have the button pressed and then be collected at the other end. That alone takes about fifteen minutes from beginning to end. It just goes on and on.

Going to bed takes about thirty minutes, which is not quite as bad. I'm more placid then, tired and ready to go to sleep. But the morning is the worst. I give Robin a bit of a hard time even though it's not his fault at all!

Robin Kinnill had joined the Williams household as full-time nurse not long after Frank returned home from hospital.

He worked in association with Penny Lilly, a long-suffering and enormously patient physiotherapist who had provided untold support for Ginny as she struggled to come to terms with the many difficulties produced by the dramatic change in circumstances. In September 1986, Iain Cunningham had been recruited to help Frank from the moment he left home by doing the driving and generally taking care of his every need while at the office. Iain and Robin would travel with Frank to the races and, typically, Frank planned to attend all sixteen in 1987. It was just as well because his presence would be required as Mansell and Piquet became even more fractious than before.

Patrick Head had produced FW11B, a development of the 1986 car, complete with Honda turbo power in its latest and most potent form. The team was amply prepared for the start of the season. On paper, Williams were unbeatable with Piquet continuing to see himself as the driver who should be allowed by the team to win the title. The thing Nelson perhaps found most difficult to deal with was the fact that, contrary to his belief when he signed for Williams in 1985, Mansell was actually much quicker than he and many others had imagined. Piquet, having proved himself with Brabham, felt he should not need to do it all over again – particularly against a member of his own team.

Nigel took pole position, with Nelson sharing the front row, at the start of the first Grand Prix in Brazil. Yet, despite the extensive testing which had got them this far, Williams had overlooked one thing when it came to planning for the race.

The back straight had a grandstand running its entire length. In the excitement generated by the relentless heat and the explosive drama of the opening lap, the Brazilian spectators had a habit of tossing paper into the air. Some of it fluttered onto the track and one or two pieces found their way into the radiator ducts on the Williams-Hondas. Rising water and oil temperatures told the drivers of the absence of the fine-mesh grilles which should have been in place to prevent occurrences such as this. Despite pit stops to have the offending scraps of paper removed, the Honda engines never fully recovered and Piquet was lucky to finish second, Mansell sixth after another stop to attend to a punctured tyre.

But, if Piquet thought that was bad luck, he was to understand the true meaning of the expression during practice for the next race at Imola in Italy. The Williams flew off the road and smashed sideways into a concrete wall after what appeared to have been a tyre failure. Goodyear took no chances and, in a mammoth operation, manufactured new tyres for the entire field and had them flown overnight by chartered aircraft from England. Piquet, who had hurt his foot, was not allowed to race. But that would not be the only legacy of the 150 mph accident. He had crashed at Tamburello, and the incident would be recalled seven years later when Ayrton Senna slammed into the same stretch of concrete wall with such devastating effect.

The race was won by Mansell, putting him into the lead of the championship. It would be the only time he found himself in such a position all year. Prost, who had won in Brazil, moved to the head of the table again after finishing first in Belgium, a race in which Mansell would disgrace himself after a collision while disputing the lead with Senna's Lotus. Both cars spun off the track, the damage to the Lotus terminating Senna's race on the spot. Mansell continued for several laps before retiring, the period spent wrestling with his hobbled car having heated his road rage to boiling point. As soon as he had climbed from the cockpit, Mansell marched into the Lotus garage and grabbed Senna by the throat. It took three mechanics to haul him off. Senna had his revenge when he won the next two races in succession to take a temporary lead of the championship. Mansell responded by scoring maximum points in France and Britain, the latter victory sensational and typical of Nigel's turbulent career.

In France, Mansell had beaten Piquet through sheer speed and clever pit stop tactics; in Britain, he would destroy Nelson through barely controlled aggression of mind-blowing proportions. It would be a suitable reply to Nelson's waspish pre-race assertion that he had won two championships whereas Nigel had lost one and was clearly a driver of no consequence.

With thirty laps to go, Piquet appeared to have the race in his pocket. Mansell had been forced to make an unscheduled pit stop for tyres, and he rejoined twenty-eight seconds behind. Then, two things happened: Piquet's tyres lost their edge and Mansell began to drive like a man possessed. Each second gained raised the anticipation of the 100,000 fans as they worked themselves to fever pitch in the heat of a perfect summer's day.

With ten laps remaining, the gap was 7.6 seconds. At the end of the next lap, it was 6.5 seconds. With three laps to go, Mansell was on Piquet's tail. Approaching Stowe corner at 180 mph, he sold Piquet a perfect dummy. As Piquet moved to cover it, Mansell dived the other way and swooped down the inside. The two cars almost touched. But Mansell was through.

Piquet had run non-stop, a tactic decided by Nelson and the team beforehand on the best advice available. His stunned expression at the post-race press conference said that his relationship with Williams was as good as finished. In Hungary, a month later, he would slide a piece of paper beneath Frank's bedroom door. The note said he would be leaving at the end of the year. Frank was not unduly surprised. Once again, Piquet had asked for unequivocal number one status in 1988. Frank could not have granted Nelson's wish even if he had wanted to: he had already signed up Mansell for another season as joint number one.

The win at Silverstone moved Mansell into joint second place with Piquet in the championship, the Williams drivers one point behind Senna. The team, meanwhile, had opened a healthy lead in the constructors' championship. Piquet took the initiative in the drivers' series thanks to wins in Germany, Hungary and Italy, Mansell responding with victories in Austria, Spain and Mexico. When they reached the penultimate round in Japan, Piquet led Mansell by twelve points; no one else was in the reckoning, but Mansell was about to crash out of the title race in spectacular fashion.

There had been an intense verbal exchange between the two Williams drivers after the previous race and Piquet wound up Mansell even further by setting the fastest time during the first qualifying session in Japan. Although he would not admit it, the physical effects of that massive accident at Imola had taken their toll on Piquet. He had been running slightly below par throughout 1987, but he turned that to good effect when dealing with the more boisterous ways of his team-mate. Piquet had said that he would win the title by consistently gathering points; Mansell's all-or-nothing style, he claimed, was not the answer. Nigel was about to prove that as he took to the track at Suzuka.

In an attempt to regain pole position, Mansell spun and crashed backwards into the barrier at high speed. Although he was not to know for certain at the time, Nelson Piquet had just become the 1987 world champion while standing in the Williams garage watching Mansell's vain efforts on the television screen.

The impact inflicted severe bruising. Mansell said he had

never known pain like it — which was quite something, given his history of injuries in motor sport. The muscular strain and the extent of shock was such that Professor Watkins ruled Nigel out of the remainder of the weekend. Mansell was taken by helicopter to Nagoya's University Clinic, where there was concern over the possible build-up of fluid between his lungs and heart. That proved not to be the case and, after being kept under observation overnight, Mansell was flown back to England, out for the rest of the season.

He was not sorry to see the back of it. For weeks, Nigel had been complaining about his treatment by Honda. He genuinely believed he was being short-changed thanks to his engines being down on power when compared with those supplied to Piquet. Even allowing for Mansell's persecution complex, it was an interesting point in the light of developments which had been brewing backstage for the best part of a year.

In November 1986 Soichiro Honda, the company's founder, had paid a rare visit to a Grand Prix. He had travelled to Adelaide in the understandable belief that he was about to witness a Honda-powered driver win the world championship for the first time. He was more than disappointed when circumstances conspired against Mansell and Piquet during that dramatic race. This was almost a matter of honour. Honda's dignity had been affronted when Prost's McLaren-TAG-Porsche had sailed through the middle and snatched the title at the eleventh hour.

How could this have happened? The combination of almost freak circumstances that afternoon was of no interest. Honda had not been impressed by the manner in which Williams had allowed their drivers to fight among themselves during the season, ultimately to the detriment of the team as a whole. But, worse than that, Japanese business methodology could not come to terms with the fact that the team was being led by someone who was disabled.

Despite the run of success which demonstrated clearly that Williams Grand Prix Engineering had a first-class management structure capable of coping without its leader for several months, the Honda management could not accept that such a thing was possible. In their opinion, Williams should have found another managing director as a matter of course. Winning races was all very well but the Japanese view, although never articulated as such, seemed to be that the company should have a recognisable and respected figurehead. The subtext was that a man in a wheelchair did not provide the correct image.

There was a further complication. Honda had fallen in love with Ayrton Senna. Quite rightly, they saw this man as the future and a deal had been done to supply Senna's team, Lotus, with Honda engines, starting in 1987. The expectation was that Senna and the Lotus-Honda, with a new so-called active-ride suspension system, would blow the doors off the Williams-Hondas. They reckoned without the fact that the Lotus designer, Gerard Ducarouge, could not hold a candle to the more pragmatic methods of Patrick Head. The Lotus won just two races, a poor return compared to the nine scored by Williams. This had the unfortunate effect of alienating Honda even further.

By May 1987, Frank Williams had begun to realise that Honda were thinking about terminating their arrangement even though the contract was due to run until the end of 1988. When he confronted his engine suppliers on the matter, there was neither a confirmation nor a denial. Then events began to move quickly.

At the end of July, Honda said they would not be continuing with Williams. (Williams had been offered the opportunity to carry on if they gave a seat to Satoru Nakajima, a journeyman Japanese driver. Frank and Patrick rejected such a poor alternative almost immediately.) Shortly after that, Piquet made the announcement that he would be staying with Honda by joining Lotus, thereby fuelling Mansell's belief that Honda were favouring 'their' man by giving Nelson decent engines in the hope that he could take the title of world champion with him when he moved to Lotus. And, as if that was not enough, Senna announced that he would move to McLaren and take Honda engines with him, in effect the Honda engines which had previously been earmarked for Williams. In the space of four months, Frank's world had simply fallen apart.

'With hindsight, I suppose one could have taken a more aggressive legal stance with Honda,' said Frank in an interview with Alan Henry. 'But a settlement was duly reached although, again with hindsight, it was grossly inadequate.' It was grossly inadequate because Honda's action would precipitate one of the worst seasons in the team's history. Turbocharged engines were about to be phased out and Williams switched to a normally aspirated V8 built by John Judd, a talented engineer who ran a comparatively small engine business in Rugby. For all his efforts, the power of Judd's V8 was no match for the latest Honda, Senna and Prost winning all but one of the season's sixteen races for McLaren. For the first time since running FW06 in 1978, Williams did not score a single win. By their standards, 1988 was a complete disaster. The only high point for Frank had been the CBE, awarded in the New Year's Honours for the team's efforts in 1987.

The introduction of an active-ride system during 1987 had been reasonably successful, Piquet having used it to win at Monza. However, a transfer of the system to the new Judd-powered car merely served to complicate matters. The

FW12 was much smaller than its predecessor, which made the packaging of the active-ride components more difficult, particularly when attempting to keep the electronic components away from the hotter parts of the car. In addition, the Judd V8 vibrated more than the Honda V6.

All told, the active suspension components did not like their new environment as they became all hot and bothered – rather like the drivers as they tried to wrestle with the car. Mansell became so disillusioned with the inconsistency of the active-ride that he brought his clubs with him to the race track in Mexico in the belief that his time would be better served on the golf course. Attempts to remove the active-ride from the FW12 halfway through 1988 resulted in what Head referred to bluntly as 'a bit of a pig's ear'. No one was in the least surprised when Nigel succumbed to Ferrari's blandishments and signed a contract for 1989.

Williams had replaced Piquet with Riccardo Patrese, a quick Italian who was at his very best only when the car was capable of winning. That was patently not the case in 1988, although things were looking up the following year. Having decided that it was essential to have a relationship with a major manufacturer, Frank had entered preliminary discussions with Renault almost as soon as he knew the association with Honda was about to end. Renault had not been directly involved with Formula One since the move by Lotus to Honda engines in 1987. But there was quiet activity in the Renault Sport headquarters in Paris as a small group of engineers worked on a brand-new, normally aspirated (non-turbo) engine to suit the forthcoming change in regulations. It was clear to Frank and Patrick that they had to be first in the queue for this engine. A deal was done for 1989. It was the first step in what would turn out to be a decade of massive achievement for Williams and Renault. Having done that, Frank then had to put his personal house in order.

As the months had slipped by, Frank's limited dexterity had improved as far as it could. Nelson Piquet had bought him a hands-free telephone, which proved a boon for someone who liked to spend much of his time communicating and keeping abreast of developments worldwide. Gloves with a mildly abrasive surface allowed the moving of pieces of paper across his desk, and special splint for his hand permitted Frank, after endless practice, at least to scrawl his initials. But, even though the recovery had reached its limit, Frank shunned devices designed specifically for the disabled, just as he refused point blank to have a badge for disabled parking displayed on his car. It was as if he wanted to be treated as normally as possible. But there was only so far his friends and family could go. Iain Cunningham, Frank's chauffeur and personal helper, commented:

We thought that because he had been so fit and so determined in his able-bodied life, he would put more effort into regaining more movement and having more independence – but he didn't. He just got on with his life. He very rarely complained. Occasionally, in the car in the mornings, he would say his arms were giving him gyp. He would say he was sorry, he was not feeling that good, that there was a bit of pain. There would be a slight explanation, but he would never court sympathy.

Interestingly, when I got to know him a bit better, I made the point that he could use his disability a little bit more when it came to getting the sympathy vote when dealing with his sponsors or whomever. He said he was aware of that, but he was reluctant to use it because it could show weakness.

He never said that he missed his exercises or his running. But he did miss being able to wander off down the paddock and see people. He refused point blank to have something like an electric wheelchair. 'No way,' he would say. 'I'm not going to look like an effing Dalek!'

He wanted to look as normal as possible. He was fastidious about his appearance. I remember on one occasion we went to Renault for the launch of an engine and I hadn't straightened his trousers. As they were taking the photos, I suddenly realised. Even now, when I see that photo, I get so angry about it. Something like that was important to Frank. It was important to me as well. It was the little details which mattered.

The biggest difficulty – for Ginny, if not for Frank – came at Boxford House. It was no longer a home in the sense of a bolt-hole from the rest of the world, a private place of intimacy and secrets, somewhere to share both frustration and affection with a partner. It was now no more than a private nursing home, a resting place for Frank at night. Frank and Ginny were part of a domestic situation which was, perforce, no longer what it had been. The strain was made worse by outsiders, albeit well meaning and extremely helpful, looking on as Frank and Ginny tried to come to terms with a complete change in roles, the once fiercely independent husband now having to rely totally on his wife, and vice versa. Ginny, in particular, found she was living with a different person. It was an impossible task, even for someone with her steely determination and utter devotion.

In the summer of 1988, they decided to sell Boxford House. Two properties were purchased: a former rectory near Newbury and a flat in London. Leaving Boxford was a terrible wrench for Ginny since this wonderful house had represented both her happiest and saddest moments. And yet, when Frank was wheeled through the door for the last time, the occasion appeared to have no meaning. When asked if he had no feelings at all, Frank looked Ginny straight in the eye and replied simply: 'Emotion is weak.' Cunningham recalled the moment vividly:

That really shook me. I thought, 'Steady on, Frank.' It was very unusual but there were times when he could be quite cruel – and I don't think that had anything to do with the accident. I think there were times when he could derive an element of what might be called perverse pleasure in using the power he had over others to inflict a little bit of pain or discomfort. I think he did that with Damon [Hill] in 1996, for example.

But the one thing he always had control over – and always used – was money. It was a constant battle with him over money and he would fall out quite frequently with people in the team over salaries. It wasn't the result of having been broke in the past, because it was quite controlled. He would quite happily spend a lot of money on expensive suits and there would be no question of taking the helicopter at £200 per hour. He was not afraid to spend his money.

The purchasing of the two properties was a case in point. Ginny used the apartment as a place to regain her independence and recharge for a couple of days each week before joining Frank at the house in Newbury when the children returned from school. The new arrangement worked well. It allowed them both to accept and adjust fully to the implications of Frank's moment of stupidity on 8 March 1986.

CHAPTER TWELVE

Nigel: gone today, here tomorrow

While en route to the 1987 French Grand Prix, Frank had returned for the first time to the scene of his accident. Peter Windsor was waiting by the roadside when Frank's hire car drew up. Together, they talked through the build-up to a brief incident which had changed almost everything. Then Frank asked Iain Cunningham to press on. There was business to attend to at the race track.

If the remainder of the journey was spent in angry contemplation of an event which would drive many a man to despair, there was no sign of it, as Cunningham confirmed:

He just took it all in. One of those things. Now let's get on. I drove him quite a lot at the time and he would say I was very smooth, but not quite quick enough! On a number of occasions, when on our way back to Boxford at night, he would tell me that he used to turn the headlamps off so that he could see other cars coming. He knew the road so well that he would drive without lights and he used the earth banks to control the car. 'So, I have no regrets,' he said. 'It was only a matter of time before I was going to have an accident.'

It was a point which he quietly reiterated after being wheeled into the shade beside the team's motor home at Paul Ricard. What was his verdict on the cause of the accident?

I cocked it up. It was entirely my fault. I can blame no one else. In fact, it reinforces my opinion that I have been extraordinarily lucky to have survived and continue doing what I enjoy most. If I'm completely honest, I had an accident coming at some point, and I didn't do anything about it. It got me in the end. I didn't drive stupidly – by that I mean, I didn't make any rash overtaking moves when I was driving. But, for me, every corner was a challenge.

The trouble is, I love racing. I just had this urge to go quickly, to handle every corner – provided the road was clear, of course – with a high-speed drift. That's why I love racing drivers, the really good ones. What they do in a racing car is just brilliant. I love it.

Whether or not he felt that way about his drivers when he travelled to Paul Ricard two years later is a matter for debate. Mansell had been replaced by Thierry Boutsen, a placid Belgian with a great deal of natural talent. Patrese, free from an overbearing number one, had come into his own, the Italian maturing and driving brilliantly. Unfortunately, he did not always have the equipment to go with it, the liaison between Williams and Renault taking time to iron out the technical wrinkles.

To be fair to Boutsen, he had got off to a terrible start when he crashed heavily (through no fault of his own) during pre-season testing in Brazil. It had taken him three months to get his breath back, but he was fit enough to score his maiden F1 victory in a wet race in Canada. Similar conditions during the final Grand Prix of 1989 in Australia allowed Boutsen to display his delicate skills once more as he gave Williams only their second win of the season. At least that was two more than the previous year and, at the end of the day, Williams were second in the constructors' championship. However, the table, showing McLaren-Honda with almost twice as many points, told the true story of a season dominated once more by Senna and Prost, with the rest struggling miserably in their wake.

The competitiveness of the car/engine combination took a step forward in 1990 when Renault introduced a new V10 which could be mounted lower in the latest chassis, the FW13B. If McLaren looked like being beyond reach, Williams were at least determined to keep Ferrari in check, even though the Italian team now had Prost on their payroll, alongside Mansell. In the event, not only would they fail to keep up with Ferrari's total, Williams would drop to fourth place when Benetton racked up fifteen points after finishing first and second in the very last race of the season.

Patrese and Boutsen had scored a win each but the feeling was that neither driver was cut out to be the thrusting number one the team expected, Boutsen a particular disappointment to Frank. It was no surprise to discover that the Belgian driver's contract had not been renewed.

Michael Cane, the team manager since the start of the 1989 season, was coincidentally leaving at the same time. His memories of working with Frank, although brief, would nevertheless be pleasant:

I found my time there, particularly getting to know Frank, very enjoyable. He was in his wheelchair all the time of course, but there was never an ounce of self-pity. He was a charming man. He had the ability to talk to anyone, no matter where they stood in the organisation. He's obviously very intelligent and he had this drive just to keep going to get back to the top.

We never had a cross word. The only disagreement we had was over someone who had worked in the team for many years. It suddenly didn't suit the structure of the team for that person to be there and Frank told me to get rid of him. But, since this person had been there for so long, I felt that should be Frank's job, and said so. To the best of my knowledge, the person concerned is still there.

Frank has a great sense of humour, but that will not be evident unless you know him. The pictures you see of Frank on television are of someone who is concentrating totally on something at that particular moment. He's massively focused but, if you look at people in a similar position in the pit lane, they are exactly the same. When it's all over, he would relax.

Frank is very good at taking any misfortune that comes along. He doesn't seem to look backwards; he's always looking towards the next objective. There was a clear division between the technical and commercial side, and it worked very well. Patrick didn't want to get involved with the commercial aspect and he was free to do whatever was necessary to make the cars competitive. Frank worked with Sheridan [Thynne] on the commercial side and it seemed to be a very good arrangement.

Frank had his own private plane by that stage and I would travel with him to a lot of the races. We didn't say a great deal either then or at any other time. I am not a great conversationalist myself and we would maybe chat about the tyres we were going to run, or something like that. But, otherwise, not a lot was said, and that seemed to suit us both.

A lot of the criticism to come his way in recent years is because of the way he appears to fire his drivers for no good reason. I haven't been surprised at all to see him let some of the drivers go because he is very pragmatic about these things. Team owners know the graft that has gone on behind the scenes. The team wins and they see drivers taking most of the glory. The team owner knows what it's like to run a business, with a great number of people working very hard, and suddenly the media is only interested in the driver. I'm sure that can be irritating at times. Certainly, Frank tends to see most of his drivers as no more than another employee. But, above all, he likes a driver with fire in his belly, one who has it there every time he gets in the car.

And there was the rub. Patrese and Boutsen, for all their skill, did not excite Frank; Nigel Mansell, for all his emotional baggage, most certainly did. As Frank and Patrick cast around for someone to drive for the team in 1991, Mansell was on the short list of likely candidates. And he was willing to talk. Or, to put it another way, he was willing to have his ego massaged and to be tempted to think about it.

Officially, Mansell was going to retire at the end of 1990. He had said so in an emotional off-the-cuff announcement at Silverstone in July. Life at Ferrari had got that bad. The relationship had started off remarkably well in 1989 when he won his first race for the Italian team. The victory in Brazil had ended a lean period; Nigel was hailed as the new hero. Thanks to a team-mate who was no match, Nigel had the place to himself. He could do no wrong and, truth to tell, he had never driven better. He was relaxed and happy. Then Ferrari signed Alain Prost for 1991. Mansell knew the Frenchman, a master politician, would be no pushover.

By mid-season, Nigel was very unhappy with his lot. He was thirty-six and yet another year seemed to be slipping by without the championship he craved. There were no team orders within Ferrari, the only rule being that whoever was in front should be allowed to stay there. At Silverstone, Mansell was in the lead. Prost, employing his usual stealth, gradually moved forward and slotted into second place. He was quite content to adhere to the rules and stay there.

Mansell was struggling with a gearbox which would play up intermittently. A bout of trouble just after half distance allowed Prost to take the lead. Mansell's mood darkened each time the transmission faltered. When the gearbox finally refused to budge from neutral, Nigel rolled to a halt on the inside of the first corner. This was the final straw. He walked back to the paddock, discarding his gloves and balaclava and throwing them to the crowd as he went. Then he wondered out loud in front of a BBC Television camera why it was that his car should always be the one to break.

The chucking away of his working gear was a symbolic act. Convinced that Prost was conspiring against him and that he no longer had the full support of the team, Nigel discussed the possibility of retirement with his wife, Rosanne. The time seemed right. Not long after the race had finished, he called the media to the Ferrari motor home and announced that he was going to quit at the end of the season. Now began a game of cat and mouse.

The stories soon surfaced, to the effect that Williams were making a pitch for his services in 1991. When the rumours began to get out of control in September, Mansell gathered the British press together in the paddock in Monza and stated categorically that nothing had changed. He was going to retire. If this was designed to increase the pressure on Williams to agree to Mansell's demands, then the tactic worked. A few weeks later, a press release from Mansell's home on the Isle of Man said he would be driving for Williams in 1991. He cited huge support from his fans as they pleaded with him not to stop racing. There was doubtless some truth in that, for Nigel had captured the imagination of the public like no driver since James Hunt fifteen years before. But the members of the media, who had no reason to doubt his earnestly articulated denial at Monza, were more sceptical. It seemed the offer of £4.6 million for a one-year contract had something to do with it. It made Mansell Britain's most highly paid sportsman and put him on a par with Ayrton Senna, the reigning champion.

The deal was a measure of just how serious Williams were about returning to the top; so serious, in fact, that Frank had tried to tempt Senna. Ayrton had played along with Williams, but the cynical view was that the Brazilian was merely using the contact as a lever in his negotiations over new terms at McLaren. Whatever the interpretation, Frank had no hard feelings:

Quite apart from Ayrton's driving ability, I was very impressed with him as a businessman; his attention to detail is meticulous. And I must admit that, yes, I thought we'd got him. At Spa, at the end of August, he came to the motor home on the Friday evening and told me that he had informed Ron Dennis he would be leaving McLaren. The contracts were all drawn up and everyone was happy. But then Mr Kawamoto of Honda came up with more money, so Ayrton's demands were met, and he stayed where he was. I was immensely disappointed of course, but I don't regret having tried to get him, whatever it cost.

Frank then spoke to Jean Alesi, who subsequently changed his mind after having signed an initial agreement. Given Alesi's suspect temperament which would emerge in the seasons to come with Ferrari and Benetton, that was a lucky break for Frank.

Despite Mansell's cloak and dagger routine and the inevitable histrionics he would bring to the team, it could not be denied that he was ready to win the championship. He would have undisputed number one status, Patrese accepting the role of support driver. And, as if to answer any remaining doubters in the team, Nigel climbed aboard an FW13B at Estoril during a winter test and took the 1990 car around the Portuguese track faster than it had ever gone before.

Frank, meanwhile, had been parrying questions from the British press when they met for their annual pre-season lunch at the Didcot factory. Naturally, some of the more truculent hacks were keen to remind Frank of how relieved he had been to see the back of Mansell at the end of 1988.

Tactful as ever, Frank agreed that Nigel had his negative side. He then employed the catch-phrase he liked to use most when defending a U-turn in company policy. 'I'm a realist,' he said. 'Circumstances change.' Then he flashed the winning smile.

The fast-moving world Williams was trying to dominate had dictated continuous change at the Didcot factory. The team was in the process of installing a new wind tunnel capable of accommodating a 50 per cent size model. The older 40 per cent tunnel, which had outlived its usefulness, had been sold to Lotus. The new facility was so large, it would not fit inside the existing building. The massive structure would require concrete pylons twenty feet deep to support it. Britain was in the grip of a recession, but there was little sign of it at Basil Hill Road. Frank countered:

That doesn't mean to say we are flush with money. Far from it. We are feeling the pinch just like everyone else. We would like to have cutbacks, but you can't, can you? Or, at least, not if you want to win races. When you are taking on people like Fiat [the owner of Ferrari], then you can't cut back. We now have about 170 people on the payroll and I would like to be able to say, 'That's it. We're not employing anyone else.' But it doesn't work like that. If a department needs someone, and you know that's true, then you can't cut back.

One such example had been the decision in 1990 to recruit Adrian Newey, an aerodynamicist and designer who had cut his teeth in Indycar racing, and with a small F1 team, Leyton House. Patrick Head was quick to realise that Newey's talent had not been exploited fully. It was a shrewd move which would have much to do with WGPE's outstanding success a few years later. In the meantime, Frank was examining the bottom line: 'It is costly,' he agreed. 'You have to say that if Fiat and Honda weren't involved in Formula One, then it would be cheaper. But, so long as companies like that are involved, then those are the rules you play by. There's no point in complaining about it.' Frank went on to give another example of the growth within his company, albeit on a smaller scale:

We had one area of the factory which we used for storage and for packing up the cars when we went on the so-called flyaway races in Brazil, Mexico, Australia and so on. Now, that space has been taken over purely for the manufacture of stickers for the cars. We have two guys doing that full time. Before, we contracted the stickers to an outside firm but we wanted to do the job properly ourselves. So, you need more space and two more employees.

The press lunch was being held in the Williams Conference Centre, a building constructed in 1989 on land at the back of the factory. Apart from providing additional revenue through the hiring out of the two meeting rooms (the Piers Courage Suite and the Alan Jones Room), the 10,000-square-foot building also served as a display centre for the seventeen Williams Formula One cars the team had gathered over the years. Frank explained:

The original requirement was to find somewhere satisfactory – long-term – for our ever-expanding collection of Williams cars. Previously they had been shoved in various corners, literally one on top of the other. But we needed a good sound business reason to spend a lot of money on the building. Colin Cordy, our commercial executive at the time, came up with the proposal because he could foresee a useful amount of business from the outside world. His research showed that there was nowhere within a considerable distance which had the sort of conference facilities we had in mind. Equally, it would be a means of pleasing our sponsors – Camel, Canon and

Labatts, as well as our technical partners, Renault and Elf – and demonstrating to them that Williams is very professional in its business attitude towards them and their requirements.

It was self-evident that the sponsors would expect an improvement in performance, and Williams was upbeat about his chances of delivering the results:

I must say Nigel's presence has done a tremendous amount for motivation round here. I think he's changed considerably from the last time around. I find him much more mature than he was, but at the same time he's every bit as aggressive as before. There's no question about his will to win the title – he really doesn't want to retire without a world championship. I'll admit I was a bit worried about his motivation in the last couple of races in 1990, but he wasn't really in my focus at the time – I was too busy trying to get Mr Alesi to honour his contract.

Williams went on to praise Patrese in the highest possible terms considering the Italian was the unequivocal number two. 'He communicates well with Patrick on a technical level,' Williams commented, 'and he's always willing to test. He never badmouths the team, either. I think Riccardo is a very good man as well as a very good racing driver.' Patrese was to prove that by qualifying faster than Mansell in the first seven races of the 1991 season, no mean achievement given Nigel's bullish commitment at the wheel. Neither driver, however, was able to translate promising practice performances into top-line results.

This was to be a difficult period for everyone on the team as they came to terms with the technical developments introduced on the latest car, FW14. An electronically controlled and hydraulically activated six-speed gearbox meant that drivers could change gear by flicking little paddles mounted behind the steering wheel spokes. It did away with the need for a gear lever and, once the car was on the move, a clutch pedal. The problem in the first race of the 1991 season was to keep the system working for the duration of the 190-mile Grand Prix in Phoenix, Arizona. Mansell's gearbox played up again in Brazil, but second place for Patrese opened the Williams championship account. Neither driver finished at Imola, but second place in Monaco not only gave Mansell his first points, it also backed up a fine performance by Patrese which had ended when he crashed on someone else's oil. The gearbox maladies appeared to have been fixed. A win was on the cards.

That seemed to be the case at the next race in Canada as the Williams drivers occupied the front row of the grid. Mansell shot into the lead and never looked likely to be beaten. As he started the final lap, Mansell led Nelson Piquet's Benetton by forty-seven seconds. It was all over, bar the shouting. It was clear Nigel was revelling in the thought that he was about to win a race for only the second time in almost as many years. He began waving to the crowd, even though there was more than a mile to go before the chequered flag. As he reached the hairpin at the far end of the circuit, the semi-circle of tightly packed grandstands rose to greet him. Mansell responded. The waving continued.

He began to change down through the gearbox and, as he rounded the tight corner, he allowed the engine revs to fall too far. The transmission baulked between gears. The low revs meant there was insufficient electrical charge left in the system to enable the hydraulics to engage a gear as Mansell began desperately to flick the paddle. At the same time, the engine died. Unable to find a gear, Mansell could not bump-start the car. The Williams rolled to a halt. Piquet almost laughed himself sick as he cruised past his old enemy to take a win he had never expected.

Mansell, naturally, was outraged, describing it as 'one of the worst mechanical failures I have ever suffered'. Frank Williams said nothing. Patrick Head opened his mouth, as if to speak, and then shut it. Finally, in a quiet moment, he later admitted that instructions about how to handle the equipment had not taken into account the fact that a driver might be using one hand to wave to the crowd. There was a smile playing on his lips as he said it.

More important was the fact that Ayrton Senna led the championship with forty points; Patrese had ten, Mansell seven. McLaren had fifty points in the constructors' championship, Williams seventeen. The respective gaps were reduced in Mexico when Williams scored their first one-two since 1989 as Patrese stormed home ahead of Mansell. Nigel began to redress the balance with victory in France but, more than anything, he needed to confirm his belated championship momentum in front of his fans at the British Grand Prix.

The immediate task was to be faster than Patrese during qualifying for the first time in the season. Nigel was positive from the outset, claiming the revised circuit at Silverstone was the best in the world, a pugnacious sign that he was going to defeat it just as readily as the opposition. Sure enough, he was fastest in every practice session, quickest in the warm-up on race morning and, apart from a brief intervention by Senna at the start, Nigel led all the way. Into the bargain, he set the fastest race lap and Senna, on course to take second place, ran out of fuel on the last lap. The Brazilian led the championship with fifty-one points, Mansell was second on thirty-three. Williams had moved into second place in the constructors' race.

McLaren's advantage was reduced further when Mansell won in Germany, Senna fighting back in Hungary and Belgium, Mansell responding with a fine victory in Italy. As they moved on to Portugal, Senna led Mansell by eighteen points.

The tension was building as Patrese once again claimed pole position with Mansell fourth fastest, the Williams drivers separated by the McLarens of Gerhard Berger and Senna. Mansell, in typically aggressive form, stunned the McLaren drivers as he swooped past them both on the first lap and fell in behind his team-mate. By lap eighteen, Mansell was leading. Senna was fourth. Everything was in order as Nigel made a scheduled stop for tyres.

The pit crew had the Williams on the move again in 7.75 seconds. Unfortunately, the mechanic working on the right-rear wheel hadn't quite finished when Mansell was waved away. He had motored a few yards when the wheel flew off, leaving the car stranded in the outer lane of the pit road. The answer would have been to place a trolley jack beneath the rear of the car and haul it back to the Williams pit, where a replacement wheel could have been fitted. But the error was compounded when the mechanics were instructed to run to the stricken car and attend to it where it sat forlornly on three wheels. That was clearly against the regulations but, unforgivably, the officials allowed Nigel to drive his heart out for twenty laps before informing the team that he had been disqualified. This time, Mansell was perfectly entitled to be outraged. He had driven brilliantly and done nothing wrong.

Who was at fault? Peter Windsor, now the team manager, bravely took full responsibility, although there was no vituperative condemnation from anywhere within the team. Nor, for that matter, from Mansell. Williams were quick to put out a press release stating that nobody would be made a scapegoat for a failure which had cost Mansell ten points. The statement said that 'the car departed prematurely and that was not the driver's fault'. That much was self-evident.

Patrick Head was prepared to elaborate more when interviewed by BBC Television.

In the sequence that occurs when the nuts are undone, the wheels come off and the new ones go on, there is a position where the chaps on the [air] guns stand up in the air holding the guns above their heads. That is the signal to the jack men that their job is complete, the nuts are tight and the person controlling the pit stop [Windsor] can step away and let the car out. In that process there was a breakdown. The right-rear wheel was not complete and the guys had not given the signal that they had completed their job, but the process that allowed the car to leave the pits was allowed to occur.

Windsor, as planned, had taken his cue from the rear jack man and, once he saw the rear wheels back on the ground, Windsor had assumed everything was ready at that end. But, having waved Mansell away, the situation would have been redeemable had the subsequent work not been carried out in the so-called 'fast lane' of the pit road. But that was impractical, not to say dangerous since other cars were hurtling into the pit lane at speeds in excess of 100 mph. To drag a hobbled car into their path would have been asking for trouble. There were other anomalies concerning the poor layout of the pit lane. Windsor, with adequate justification, raised the point with officials, but they would have none of it. Mansell was disqualified. Frank was typically philosophical. 'We can't appeal against a stewards' decision,' he said. 'We changed the wheel in the wrong place, and that's all there is to it.'

As far as Windsor was concerned, Frank supported the team's public stance by refusing to blame anyone once they were behind closed doors. On the other hand Windsor felt he could have been given more support since the system of watching the two jack men had been devised as a means of making up time, a saving which was necessary because the design of certain parts of the car placed the team at a disadvantage during the pit stops. Windsor offered his resignation, but Frank refused to accept it.

That was a vote of confidence, but I needed Frank to say: 'You are one of a team, there was a cock-up, so let's move on and do a proper analysis.' That didn't really happen.

Also, I didn't agree with Frank when he said we could have pulled the car back into the pit and put the wheel on. To me, that was an insane reaction. I remember one car coming past and I barely saw who it was because it was going so fast – down the inside! If we had started pulling the car back, someone would have been killed, for sure.

Frank did not protest afterwards, and I thought we should have. Frank seemed very down about the whole thing. After that race, I drove alone across the mountains to the next race in Spain. I needed someone that I could have talked to; it was a pretty lonely time. But I think if that had happened to Frank, he would have done the same thing. He would have expected to be on his own and dwell in his misery.

Frank is a loner but I wouldn't say he has a mean streak. I don't think there is anything mean about Frank. He's a very hard person sometimes but he is no harder on anyone than he is on himself. Therefore he is very fair as a result. If he behaves in a way that makes you think 'What a bastard!' then nine times out of ten he has probably been in the same situation himself and he knows what he's doing.

I have been asked what sort of relationship we have because of the accident. I can say that I know Frank pretty well, but he's not one of those people you can get under the skin of. I think there is some sort of bond between us, but it is never spoken about and never allowed to come to the surface – on either side. That's because Frank's way of getting on with his life is to forget about the accident when possible. That's why I think he resisted some of the rehabilitation work. The reason he has survived so strong mentally is because he has the motor racing infrastructure which he could switch to and concentrate on. If, say, Frank was a farmer and had the same accident, I don't think he would have recovered mentally the way he has.

Certainly, there was plenty to occupy his thoughts at Estoril since there had been good news as well as bad. Patrese had won the race, but Senna had finished second. As discussion about Mansell's unfortunate exit continued into the evening, Riccardo put the day's events into perspective. 'Don't say it's a shame again!' he smiled. 'I think I deserved to win this race.' At least he had prevented Senna from scoring another four points. With three races to go, Mansell was twenty-four points behind. At least that simplified the tactical thinking. He had to win the next race in Spain. Second place would be of no use.

When the drivers arrived in Barcelona, Senna was still upset about Mansell's tactics on the first lap in Portugal. Given Ayrton's naked aggression in the past, it was a classic case of the pot calling the kettle black. Senna seemed uptight and uncertain. While Mansell went out and got rid of his frustrations with a vigorous game of football with the media (hurting himself in the process), Senna was working himself into a lather which spilled over at the drivers' pre-race briefing.

The mood was set when Berger playfully tapped Mansell's left ankle, the one Nigel had injured during the football match. Mansell got to his feet and grabbed his former team-mate. Some reports say it was a gentle shove; others, that he had Gerhard by the throat. Either way, tension was mounting. An official then said that he would be watching certain drivers in the light of what had happened during the first lap in Portugal. No names were mentioned, but Mansell was on his feet again saying that, if that was the case, they ought to look at some of Senna's misdemeanours in the past. Whereupon Senna angrily retorted that Mansell had been involved in more accidents than anyone else. According to Mansell's account of this exchange, Senna then called him a 'shit'. Piquet weighed in with the observation that the officials were wasting their time because they made a lot of noise and never followed up their threats. The meeting descended into chaos, but it was clear that there was no love lost between the championship contenders as they made their way to the starting grid.

Berger took the lead with Senna second and Mansell third. When Mansell, who was in no mood to wait for anyone, drew alongside Senna at 190 mph on the main straight, everyone held their breath. On and on they went, the two cars veering dangerously close, two hard men intent on out-psyching each other. In the light of what had happened in the briefing, no one dared look. It was one of the most dramatic pieces of motor racing of recent times.

Mansell emerged in front. And won the race. Senna was a dispirited fifth. They were sixteen points apart. Again, Nigel had it all to do at the penultimate race in Japan, the only certainty being that he would not give up until the championship was completely out of his reach.

The battle would last for just another seventeen minutes of racing. Before the start, Nigel had visited the Canon hospitality area above the pits at Suzuka and addressed his sponsor's guests. 'I hope you enjoy the race as much as I will,' he said. 'And watch the start; it will be very interesting.' Mansell was referring to the fact that the start would be his only chance to get ahead of the two McLarens on the front row of the grid. In the event, his plan failed and he had to take up station behind Berger and Senna, a perfect situation for Ayrton since he knew Mansell simply had to win.

Blasting past the pits to begin lap ten, Mansell radioed to his team that everything was under control. It was an unfortunate moment to make such a remark because, when he reached the bottom of the hill and swept into the right-hander, the nose of the Williams suddenly veered sharply towards the inside. Mansell caught the car but the moment had taken him off line as he accelerated towards the exit. Drifting wider and wider, the Williams slid towards the kerb, and then up and over it, and off at high speed into the gravel trap, where he became stuck fast.

Mansell said later that his brake pedal had given trouble. Then he claimed Senna had backed off early, causing him to veer off line. Whatever the reason, his campaign had ended. And Williams would finish second in their championship behind McLaren. Typically, Frank was not satisfied. The team had improved enormously, they were almost back to their winning ways. But it was not good enough. And the feeling was that for Nigel Mansell, it would be now or never in 1992.

CHAPTER THIRTEEN

A champion's fast farewell

Patrick Head was typically blunt: 'We won't beat McLaren by making a more reliable car, or by operating it better – that's something they do superbly. We need to beat them by producing a faster car, and that's all there is to it.'

So saying, he wheeled out FW14B, a revised version of the 1991 car but featuring the latest form of computer-controlled active suspension. Despite the torrid time experienced with the system on the Judd-powered car in 1988, the benefits of the active-ride, when it worked, had been sufficient to persuade Williams to continue with his line of development.

Throughout 1990, a test car driven by Mark Blundell had carried out further experimentation. That work had been continued into 1991 by the team's new test driver, Damon Hill. The reliability and performance during 7,000 miles of running was good enough to persuade Head to race the system in 1992. Nevertheless, with Mansell and the team expecting nothing less than the world championship, this had to be a gamble. Frank remarked:

Maybe. But you've got to try these things because it is much harder now to find a technical advantage. The rules are so tight these days. There is no comparison between now and ten years ago. It's like night and day. Today's racing cars are incredibly more complex than they were in the eighties. Gaining a second a lap is a giant task. We have to keep coming up with something new all the time.

Anyway, I like taking gambles! When I signed Nigel at the start of 1991, plenty of people were ready to have me certified. So what? I've never attached any importance to what people think about what I say and do. All I know is that the combination of Nigel and Riccardo is as good – if not better – than any pairing in most teams today. As they have both become more competitive there is a slight arm's length relationship, but there is zero aggravation. There is trust. They swap information. They try to keep their cards close to their chests, but they know that doesn't work because the engineers talk. We try to give them both the best equipment and they just get on with it. From my point of view, life is easy.

A lot of the credit for this must go to Riccardo; he is pretty damned apolitical. Nigel is an immensely tough bastard and, if things are going wrong in the car, he will give me or – more usually – Patrick a very hard time. He's not slow in coming forward. But I think Nigel is going to show everyone what he is worth this year.

Mansell was reputed to be taking £5m from the Williams budget and perhaps doubling that figure thanks to personal sponsorship deals. Frank would receive value for money but, before the season had finished, he would also brush against the prickly edge of Mansell's complex character.

The team was better prepared than ever before. Renault and their fuel suppliers, Elf, had between them made the performance of a new V10 more than a match for anything produced by Honda. Meanwhile, Adrian Newey had been busy in the wind tunnel, which had finally come on stream – at a considerable cost. Frank would not divulge just how much: 'Let's say it cost a lot less than Mansell or Senna,' he smiled. 'But it still amounted to many millions of pounds.

It's been worth it. It is more accurate, runs at a higher speed than our old one and it also has greater repeatability. In other words, you can put the same stuff in this week as, say, last week and you get the same figures from it. That was always a problem before.'

The overall performance gains were immediately apparent. Mansell claimed pole position for the opening race of the season and led every lap. Patrese finished second. The active suspension came into its own on the bumps of the spectacular Autodromo Hermanos Rodriguez in Mexico City, the Williams pair repeating the domination shown in South Africa three weeks before. There was a slight internal hitch in Brazil when Riccardo got the jump on Nigel at the start. When Mansell tried to assume his usual place, Patrese would have none of it and chopped across the front of his team-mate. Nigel got his revenge when, after having made his pit stop for tyres, he flicked off the engine rev-limiter and drove absolutely flat out. Riccardo found himself in second place when he emerged from his pit stop two laps later. The pace of the Williams pair had been such that they lapped the entire field, but this was the first sign of a simmering internal rivalry.

On to Spain, where Mansell would score one of his finest victories on a saturated track. Half the field spun into retirement, including Patrese and no less a person than Senna. Unfortunately, Nigel was to taint a great drive by berating a questioner who had the temerity to suggest during the post-race press conference that the car might have, in part, had something to do with such a flawless performance.

Never mind. Mansell had no reason to feel put upon when he set a new record by becoming the first driver to win the first five races of the season when he took another copybook victory at Imola. Second place for Patrese meant Williams had seventy-four points in the constructors' championship. The rest of the teams could only manage fifty-six points – between them. Nigel was streets ahead in the drivers' race. It was becoming monotonous. All that would change during the next two races.

A stunning pole position lap for Mansell – almost a full second faster than Patrese in second place on the grid – appeared to have locked up the Monaco Grand Prix before it had started. Certainly, that was the way of it as Mansell streaked into the lead. Senna, holding a comfortable second place ahead of the other Williams, could merely hope for some misfortune to befall the leader. That moment came with seven laps to go.

As he came through the tunnel at 160 mph, Mansell had a sideways moment which seemed to increase in drama each time he spoke about it after the race. Certainly, there was a problem of some sort and Nigel limped into the pits, where all four wheels were changed. He rejoined to find that something other than a Williams-Renault was leading a Grand Prix for the first time in 1992.

Mansell set out after Senna, slashing the lap record as he went. The Williams was on the tail of the McLaren with three laps to go. At any normal circuit, the benefit of the fresh tyres, coupled with Mansell's pumping adrenalin, would have taken him into the lead with barely a moment's hesitation. But by no stretch of the imagination could Monaco be referred to as an 'ordinary' circuit.

With overtaking almost impossible without the cooperation of the man in front, there was little opportunity for Nigel to get by. Senna was tired, his tyres were finished. But he was not feeling charitable. Despite Mansell's dramatic movements and theatrical thrusting into gaps which were never big enough, Senna remained calm. He was not about to give up the chance of winning the Monaco Grand Prix for a fifth time and equalling Graham Hill's record.

Once again, Mansell would be denied his first victory in the principality, despite having come closer than ever before. His championship advantage was still considerable but the inability to take what he felt was rightfully his, and criticism which suggested he had not formulated a clever plan of attack, would continue to rankle as he travelled to Canada for the seventh round. If Nigel thought some of the post-race comments in Monaco had been unfair, he was in for a pasting in Montreal.

A photograph in the Monday morning paper showed a Williams shedding nose wings and bodywork as it bounced off a kerb and plunged into a gravel trap during the previous day's Canadian Grand Prix. The headline said: 'Going to Pieces'. It was an apposite summary in every respect. Doubtless the headline writer was referring to the spectacular mayhem as Mansell committed his car to such harsh treatment, but there was a touch of unconscious humour about the choice of words. Although very few people witnessed the critical moments leading to Mansell's departure from the race, those who did were in no doubt that the leader of the championship had momentarily lost his composure. Gone to pieces, you might say.

Nigel was attempting to snatch the lead from Senna. He claimed the Brazilian had bundled him off the track as he drew alongside the McLaren. Whatever the reason, it did not lighten Nigel's mood. His displeasure with life in general had not been helped when Senna produced the fastest time during first qualifying. Mansell's disposition was palpably thunderous the following day when the track conditions were slower and, although the Williams was clearly the fastest car on the track, all he had to show for his good work was a move from fourth to third on the grid. Nigel had won pole position at the previous six races. Now he wasn't even on the front row. Unhappy did not begin to make a start to describe his general demeanour.

Mansell had been complaining that the Honda had found more power for their engine. That seemed to be the case when it came to punching the cars out of the tight chicanes which dominated the Montreal track. Senna had described his car as being like a rocket, although he was less complimentary when discussing its behaviour through anything resembling a fast corner. Mansell could see that for himself and he knew if he was to win this race, he would have to get ahead of Senna at the start.

And that was another thing. Riccardo had been faster than Nigel during qualifying for the first time in 1992. No matter. On the green light, Mansell dealt quickly with Patrese but the layout of the track was such that the straight leading to the first corner was simply not long enough to give Mansell time to overtake Senna as well. For the first fourteen laps, the leading bunch ran nose to tail. It was clear that Senna was holding everyone up but there was no law against such a thing. Once or twice Berger thought about taking third place from Patrese but decided against it. 'It was too risky,' he would say later. 'The track was just too dusty and bumpy off line.'

Indeed it was. But Mansell switched off the rev-limiter and launched an attack as the leaders reached the chicane preceding the pits. Senna saw him coming and left the minimum amount of room. Late braking off line was never going to work. Mansell had no alternative but to attempt to straight-line the chicane. The kerb did its work and the photographer from the *Montreal Gazette* was there to record the destruction of the Williams.

Mansell spun to a halt at the exit of the chicane, in full

view of the pit lane. To increase the dramatic effect, he remained in the damaged car for a whole lap. Then, once on his feet, he let it be known to all and sundry that Senna had shoved him off the road. He marched to the McLaren pit and raged at Ron Dennis. Then he went to see the race officials and raged at them. But there was no official protest and that was the end of the matter since there was no video available of the critical moments. The drivers following Senna and Mansell had the best view. They were unanimous: Senna, predictably, had not given Mansell much room; Nigel was never going to make it.

The only good news was that Senna and Patrese would both retire, thus leaving Mansell's championship lead intact. He continued to have a twenty-eight-point advantage but there was concern that the Williams driver might fritter away his huge advantage if he continued in this manner when things were not going right. James Hunt, commentating on BBC Television, summed it up: 'Nigel must make up his mind whether his priority is to win every race or win the championship. His instinct is to race as hard as he can. However frustrated he may feel at being stuck behind a slower car he must curb his natural instinct and bide his time. His position in the championship now is that he need take no unnecessary risks. All he needs to do is accumulate points.'

Frank said nothing. Neither did Patrick. However, Head did have a few words to say a few weeks later at Magny-Cours. Patrese had been told by Frank that his services would not be required in 1993. Driving as if he had a point to prove, Riccardo took the lead and did everything to keep Mansell at bay until the race was stopped after nineteen laps because of a light shower. During the lull, Head spoke to Patrese in words of one syllable. It was made clear to Riccardo that he was free to defend his position, provided he did not put the chances of the team in jeopardy. Patrese's mechanics, who overheard the lecture, were shocked by the severe manner of its delivery. But the point had been made. Patrese knew that Mansell was likely to stop at nothing and, if contact was made between the two then, in view of Head's comments, Riccardo would shoulder the blame.

Patrese assumed the lead once more at the restart, Mansell launching an immediate attack. They ran side by side for a period, no quarter being asked or given. What on earth was Patrese up to? At the end of the lap, it became clear. As the cars accelerated onto the pit straight, Patrese pulled over to one side and raised his arm high in the air to make it clear he was letting Mansell through. Under sufferance. That was the end of the challenge.

Nigel needed no help to win the British Grand Prix. In his most crushing display yet, he set a pole position time which was almost two seconds faster than Patrese. He then backed that up with a truly dominant performance in the race. It was too much for a capacity crowd, fed by the media on Mansell mania and aware that they were witnessing a gritty Brit on his way to the world title. As soon as Nigel took the chequered flag, Silverstone went berserk as spectators burst onto the track before the rest of the field had finished. Fortunately, no one was hurt, but a great day for the man in the red, white and blue crash helmet came close to being tarnished unnecessarily. Meanwhile, finishing sixteenth and last, four laps behind the victorious Mansell, came Damon Hill's Brabham at the end of the Englishman's first Grand Prix.

Another win in Germany, Mansell's eighth of the season, brought the title within his grasp even though there were still six races to run. Second place at the next race in Hungary clinched it. Nigel Mansell had finally become world champion after a dogged and frequently heroic campaign which had lasted several years. No one deserved it more. Williams-Renault had provided the equipment, but Nigel had delivered. He had made it look easy at times but Patrese's occasional struggles told a more realistic story, one which was clarified by Riccardo's engineer at Renault, Eric Faron. Having studied the telemetry printouts from both cars, Faron was able to pinpoint a telling difference between the driving styles of the two drivers: 'Riccardo finds driving the car on the limit less easy than Nigel. That is quite simply because Riccardo drives a great deal with his body. Unfortunately for him, the reactive suspension filters out many of the physical sensations which are traditionally transmitted to a driver. The FW14B demanded a different driving technique from that of a more classical car and that doesn't really suit Riccardo's style.'

In effect, Faron was saying that Mansell would keep his right foot hard on the throttle, even during a high-speed slide of the kind which would prompt Patrese to back off momentarily. That little confidence lift by Riccardo would make all the difference when it came to measuring a lap time in tenths of a second. Whatever may have been said about Mansell's personal qualities, no one could deny that he had taken the FW14B and wrung its neck. Just as Frank had hoped he would do. Meanwhile, Frank would have been forgiven for wishing to wring Nigel's neck – and vice versa – as negotiations over a contract for 1993 reached a fraught conclusion.

As early as the previous May, Frank had begun to probe Mansell for his feelings about remaining with the team in 1993. Mansell was more than willing, saying he would stay on the same retainer (£5m), with one proviso: Patrese would have to remain on the payroll as number two. It was a logical request; from Mansell's point of view.

As Williams had reiterated at the beginning of the season,

the two drivers worked in reasonable harmony, part of the reason being that Riccardo was a gentleman player and Nigel did not see him as a threat. And therein lay part of a growing problem for Frank. Almost half his annual working budget (reputed to be in the region of £25m) was supplied by Renault and Elf in the form of engines and technical support. It had not escaped their notice that Alain Prost, a triple world champion, was sitting around doing nothing as he spent a sabbatical year in 1992. It was intimated to Frank that Prost's presence in a Williams-Renault would be most welcome.

Frank listened to what Nigel had to say. Then he asked for his thoughts on having Prost as a team-mate in 1993. Understandably, Mansell asked why a team which was scoring one-two finishes left, right and centre should need Alain Prost. It made no sense to Nigel, but he was quick to appreciate that the team's French partners might think otherwise. In that case, he said, he would want an extra fee to compensate for having to relinquish undisputed number one status. In return, he would require a written guarantee from the team and its technical partners that he would receive equal treatment.

Nothing further was said. As the season reached the midway point at Silverstone in July, Mansell could not ignore mounting rumours that Prost had actually been signed. According to Mansell's version of what happened next, Frank admitted two weeks later that it was 'likely' that he would sign Prost, whereupon Mansell was apparently informed by a source inside the team that an agreement had, in fact, been reached. Mansell said he was 'utterly devastated'. Williams claimed that he had merely told Mansell to bear in mind, when deciding on his future plans, that Prost might be a part of the team in 1993. Mansell's discomfort was then intensified when he learned through his private source that

Prost would have the power of veto over the choice of second driver. In fact, Prost had been referring to Senna since he was anxious not to have his nemesis driving alongside and shaping up for a repeat of their tempestuous partnership at McLaren. Mansell was of the opinion that Prost was keen to rule him out as well.

The increasingly bizarre negotiations returned to a more acceptable level in Hungary. On the weekend that Mansell would win the championship, he had also made progress by sitting down with Frank and thrashing out a deal. He said he would accept an additional $1.5m (£937,000) as compensation for having to share number one status with Prost. Frank apparently agreed.

Then they got down to minor points, one of which covered the provision of hotel rooms by the team. The precise details were never made clear to the outside world. The Williams viewpoint seemed to be that Mansell wanted three rooms at each race, whereas Williams wished to limit the number to one. Nigel's version was that Williams had always provided three rooms for Mansell's family and friends, and Frank wished to bring that to an end. Mansell had asked for at least one room, 'as a sign of good faith, if nothing else'.

That aside, everything seemed to be agreed. Frank said a contract would be sent to Mansell's home on the Isle of Man the following day. When the fax failed to appear, Mansell grew concerned. He called Frank, who said he had a few points to iron out with his sponsors. All of which added to Mansell's unease, particularly in view of the story which concerned an absurd offer from Senna when he said he would drive for Williams for nothing. It would turn out that this was Senna's way of expressing his annoyance when he heard that Prost was blocking his presence, should he have wished to sign for Williams. Nevertheless, it added to Mansell's fears as he went about his business on the Isle of Man.

On the following Wednesday, Mansell set off for a round of golf. He was halfway through the game when his mobile phone brought a call from Sheridan Thynne, still the commercial director at Williams and a staunch supporter of Mansell. Thynne had devastating news. Frank was offering a new deal which was worth much less than had been agreed in Hungary. Mansell said later it was a cut of 50 per cent. Whatever the figure, he was deeply aggrieved. It was an insult to be treated in this way after all he had done for the team. Money, he would insist later, was not the overriding factor. It was only a small part of the package. It was the principle which counted.

The Williams side of the story was, not surprisingly, slightly different. According to other sources inside the team, money was *very* important to Mansell. Williams in the meantime had come under pressure to control his budget. There was no firm news on how much Elf would be able to bring to the table in 1993 since the oil and petroleum company had just suffered a 23 per cent drop in profits for the first six months of 1992. Under such circumstances, Frank's view that the driver is nothing more than an employee would come into serious play.

There was no further progress in the discussions at the next race in Belgium. Two weeks later in Italy, Mansell had had enough. There had been meetings between various parties but, in Nigel's view, they were getting nowhere. On race morning at Monza, Mansell convened a press conference.

At eleven a.m. on Sunday, 13 September, Mansell entered the packed media centre and sat centre stage. Just as he was about to begin reading from a prepared statement, Gary Crumpler, a member of the Williams commercial team, pushed his way through and, in whispered tones, passed on a message from Frank to the effect that Nigel should hold back on what he was about to say. Renault (who had been

very keen that Mansell should stay) had come to an arrangement with Williams to make sure Nigel would receive
whatever had been agreed in Hungary. But it was too late.
With the media at his feet and his adrenalin running,
Mansell launched into his speech. The thrust of it was that
he would be retiring from Formula One at the end of the
season – 'due to circumstances beyond my control'.

The entire affair had degenerated into a farce, a hopeless
breakdown in communications forcing the dramatic departure of one of the sport's most popular drivers. It made
headline news and the reaction among Mansell's fans in
Britain was swift. The newspapers and magazines were
bombarded with letters of protest, although a demonstration
outside the gates of the Williams factory, orchestrated by
the *Sun* newspaper, fell surprisingly flat.

Inside the team headquarters at Basil Hill Road, Frank
was marshalling his troops in response to Mansell's
announcement, which appeared to have caught them on the
hop. A statement – surprisingly long for Williams – was
signed by Frank and issued to a press corps, anxious to hear
the other side of the story. The statement read:

Williams Grand Prix Engineering would like to reemphasise its deep
regret at Nigel Mansell's decision to retire from Formula One at
Sunday's Italian Grand Prix.

His 26 wins while driving for Williams allows him a special
place in our history having won considerably more races than any
other of the team's drivers.

To ensure the team has the best chance of winning races and
world championships, fellow director Patrick Head and I have
always sought to employ the best drivers and engineers.

To allow us to express our skills as engineers we have had to
raise significant funds to invest in world championship winning
technology and world championship winning drivers. This only

comes from many long hours of considered negotiations which are dependent on many variables, some known, some unknown. Our strategy for 1993 included ensuring we had Nigel in the team, a strategy we pursued right up until Nigel's announcement on Sunday.

Without going into details of the long and protracted meetings, we had made several offers to Nigel, all of which were rejected. Some criteria for the decision-making process have changed throughout the year, but we repeat Nigel was the focus of our efforts for the 1993 season.

In parallel with the driver negotiations, we obviously have to ensure the team's future, which in a world recession is difficult even with our team's world championship winning status. It is noteworthy that despite the enormous support for both the team and Nigel from many British fans, we are still unable to raise any significant sponsorship from the UK.

Our first responsibility is to Williams Grand Prix Engineering and its 200 employees and, therefore, regrettably we could not meet Nigel's demands in the time-frame required. We are obviously aware of the disappointment that Nigel's retirement generated in the UK, but Williams Grand Prix Engineering is an international company that operates on a global basis and must continue to do so.

In the meantime, we would like to thank Nigel for all his efforts for the team and the sponsors and wish him and his family well in America. Nigel returned to the Williams team with the sole purpose of winning the world championship and he has now achieved his goal. In doing so he has won a further 13 races with us, and this year has equalled the record number of eight wins in one season with three races still to go.

We know that in the early months of his second period with us he said he would retire if he won the Championship. This could obviously have been a stronger consideration than we originally thought and whatever the final reasons for Nigel's retirement we are glad he has won the Championship he richly deserved.

Peter Windsor had watched the drama unfold and was saddened that it had reached such an unnecessary end:

The bottom line is that Nigel was annoyed that Frank had signed Prost. The only way he was going to stay was if he got twice the amount of money Prost was getting. I don't think Nigel was in the mood to spend three months negotiating. He was world champion, he was king of the castle and he wanted an instant response from Frank. He wasn't going to get it because Frank would never give in that quickly. He wasn't being mean. He was trying to do the best job for himself and his company. There were a lot of people around who were fanning the flames. To me, it was simple: Nigel wanted the money and Frank was either going to pay it or he wasn't. He did offer it in the end and, to this day, I don't understand why Nigel didn't accept that very late offer and stay. Okay, you could argue that Frank was asking for trouble by bringing Prost into the team, but I think he genuinely felt that Mansell and Prost were the best driver combination for 1993 and, from Renault's point of view, it was the right thing to do. If Frank had made that final offer a couple of months before, the deal would have been done.

Nigel would win one more race for Williams (in Portugal) to establish a record which is unlikely to be beaten. In that same race, Patrese was very fortunate to escape unhurt from a spectacular accident when a misunderstanding with Gerhard Berger led to Riccardo running into the back of the slowing McLaren. The 160 mph impact caused the Williams to take off like a rocket. Just as it looked like flipping over backwards, the car began to fall to earth again, narrowly missed a bridge in the process and walloped onto the track.

The wreckage tobogganed for a considerable distance and rattled to a halt along the pit wall. Patrese was able to climb out of the cockpit, which had remained perfectly intact, and walk away.

Proof that he was completely unharmed came a few weeks later when he won in Japan, leaving the Williams-Renault team a massive eighty points clear of McLaren. Just before retiring with mechanical failure, Mansell had made a generous gesture by giving up his lead and allowing Patrese through as a means of helping Riccardo in his battle with Senna for second place in the drivers' championship. Nigel, in fact, was to contribute to Patrese's cause once more, but in more controversial circumstances as he disputed the lead of the final race with Senna.

Both drivers retired from the Australian Grand Prix when the McLaren ran into the back of the Williams as they braked for a hairpin. There were, predictably, different views about the cause: Senna claimed Mansell had braked earlier than normal; Nigel blamed the Brazilian for crashing into him. Interestingly, Mansell did not wait to remonstrate with his rival after climbing out of his car, Nigel's usual *modus operandi* when certain he was in the right. The last anyone heard of the Williams driver was a bitter complaint that the officials were unwilling to act on his protest over Senna's driving. With that, Mansell packed his bags and left for pastures new. He would never see Ayrton Senna again.

Frank, meanwhile, had become more direct in his assessment of the breakdown of negotiations with Mansell:

Put simply, I think it was a matter of two hard-headed idiots who couldn't make a deal, couldn't communicate at the right time. It's still my firm opinion that if Nigel hadn't had that press conference at Monza, announcing what I thought was a grossly premature decision to retire, by Monday evening or so – away from the race track – both of us would have calmed down. He'd have been away from all his sycophantic followers, who were advising him badly, in my opinion, and we'd probably have made a deal.

As could be gathered from the reference to 'America' in Frank's official statement in the days following the Italian Grand Prix, Mansell had already organised an escape parachute by signing (for less money) with the Newman/Haas Indycar team. Sheridan Thynne would abandon his long-standing association with Frank and travel with Mansell to the United States, where Nigel would go on to score a remarkable double by winning the Indycar Championship at his first attempt.

The contract fiasco became a standing joke during the winter. Nigel Roebuck, writing in *Autosport*, summed it up when he quoted from a Christmas television sketch in which the impressionist Rory Bremner played the part of Mansell with typical aplomb, not to mention a flat-vowelled accent:

Well, basically, Frank called me, and he asked me how many sugars I wanted in my tea. I felt totally insulted, you know. As far as I was concerned, we had an agreement on the number of spoonfuls, and then I suddenly discovered that Frank had spoken to Alain Prost, and secretly agreed how many sugars he'd have. Plus, you know, Prost had been offered whatever he wanted – basically, you know, his own mug, even with one of those little plastic stirrers . . .'

To all intents and purposes, Mansell's long and sometimes turbulent association with Williams Grand Prix Engineering appeared to be well and truly over. Typically, however, he would be back for one last shout. In the meantime, his dramatic departure had left a golden opening for a decent and industrious thirty-two-year-old waiting quietly in the wings.

CHAPTER FOURTEEN

Working towards a nightmare

On Sunday, 29 November 1992, Damon Hill caught the early evening flight from London to Lisbon. On the face of it, there was nothing unusual about this trip. He was on his way to Estoril and another test session in which he would add to the 18,000 miles already logged for Williams-Renault. He was competent and highly regarded. But he was not a fully fledged Grand Prix driver. Or, at least, not yet.

When Hill realised that Mansell and Williams could not reach agreement, and that Patrese would be joining Benetton, he had begun to push for promotion from the role of test driver. He had paid out of his own limited funds to travel to the last race in Australia, simply to be around while Frank and Patrick assessed the likely candidates. Mika Hakkinen, a Formula Three champion and a driver with the sort of flair which appealed to Frank, headed the short list. Martin Brundle, experienced and professional, was also in discussion with Williams. But Damon could see no reason why he should not be considered. There had to be a way of finally proving his worth.

When he received the call to travel to Portugal, he was tipped off that the test could be vital to his future. Although no one said as much, it was clear to Damon that his progress over the next four days would be scrutinised closely. He knew he would never have a better opportunity to impress. That prospect occupied his thoughts as he boarded the aircraft.

But there was an added poignancy to the trip. It was seventeen years to the day since his father had been killed. Graham Hill, one of the most universally respected and admired drivers to have won the world championship, had been flying his light aircraft back to Britain following a test session with his team in France. The Piper Aztec had crashed on 29 November, at around the same time in the evening as Damon's flight was lifting off from Heathrow. One career had ended and, seventeen years later, it was as if another was about to begin. Hill somehow knew he was going to do enough to win the drive he cherished most.

At the end of the test, Damon's name was at the top of the list of lap times. He was a tenth of a second faster than Prost and almost a second quicker than anyone else. Frank, who did not travel to test sessions as frequently as before, had made a flying visit. Two weeks later, he announced that Damon Hill would partner Alain Prost in 1993.

Speaking to *Autosport* magazine, Williams explained why he had gone against established form by selecting a driver whose Grand Prix experience had been limited to just two races with a back-of-the-grid team:

It's an unusual move for us, but F1 racing is changing rapidly and we must flow with the times. Damon is very, very fast and he has a lot of experience with our active-ride car. During testing, he has been able to help Alain out of some of the technical difficulties setting up the car.

Patrick and Adrian have been very impressed with Damon for a long time. They have always felt he was good – and getting better. Alain has been very much in favour, too. They get on well together, and he also feels the continuity is important: Damon knows the car very well, after all. I'm very hopeful that he'll do well.

That assumed, of course, that Williams Grand Prix Engineering would be taking part in the races, something which was no longer an automatic right following an increasingly absurd stance taken by the sport's governing body, the FIA, and its president, Max Mosley. Simply put, Williams had been a day late in lodging their entry form for the 1993 FIA Formula One World Championship. The overdue paperwork had since been accepted but, when the official entry list was published, neither Williams driver was on it.

Politics were at play here and, thanks to the late delivery of the entry form, Williams had weakened his hand. The price of such outstanding success in 1992 had been the wish of rivals not to be thrashed again. Frank could understand that but he could not accept a proposal from some leading teams which would rule out many of the technical advantages exploited so brilliantly by Williams. In Frank's opinion, he had never complained when the odds were stacked against him; it was part of the game. Why should he want to help his rivals now? The only problem was, the situation might be reversed. In order to have his late entry accepted, he needed the full approval of every team. And, to no one's surprise, not everyone was willing to give the nod while Williams (and McLaren) held out against the proposed changes to the technical regulations.

The unavoidable feeling that the Williams team was being put upon strengthened in January 1993 when Mosley suddenly took exception to Prost's behaviour when acting as a media analyst during his sabbatical the previous year. In a long letter to Frank, the president of the FIA catalogued his grievances, and then stated: 'Frank, we really have to ask ourselves if the best interests of Formula One and the FIA World Championship are served by allowing a man like this to participate. He really thinks he should be running everything. He pontificated about things he does not understand and he describes the entire governing body in contemptuous and offensive terms.' It was an unprecedented attack on a driver, one which made Williams wonder briefly if there was any point in carrying on. Prost took care of the complaints against him by appearing in front of representatives of the governing body and explaining that he had been misquoted. Meanwhile, Mosley used his power to the full by allowing Williams to enter the championship, and then announcing sweeping reforms which would remove much of the complex technology from the cars in 1994.

Thus far, the 1993 season had been very hard work before a car had so much as turned a wheel in anger. And what made it worse, particularly from Prost's point of view, was the fact that everyone expected him to walk off with the championship in what had to be the best car.

Patrick Head and Adrian Newey had produced FW15 the previous year, with the intention of introducing it during the season. But, since FW14B had been so effective, it seemed foolish to risk bringing on a new car when there was no need. It is not often a team finds itself in such a comfortable position, all of which, of course, was helping to stir up the petty jealousy being shown towards the reigning champions. That said, Frank and Patrick were not being complacent. A busy schedule of winter testing saw FW15 updated in readiness for the start of the season in South Africa. All that hard work came close to being written off ten seconds into the race.

Prost claimed pole position and then wasted it when he made a poor start. Hill, starting from fourth on the grid, could not believe his luck when he found himself in second place – and close enough to Senna to challenge for the lead. The sense of occasion became too much for Damon. He promptly spun, and almost took Prost with him. Hill eventually got going again and then went off for good after tangling with the Lotus of Alessandro Zanardi as they disputed twelfth place. It was the worst possible start for Damon, but the potentially cool mood in the Williams garage was thawed by a copybook victory for Prost.

Alain's lead of the championship would disappear as Senna scored two exceptional wins in Brazil and at a wet Donington Park in England, but Prost was in command once more thanks to victories at Imola and in Spain. The struggle continued in Monaco, where Senna finished first and Hill produced an impressive and mildly emotional result by taking second place and stepping onto the rostrum visited on five occasions by his father. Senna, in fact, had just beaten Graham Hill's record and Damon, with typical good grace, was quick publicly to recognise the fact. 'It's thirty years since my father's first victory here,' said Hill. 'I'm sure he would have been the first to congratulate Ayrton on breaking his record. It's a tribute to my father as much as to him that it has taken someone of Ayrton's calibre to do it.' Senna was clearly moved by a gesture which would do much to pave the way for a brief but amicable working relationship between these two in the future.

Prost, meanwhile, was not entertaining charitable thoughts of any kind after finishing fourth. It seemed that the hostility towards him was continuing as he recovered from a ten-second penalty imposed for allegedly jumping the start. Senna was now five points ahead in the championship, although Williams were continuing to maintain their advantage in the constructors' series.

Prost was back on top once more thanks to victory in Canada, and he would extend that lead to twelve points following the first one-two finish of the season for Williams when Hill dutifully followed his team-mate in France. Having put the *faux pas* of the first race behind him, Damon was driving with increasing confidence and it seemed only a matter of time before he would win his first race. Where better than at the next Grand Prix in Britain.

Prost claimed pole position for the eighth time, but Hill was alongside on the front row and perfectly positioned to shoot into the lead when Alain made a poor getaway. This was not a new experience for Damon. Seven days before in France, he had started from pole for the first time and looked to have control of the race until a slow pit stop dropped him behind Prost. This time, however, he had an added advantage in that Prost was held up behind Senna, the McLaren driver engaging in particularly hostile tactics as he kept his old sparring partner at bay.

Prost expected no less. At the end of the previous year, Senna had been affronted when he discovered that Prost had put the block on his plans to join Williams. Senna's mood had not been improved when Honda announced their intention to pull out of Formula One, leaving McLaren to race with a customer version of the Ford V8, the latest works engines being entrusted to Benetton. Senna's sense of outrage had spilled into print:

I don't accept being vetoed by anyone in the way this has been done. This is supposed to be the World Drivers' Championship. We had two fantastic championships in 1991 and 1992. In 1989 and 1990 [Senna having clashed on the track with Prost on each occasion] we had two very bad ones. They were a consequence of unbelievable politics, and bad behaviour by some people. I think that now we are coming back to the same situation.

If Prost wants to come back and maybe win another title, he should be sporting. The way he is doing it, he is behaving like a coward. He must be prepared to race anybody, under any conditions, on equal terms. He now wants to win with everything laid out for him. It's like going for a 100-metre sprint in running shoes while everybody has lead shoes. That is the way he wants to race. But it is not racing.

Senna continued to feel deeply aggrieved if his tactics at Silverstone were anything to go by. His 'lead shoes', the comparatively underpowered McLaren-Ford, was no match for Prost's swift Williams and it was not often Senna would get the chance to run ahead of his old enemy. He held out for several laps. Once he had squeezed past the McLaren, Prost closed on the leader but Damon seemed capable of maintaining a two-second gap. The crowd sensed he was on course for a memorable first victory at home. Then, with eighteen laps to go, an enormous cloud of smoke from the back of the car announced a rare failure of a Renault engine. Hill rolled to a halt on the edge of the infield behind the pits. He climbed from the car, acknowledged the applause from the towering grandstands on all sides and headed slowly towards the Williams garage, stopping on his way for a pint at the British Racing Drivers' Club.

Prost cruised home to his sixth victory of the season. Compared with the pandemonium which had greeted Mansell twelve months before, this win was received with polite applause. Frank's stern expression had remained unchanged for the hour and twenty-five minutes it had taken to run this ninth round of the championship. It was hardly a perfect ambience for Prost to celebrate his record-breaking fiftieth win.

The mood within the team was not much better two weeks later in Germany. With two laps to run, Hill was ten seconds ahead of Prost and not remotely under threat. Then a rear tyre punctured and he was out of the race. Prost won again, but he was not happy. Once again, the officials had applied a heavy hand by giving Prost a ten-second penalty for taking to the escape road on the first lap. Prost claimed that, had he not done so, he would have been hit by the spinning Ligier of Martin Brundle. Certainly, he had gained no advantage through his action. 'They've just got it in for Alain, haven't they?' was Patrick Head's summary. But at least his man was twenty-seven points clear of Senna in the championship.

If Prost's mixed fortunes were to continue in Hungary – where he stalled on pole position, was obliged to start from the back of the grid and then had a lengthy pit stop for repairs while on his way to twelfth place – Hill's luck would change dramatically. He led from the start and this time nothing would prevent a long-awaited maiden victory. Frank quickly seized the moment to take a friendly jibe at the British press. 'You can disconnect the phone lines to Florida,' he grinned. 'England has a new hero.' It was a direct reference to the incessant headlines covering Mansell's successes in North America, where he had also established a home in Tampa, Florida. Moving on to more serious matters, Williams said: 'Damon has been a really quick learner. After his first three races for us, it was obvious he could cut the mustard. He drove a near faultless race.' Frank's mood was also lifted by the thought that, fortunately for Prost, Senna had retired early on.

Having got into the winning habit, Hill rattled off two more, the latter coming at the expense of Prost just as he was poised to clinch the championship in Italy. Fewer than twenty miles from the chequered flag, Alain's engine failed, leaving a delay of two weeks before he finally claimed the title by finishing second in Portugal. Hill moved into the runner-up slot in the championship but, despite such a commendable effort in his first full season, Damon was becoming increasingly concerned about his future. The name Ayrton Senna continued to be linked with Williams far too often for Damon's comfort.

Prost, meanwhile, had become even more disillusioned as he headed towards a title which had been devalued by the widely held view that it was there for the Frenchman to win as he pleased. It had not been that simple. Apart from the menacing presence of FIA officials and their willingness to distribute ten-second penalties at the drop of a hat, Prost had been unsettled by the attitude shown by Frank Williams in the aftermath of the wet race at Donington the previous April.

Hill had finished second with Prost struggling home third in the atrocious weather. Prost had done a reasonable job on a day when over half the field had either spun off or crashed, but his performance had been made to look second-rate by the unbelievable genius of Senna as he claimed one of his greatest victories. It was just the sort of extrovert drive of which Frank approved. After the race, which had been run in continually changing conditions, Frank made an uncharacteristically ill-advised comment to the media: 'It is obvious that Alain made a very tactical [first] change onto dry tyres, but threw it away with a vastly premature switch back to wets, and that was the end of the race. It surprised me that a driver of Alain's ability should make those mistakes, but he doesn't like the wet and is cautious.'

It was true that Prost was circumspect in wet conditions, but only because he railed against the stupidity of ploughing mindlessly into spray. The result of that particular folly had been all too evident when Didier Pironi had rammed the back of Prost's Renault in 1982 and crashed so severely that the Ferrari driver would never race again. Deeply offended by the tone of Williams's remarks, Alain returned to Switzerland and contemplated his future. 'I just stayed at home,' he later told Alan Henry. 'I didn't move. Even though I had a lot of support from the team and from Renault, I really seriously thought that I would stop, perhaps even immediately. I didn't, of course, but the more the season went on, the more convinced I was that I would retire at the end of the year.'

In September, Prost intimated to Williams that he was going to stop racing. Frank was continuing to talk to Senna. Hill did not know where he stood. The precise sequence of these events remains blurred to this day.

Prost had a two-year contract with Williams and, despite his misgivings, there seemed no good reason to stop racing since it was likely that Williams would produce another race-winning car. Speculation in the paddock suggested that Williams was determined to achieve his long-held ambition of signing Senna. And if Prost was on board as well, then such a Dream Team would be a bonus. But the only certainty was that, after all they had been through, Alain could not cope with having Ayrton in the same team. Whether that prompted his final decision, or whether he had simply had enough, has never been made clear. But, at Estoril, he announced his decision to retire at the end of the year. 'The sport has given me a lot,' said Prost. 'But I decided that the game wasn't worth it any more. I have taken too many blows. I will not drive for Williams or anyone else. That goes for Formula One and all the other formulae. There will be no comeback.'

Whatever the reason behind Prost's decision, there was no getting away from the fact that Frank, who had sat with Alain during the press call, had lost another reigning world champion. As usual, he did not seem unduly concerned even though his respect for the Frenchman had never been greater. He rejected completely the suggestion that his team had missed the more confrontational atmosphere produced by a driver such as Nigel Mansell. 'Absolutely not,' he replied. 'There's an immense respect for Alain and his talents. Alain's a charming individual, never makes waves. His approach to life – and to racing – is different from Nigel's. Nigel was terrific in the car, but a tough man out of it. He knew what he wanted and he pushed to get it. Alain is very easy to get on with, very straightforward, and has a very good relationship with the team, and with Renault.'

At least Hill could be fairly confident that his seat was now safe. A few days later, Senna announced that he would be leaving McLaren after six seasons. It was the work of a moment to guess which team he would be driving for in 1994. Senna's two-year contract with Williams was formally announced in October, and the Brazilian was ecstatic:

I feel comfortable saying this is a dream come true. Frank Williams is the man who gave me my first opportunity to drive a Formula One car and, with a Renault engine, I won my first Grand Prix. We have been so close to doing the deal in the past. This year we finally made it.

I'm really looking forward to driving the Williams-Renault in what I consider the beginning of a new life in motor racing for me. I have been waiting for this move for so long, from the moment I decided to change direction. A new team; new people to work with and to get to know. It's a big challenge for me because I am the newcomer here; I am the one who has to adjust. I've been waiting impatiently for this. I need it for motivation.

Frank could barely contain his excitement. A rare bond had grown between the two ever since the day Frank had given Ayrton that test drive in 1983. They would talk frequently on the telephone about their abiding passion for racing. As the years went by and Senna's remarkable deeds underscored his exceptional talent, Frank knew he would not be satisfied until they worked together. Yes, he enjoyed having Mansell at the wheel of one of his cars; his admiration for Prost's professionalism knew no bounds. But Senna was different. And now he would be driving for Williams Grand Prix Engineering. Or Rothmans Williams-Renault as the team would henceforth be known in deference to a new title sponsor. And that had been another bone of contention during the 1993 season.

As early as the British Grand Prix in July, Williams had sent a shock wave through the paddock by revealing the planned two-year deal with Rothmans. This would not only help to pre-empt the departure from Formula One of RJ Reynolds, whose Camel brand had been associated with Williams since 1991, but it would also outrage Canon and force the Japanese photographic and business machine giant to quit Grand Prix racing after nine seasons with Williams. Canon had thought they were about to re-sign for another two years as title sponsor with Williams. Masahiro Tanaka, the president of Canon Europa, was brief and to the point in his statement: 'Due to the unacceptable actions of the Williams team we have been obliged to withdraw from all sponsorship of F1 at the end of the season.' Williams were not happy about being made the scapegoat but, in the absence of an official response, Mr Tanaka's view continued to taint the team's commercial reputation for some months. If Frank had been moved to make any comment, he would probably have said he was a realist and the terms of the Rothmans deal were better for his team.

In any case, by the time the 1994 Williams had been unveiled in its Rothmans colours in February, the team had more serious matters to consider. Such as the fact that the car, FW16, was very difficult to drive. FW16 was nothing like the previous year's car. But then it wasn't meant to be. Sweeping changes to the technical regulations had ruled out computer-controlled active suspension systems and traction control devices, all of which had contributed to making the cars much easier to drive. In addition, refuelling would be permitted during the races. Hill described the effect of the changes from a driver's point of view:

These measures introduce a new set of parameters which we have to work to extract the maximum potential from our driver/chassis/ engine package. The rear tyres now suffer more from the damage caused by excess wheel spin – previously controlled by the traction devices. The critical ride height of the car above the ground, which affects its very sensitive aerodynamics, could only ever be a compromise as we were no longer allowed to use the computer to optimise the 'ground effect'. In addition, thanks to refuelling, the start weight of the cars would be reduced by running as little as a quarter of the previous season's starting fuel load, thus considerably increasing their speed.

All it meant to me and to the rest of the Williams team was that we would effectively be starting from scratch and would have to do a better job than all our rivals. So in that respect nothing much had changed – except one thing. All the hard work Williams and I had done to develop a state-of-the-art car had been negated by the new rules and we had to start all over again.

Patrick Head and Adrian Newey had revised the aerodynamic packaging at the rear of the car in an attempt to claw back some of the grip lost thanks to the rule changes. As soon as Senna and Hill drove the new car for the first time, they discovered immediately that it was on what Hill referred to as 'a knife-edge'. FW16 was extremely sensitive to change on the suspension settings. 'You don't have to be very far out with any of the settings and suddenly the car is not competitive,' said Hill. 'That's good and bad. Good, because it's working straight away. But bad in some ways because you can be out of bed very easily.' In addition, neither driver felt particularly comfortable in the cramped cockpit. Clearly, there was much work to be done before the first race in Brazil on 27 March.

Confirmation that Williams faced an uphill struggle came at the end of the first day of practice at Interlagos when Hill described the car as being 'very, very difficult to drive'. Since Hill was not given to exaggeration, this was a worry which would be graphically confirmed by Senna during the race. It was a sign of Ayrton's innate skill that he had wrestled the Williams onto pole position. Driving like that for seventy-one seconds was one thing, keeping it up for seventy-one laps quite another.

This was Senna's home Grand Prix, a meaningful occasion for a proud man carrying the hopes of an entire nation on his shoulders. It was with some difficulty, therefore, that he had to accept being overhauled by Michael Schumacher during the first round of pit stops, and then watch the Benetton-Ford pull away. With fifteen laps remaining, the unthinkable happened: Ayrton Senna spun. No one could remember the last time Senna had done that through no other reason than being unable to control the car. It was like Alan Shearer attempting a penalty kick and missing the ball completely. As Senna abandoned his car, Hill moved into second place. He was one of the few people not to be surprised by Senna's plight. 'I would describe the car as virtually undriveable in the slow corners,' said Hill. 'And, in the quick ones, it threatened to turf you off the track at any moment. It was unpredictable.' Frank Williams was not accustomed to having one of his cars described in this manner. There was not much which could be done in the limited time available. Round Two in Japan was only three weeks away.

The TI circuit in Aida, a solitary place in the hills above Okayama, had not been used before as a Grand Prix venue.

Senna became accustomed to it more quickly than most and claimed his second pole position, Hill setting the third-fastest time in a car he found better suited to the slow corners which dominated an unimaginative track. With Schumacher second fastest, Senna knew he would have his work cut out to stay ahead. Pit stop tactics – a more important aspect than ever before thanks to the introduction of refuelling – had been discussed at length as the Williams drivers and engineers gathered round the large table in the centre of the temporary office. Senna weighed up every possibility as he lay motionless on the floor for half an hour before the race.

One thing which probably never occurred to him – and, if it had, the thought would have been dismissed in seconds – was the possibility that he might not get further than the first corner. But that's exactly what happened. Schumacher made the better start. So, too, did Mika Hakkinen from fourth place, the McLaren tapping the rear of Senna's car as they braked for the first right-hander. The Williams spun sideways and was struck by the Ferrari of Nicola Larini, the pair ending their race in the gravel trap on the outside of the corner.

Hill had made a poor start but then took advantage of the confusion at the first corner and moved back to third place. Anxious not to let Schumacher get away, Hill tried an adventurous move as he tried to overtake Hakkinen, but the Finn would have none of it. Within a minute of the start, both Williams drivers had spun, the difference being that Hill was at least able to restart, albeit in ninth place. A very impressive climb to second place was halted when his transmission broke with over thirty laps to go. Hill walked back to the paddock and joined a morose gathering as the Williams team watched television pictures of Schumacher heading towards his second victory in succession. Schumacher and Benetton had accumulated twenty points apiece; Williams, fourth on the table, had six points, and, incredibly, Ayrton Senna had none. The mounting pressure was all too evident as he sat silently in that room.

The talk before the start of the season had been of Ayrton perhaps winning eleven Grands Prix in 1994 – not an outlandish suggestion given his prodigious talent and the Williams track record in recent years – to become the most successful driver of all time by overtaking Prost's total of fifty-one wins. And yet here he was, stuck in the back of beyond in Japan, with absolutely nothing to show for his efforts. In his eleven years of Formula One racing, Senna had never gone through the first two races without scoring at least one point, never mind winning, something he had savoured eight times in the opening rounds of the championship.

Senna's immense pride in his work left no room for criticism, yet, judging by his increasingly haunted look, he would have been the first to admit that he was coming under pressure for the first time from a driver nine years his junior who possessed the same brand of natural flair Senna had brought to Formula One in 1984. If he was to stop Schumacher from taking the title, then Senna knew that he simply had to win the next race at Imola.

Frank was just as deeply concerned about the turn of events. But, if there was no pressure on Ayrton from within Williams, then it was coming from all angles once he stepped outside the embrace of the team. The issue of *Autosport* dated 21 April 1994 carried a bold front cover. The headline said simply: 'Michael 20. Ayrton 0'. The front page of the next edition, previewing the San Marino Grand Prix, went a step further. Under a troubled portrait of Ayrton, the headline said: 'Senna. Can he take the heat?' The following week's magazine would carry a story of an altogether more tragic kind.

CHAPTER FIFTEEN

1 May 1994

Most people in Formula One enjoyed Imola because, as a rule, it signalled the beginning of the season's European sector. After the disruption and make-do of the long-haul races in Brazil and Japan, it was good to have what might be called the home comforts provided by the transporters and motor homes which could be brought to each race by road.

In any case, Imola was a nice place to be. Situated in a picturesque part of Emilia, the circuit offered a challenge for the drivers while the local food and wine provided adequate sustenance for those who either worked or watched. The atmosphere was always highly charged thanks to the Italian passion for motor sport and the persistently voluble support for Ferrari, a team based less than an hour away. The San Marino Grand Prix was considered to be one of the best races of the season. In 1994, it would become one of the most catastrophic of recent times.

The trouble began on the first day of practice. Rubens Barrichello lost control of his Jordan as he came through a chicane at over 140 mph. The car, launched by a kerb, looked for a moment as though it was heading for a wire-mesh fence in front of a packed grandstand. Somehow, the Jordan ran along the top of the crash barrier before landing upside down on the trackside. The following day, the

Brazilian was walking around the paddock with nothing more than a cut lip and a broken nose. It had been a close call, but Formula One people, cushioned in recent years by the enormous strides in safety, thought no more about it. There was a Grand Prix to be run and work to be done.

The Williams engineers had not been idle. Small but significant changes had been made to the aerodynamics of FW16 in a bid to cure the handling problems. The wheelbase had been changed and the cockpit surround had been reshaped in an effort to improve the comfort of the drivers. On the same note, and more significant in the light of what was to follow, the steering column design had been altered to allow the steering wheel to move slightly, to a position preferred by Senna. Such minor details could make all the difference within the cramped cockpit of a Formula One car where there was no more than an inch to spare on either side of the driver's knees and down by his feet.

The changes made a difference. But they were not the complete answer. Nevertheless, Senna set a time good enough for pole position during final qualifying on Saturday afternoon. Then the weekend delivered another blow, much more severe than the first.

Roland Ratzenberger, a thirty-one-year-old Austrian who was having his first season in Formula One, slammed into a concrete wall at high speed. The nose section of his Simtek-Ford, which was believed to have been loosened when Ratzenberger touched a kerb on the previous lap, had become detached as he reached 190 mph. Ratzenberger had no chance of controlling the car. In hospital later that afternoon, he would succumb to his multiple injuries.

It was the first time in twelve years that a driver had lost his life at a Grand Prix meeting, eight years since a driver had died while testing. During that time, a generation of personnel had come into Formula One and never known anything like this. Senna was among them. He visited the scene of the accident and then went to the circuit medical centre, where he met Professor Watkins. They had become good friends over the years and Sid told Ayrton as gently as he could that Ratzenberger was beyond help. Watkins recorded in his memoirs:

Ayrton was beside himself. He had not been close to death at a circuit before. The last tragedy we'd had at a race meeting in Formula One had been in Montreal in 1982 when Ricardo Paletti was killed at the start of the race, before Senna's career had reached Grand Prix level. Although he was totally aware of and accepted the dangers, we'd had a long run without fatality. So many accidents in the past twelve years, so many serious injuries, but nobody irrevocably lost. It was both cruel and horrible for us all that tragedy had happened again. Ayrton broke down and cried on my shoulder.

Sid comforted Senna as best he could. Then he tried to persuade him to withdraw from the race the following day. 'What else do you need to do?' asked Watkins. 'You have been world champion three times, you are obviously the quickest driver. Give it up and let's go fishing.' According to Watkins, Senna was silent for a while. 'He gave me a very steady look and, now calm, he said, "Sid, there are certain things over which we have no control. I cannot quit, I have to go on."'

Despite such a firm commitment, there is no question that Senna's mind was in turmoil. Barrichello remembers regaining consciousness in the medical centre to find Senna standing over him with tears in his eyes. In addition, Ayrton's personal life was enduring enormous highs and lows. He was deeply in love with Adriane Galisteu, a twenty-one-year-old former singer and fashion model with whom he had spent the previous thirteen months. Senna's family did not approve of the relationship and, at Imola, Ayrton was reported to have had strong words on the matter with his brother, Leonardo. On Saturday evening, Senna spoke at length on the telephone with Adriane, who was in Faro, in Portugal, in one of Senna's homes. He is believed to have said he was unhappy about having to race. Yet, for all this emotional disorder in his private and professional life, Senna refused to shy away from the task before him.

Hill was in no doubt that Senna meant to continue when he studied the warm-up times the following morning. Senna had been quickest, with Damon next.

I knew that Ayrton was out to dominate proceedings that day, I was 0.9 seconds slower and I was happy with the car; I knew exactly what I'd had to do to set that time. So it was clear that Ayrton must have tried very hard indeed to set his time. It seemed to me that my team-mate was playing a psychological game here because, when you know that someone is almost a second a lap faster, it can demoralise you before the race has even started. I was not too worried because I was happy with the pace I was running at; I knew I could keep that up throughout the race whereas I didn't think Ayrton could. It was going to be a very interesting race.

When Hill spoke about unsettling the opposition, it did not need to be said that Senna had Schumacher in mind. Significantly, the Benetton driver had been eleventh fastest in the warm-up, more than two seconds slower than Ayrton. The guesswork said that Schumacher was planning to run with a heavier load of fuel and make one stop fewer. The reality, as Senna would discover, would be quite different.

The unease which had descended on Imola turned to deep consternation when there was another incident within seconds of the start. The Finnish driver J.J. Lehto stalled his

Benetton on the grid. Most of the field managed to take avoiding action but Pedro Lamy, starting from the back, was unsighted and accelerating hard in third gear when confronted by the stationary Benetton. The inevitable collision caused wheels and bodywork to fly up and over the fencing and into the crowd, injuring several spectators. Lamy and Lehto had escaped serious injury but wreckage was strewn across the track.

Senna was unaware of all this. His attention was focused on the Benetton glued to his gearbox, a clear sign that he was not going to have this race, a race he desperately needed to win, all his own way. The Safety Car had been sent onto the track in order to take control of the race while the wreckage was cleared but, before the leaders could catch it, they had run through the chaos of the start/finish area at close to racing speed. Then followed four laps running at a crawl behind the official car.

Why the race was not stopped and restarted afresh, as allowed by the regulations, was never made clear. It was suspected that the fear of losing the television audience might have had something to do with a decision which was having a worrying effect on the cars. During the minutes spent creeping along behind the Safety Car (an Opel saloon which was hopelessly inadequate for the job) the tyre temperatures – and hence the tyre pressures which were so critical to ride heights measured in millimetres – were falling. It was a concern Senna had voiced in the pre-race drivers' briefing earlier that day. But there was not a lot he could do about it now even though the pressures had dropped by at least 50 per cent. The safety car pulled into the pits. The race was on once more.

Senna and Schumacher began to ease away from the rest, the Benetton driver continuing his mission to harry the man he wanted to beat most. As he did so, Schumacher noticed that the Williams was occasionally showering sparks from the titanium skid plates, a sign that the car was bottoming on the bumps, particularly at Tamburello, a long and very fast left-hand curve which, despite its speed, did not cause the drivers undue concern.

They completed another lap and set off for the seventh time towards Tamburello. Senna began to turn in to the bend. His Williams had reached 193 mph when it unaccountably veered right. Less than two seconds later, it ran straight into the concrete wall lining the outside of the corner. The right-front wheel was torn off by the impact and forced towards the cockpit area. A jagged part of the suspension pierced Senna's crash helmet on the right forehead.

Sid Watkins, dressed in flameproof clothes and waiting as usual in the emergency response car a few hundred yards away, was quickly on the scene. There was not a broken bone in Senna's body, but one look at the head injury told the Prof that his best friend in racing would not survive.

If the world of motor racing had been stunned by events the previous day, it was about to go into deep shock as the picture emerged. Nowhere would this be felt more keenly than in the Williams garage. And, in particular, a desperately sad figure who at once became gaunt and frail as he sat motionless in his wheelchair and studied the television monitor.

Drivers had survived accidents at this corner before. For instance, Piquet in 1987. But Frank's motor racing vibes, his experience as he watched the doctors working frantically at the scene, told him that the unthinkable had probably happened. He sat in the garage surrounded by his team. The relentless eye of television was making Ayrton's accident desperately public. Yet Frank felt terribly alone. He had wanted Senna more than anyone else to drive his car. Now this.

Senna was airlifted to the Maggiore Hospital in Bologna. The teams would go through the motions by taking the restart and completing the outstanding fifty-eight laps. Hill would finish sixth. All of that became a mere footnote when, in the early evening, news came through that Ayrton Senna was dead. Formula One went blindly about its business, packing up and getting away from this place as quickly as possible. The sport would become engulfed in a period of profound sadness. The bitter recriminations would follow soon after.

In the meantime, the Williams team had to come to terms with this shattering set-back as best they could. Iain Cunningham had been dispatched by Frank to take care of things at Bologna airport:

I actually learned that Ayrton had died when I was at the airport. I was very conscious, as I watched the McLaren people arrive at the airport, that it was much worse for them than it was for us. Ayrton had driven for McLaren for six years and won championships and races. We had done nothing with him. It was like a maiden aunt giving you that precious vase – and you've dropped it. It might have been easier for us if Ayrton had done a season with us, but we had achieved absolutely nothing and we had lost all. That made it worse for Frank, much worse. Having finally got Ayrton on board, he hadn't been able to give him anything. And as we all believed at the time, and now know for certain, Frank could have given Ayrton so much. They could have achieved a great deal together.

Everyone at Didcot was devastated. Ayrton had come round a couple of times. He'd said 'Look, we're having a really tough time but we are going to get better because there is plenty of potential.' He was so upbeat and it gave everyone a tremendous lift. I took him round the factory the first time. He had photographs taken with everyone. And I mean everyone. There was an old boy called George who swept the floors. As Ayrton went by, he spotted George sweeping up behind a milling machine. 'What about him?' he asked. George got his photo. All of that just made it so much harder for everyone to take, particularly when the photos arrived about a week after the accident.

There was no real emotion from Frank at the time but I remember speaking to Robin about a week later and asking how Frank had been. Robin said Frank did cry on the flight back from Imola. That was the only time I heard of any real emotion.

I knew how much Ayrton meant to Frank. I remember at the time of the contract, Frank had no real interest in the terms and conditions; just sign it and get it sorted. Frank even took an interest in Ayrton's overalls and sent different Nacional [Senna's sponsor] badges for him to look at. I'd never known Frank take such an interest in a driver's welfare before. It was a very genuine friendship and there is no doubt that Ayrton looked up to Frank.

It was so difficult to know what to say to Frank afterwards. I went up to him and said, 'I'm so sorry.' He said he had been through this before in his life. But this was probably the worst.

There were pictures taken of Frank as he sat alone with Ayrton's coffin in São Paulo. You could see that he was extremely distraught. I thought: 'If he manages to survive this, I will be amazed.' But he did.

CHAPTER SIXTEEN

Pressure everywhere

The FIA, under pressure to provide an answer to what amounted to a freak run of disasters, remained calm and resisted the easy option of an unnecessary knee-jerk reaction. But events two weeks later in Monaco would force their hand.

Most people could have done without this race, difficult at the best of times, but almost impossible when you simply wanted to get the job done and move on. Monaco, noted for its razzmatazz, had never been so sombre. Compared with what Frank had known in more than twenty-five years of visiting the principality, it was a different place entirely. The public address system, normally blaring from dawn to dusk, was strangely muted; the cafés and bars, while doing a reasonable trade, somehow lacked the *joie de vivre* that accompanies the Grand Prix de Monaco. The unmistakable feeling was that this was a weekend to be endured, got through as quickly as possible. Frank saw it as simply another race. 'You know you've got to do it,' he said. 'All I can remember is great sadness, but I don't remember any particular difficulty in going to work, or turning up at Monaco. There was just this huge sadness.'

The mood of the moment was exposed immediately when Gerhard Berger, a friend and fellow countryman of Ratzenberger and one of the drivers closest to Senna, held a press conference the day before practice began. There had been rumours that he was about to quit and the Austrian wanted to clarify his position. It was a brave move, witnessed by more than 400 media members, many of whom knew next to nothing about the sport but had come to Monaco in search of some dramatic follow-up to the tragic events at Imola. Berger handled the potentially explosive situation with great honesty, particularly when one buffoon asked if this weekend 'was to be the most important race meeting in living memory'. Seasoned motor racing types scoffed at such emotional hyperbole, but fewer than twenty-four hours later, that man's words came back to haunt us.

Karl Wendlinger, a young Austrian driving for the Sauber team, crashed at the harbour chicane. It was a comparatively low-speed accident, his car catching the barrier a glancing blow. It was with utter disbelief that the paddock learned that Wendlinger was in a coma. The fact that the accident was, in some ways, a fluke did nothing to lessen its devastating consequences. Formula One had just been accelerated into a crisis.

The FIA, with the media baying for answers, had to be seen to be taking some action. Technical reforms, designed to slow the cars and due to be introduced in 1995, would come into force sooner than planned, some with effect from the next race in Spain. Then, when it seemed the tense atmosphere could not be wound tighter, the drivers held a brief but moving ceremony on the starting grid, where the front row had been left clear in memory of Senna and Ratzenberger, both of whom had been residents of Monaco. 'It was hard,' said Damon Hill, describing this unique gathering, moments before the start of the Grand Prix. 'But I felt it was the right thing to do. When it was over, I was really ready to go racing, and I thought that's exactly what Ayrton and Roland would have wanted to do.'

It had been a difficult time for Hill. He had flown to Brazil and attended Senna's funeral, an occasion of massive emotion as the city of São Paulo came to a virtual standstill in order to bury a national hero. With barely time to pause, Damon returned to Britain and prepared to travel to Monaco, where he would be the sole representative of a team which, under the circumstances, would be allowed to enter just one car. Eighteen months before, Hill had simply been the test driver. Now he was carrying the responsibility of the entire team on his shoulders. Not only that, this was happening in a race Senna had virtually made his own, one which was also synonymous with Damon's father. After the events of the past few weeks, Williams and Renault desperately needed a result to give them a boost. The pressure to succeed was enormous, but Hill felt he was up to the job.

Starting from fourth on the grid, he made an excellent getaway and began to draw alongside Hakkinen's McLaren in the rush to the first corner. The two cars touched. Hakkinen was out on the spot. Hill got as far as Casino Square at the top of the town before his suspension broke. The walk back to the pits seemed endless. The team, without a second car to fall back on, had begun to pack up, almost in total silence. Hill was shattered. On top of everything else, the Renault hierarchy was on hand and their mood was not improved when arch rivals Peugeot powered home a McLaren into second place. The race was won by Schumacher. Benetton-Ford had forty points, Williams-Renault had seven.

Frank and Patrick had been giving serious thought to finding a replacement for Senna and the choice was narrowed by the FIA's decision to have the cars dramatically altered in time for the Spanish Grand Prix. Not only had the technical goalposts been moved, they were out of sight, on a pitch which was far from level. By slashing the amount of downforce available, the rule changes would make cars even more nervous to drive than before. Under the circumstances, it would be preferable to have someone who knew the team and was familiar with the FW16. David Coulthard, the Williams test driver, was the obvious choice.

The personable Scotsman at least gave the British media something different to write about. Hill was almost forgotten. Indeed, there was the feeling that one or two high rollers at Renault were convinced Damon was not capable of leading the team. Nigel Mansell's name was mentioned more than once since word was coming through that his honeymoon in Indycar racing had long since finished and the relationship with his team was rapidly turning sour. Frank, when pressed, said he had no intention of getting rid of Hill. But as one seasoned member of the British team remarked: 'He would say that, wouldn't he?'

Frank's pragmatism, his determination not to permit anything to stand in his way, would allow him to be economical with the truth to the point of parsimony. He had been known to tell many a white lie in order to protect his interests while under close questioning. When the truth would eventually come out and his words thrown back in his face, Williams would say: 'I'm sorry, I had to.' Then the sheepish grin.

Whatever may have been afoot, Hill provided the perfect riposte by winning his first race of the season. This had been one of his most difficult drives since he knew, above all else, he could not afford to make a single mistake and throw away a desperately needed victory. It was small wonder that he looked mentally exhausted as he stood with Schumacher on the podium. Dignified as ever, and resisting the temptation to score a cheap point, Hill later accepted the gushing platitudes of the Renault bosses as they sheathed their metaphorical knives for another week or two. It had been a crucial breakthrough for the beleaguered team. Frank smiled, probably for the first time in four weeks.

Coulthard, who had given a good account of himself before retiring with electrical trouble, remained on board for the Canadian Grand Prix. In view of the mounting rumours that Mansell might indeed return, Coulthard made the most of his opportunity. Having qualified a fraction slower than Hill – who was not happy with the balance of a car which remained nervous and difficult to drive – Coulthard jumped ahead at the start and remained there despite Hill's close attention. Coulthard eventually let Hill through, but not before the team had issued an instruction. Hill was slightly miffed about it, his mood after the race not helped by having finished second to Schumacher, the gap between them having stretched to thirty-three points as the season reached its halfway point.

The details of the championship became irrelevant when it was announced that arrangements had been made for Mansell to drive in the forthcoming French Grand Prix (which did not clash with an Indycar race), and then in the final three Grands Prix, which would take place after the North American season had finished. Renault had been behind a deal which would pay Mansell approximately £900,000 for each race. If Hill was put out by the thought that his annual retainer was not much more than £300,000, then he kept his opinions to himself. Coulthard would stand down and Hill said he welcomed the opportunity to be measured against the former world champion.

Certainly, there was much to be said for having Mansell in the team when a typically extrovert lap, which seemed good enough for pole position, prompted Hill to take to the track in the closing minutes of qualifying and drive out of his skin. He took pole by 0.07 seconds. Mansell was not a force for the rest of the weekend.

The race turned out to be a battle between Hill and Schumacher, one which was more or less settled straight away when the Benetton, starting from the second row, powered between the pair of Williams-Renaults as if they were standing still. When Hill returned to the motor home after finishing second, Mansell had already left, his car having stopped with hydraulic failure. Hill found Patrick Head and the team manager, Ian Harrison, running a video of the start. Schumacher's getaway, as the Benetton changed direction at will and rocketed into the lead with nary a hint of wheelspin or drama, seemed too good to be true. Head watched the pictures once more, then grunted and left the room. It was easy to read his thoughts.

When Senna had been forced, through the first corner retirement at Aida, to watch the race from the sidelines, he had suspected there might be something different about Schumacher's car, certainly when compared with the performance of the second Benetton. Later in the year, there would be suggestions that Benetton might be continuing to operate a (wheelspin-reducing) traction control system even though it had been made illegal for 1994. It was never proved. But Senna's comments, and those pictures of the start at Magny-Cours, would remain at the back of many minds as the season progressed. In the meantime, Schumacher was about to apply a self-imposed handicap as the scene shifted to Silverstone and the British Grand Prix.

Hill had recognised that, if he was to do anything about arresting Schumacher's runaway championship campaign, then he needed to win in France. The fact that he failed to do so added to a frustration which boiled over when he walked into the Silverstone paddock four days later. During the intervening period, one or two reports had suggested that the turnaround in the Williams performance had been due to Mansell's input, and Bernie Ecclestone (a prime mover in the Mansell comeback) had gone on record as saying Hill would never have been on pole in France had it not been for Mansell.

Hill was due to have his informal briefing with the British press. The hacks gathered outside the Williams motor home and prepared for the usual fairly predictable preview of the weekend ahead. What they got was far removed from anything they had expected. Damon Hill threw off his nice guy image and became Mr Angry. In a terse monologue, interrupted only by the whirring of tape recorders and frantic scribbling, Hill said he was fed up with being taken for granted by the team and by the press:

What do you have to bloody do for people to believe that you are any good? Basically, I don't get any credit for being polite and diplomatic. So I'm going to ditch that tack as it's not getting me anywhere. I'm fighting a battle here with a car that is clearly not as good as the Schumacher/Benetton pairing and, after last weekend, I have proved that I am getting the best out of my equipment. I promise you that I am here to stay. I have proved myself as a top F1 driver. And this weekend I will once again prove that point.

Talk about making a rod for your own back. Hill was exposing himself to all manner of potential ridicule if he failed, but he was clearly willing to accept the risk. He was one of the first onto the track on Friday morning. And the front suspension on the Williams promptly fell apart. Hill was stunned as he watched first the left-hand push rod, then the right, pop out of their mounting points as the suspension came under load for the first time. Any thought of limping back to the pits was cancelled by the front of the car bouncing dangerously along the track.

Hill hitched a ride back to the pits and, as he passed through the paddock, he saw Patrick Head walking to the garage, about to start his day's work on the trackside. Head was amazed to see his driver appear on foot not five minutes after practice had started. The amazement turned to consternation when he saw Hill's angry expression, and then to disbelief when he heard what had happened. It was clear that an unfortunate mechanic had put the bolts in place but had forgotten to secure them properly. Both Damon and Patrick knew there was no need to chastise the person responsible since the moment will live with the poor man for the rest of his life.

Meanwhile, Hill was under pressure. With use of the spare car not permitted during practice, he had to cool his heels until the break halfway through the session. Then it took time to repair the race car and he just managed four laps at the end. Straight away he was third quickest – a sign that his aggression had been stoked even higher by this latest turn in events. He carried that right through to the final qualifying session when he took pole from Schumacher with a lap which was, if anything, even greater than his spectacular effort at Magny-Cours.

The race was set for an epic struggle between Hill and Schumacher but, even before the appearance of the green light, Schumacher was to be the architect of his own downfall.

Hill was surprised at the beginning of the formation lap when Schumacher smoked away from his grid position and passed the Williams. This was expressly forbidden and Schumacher compounded his mistake by doing it once more halfway round the lap. Then the officials bungled by failing to follow their own rules and remove the Benetton to the back of the grid. This set in motion a sequence of events which would ultimately spoil the race.

Hill made a clean start and led into the first corner. Benetton and Williams had been attempting to out-guess each other on tactics and, in the event, they made identical decisions: to run very light at the start in order to open a lead. Thus Hill and Schumacher powered away from the rest, Hill with the upper hand throughout.

By that time the officials had creaked into life and issued a decision to penalise Schumacher by five seconds for his errant behaviour. The notice made no mention of a stop-go penalty. But then it didn't need to because that is taken as read. Now it was the turn of the Benetton team to display their ignorance and they assumed the five seconds would be added onto Schumacher's race time. So they did not call their man into the pits, as the officials had expected. Schumacher was shown the black flag and, for whatever reason – he said he didn't see the flag although it could have been that the team told him to stay out – he chose to ignore it. Eventually, the team explained their confusion and it was pointed out that Schumacher must come in for a stop-go. This he eventually did, giving up the lead in the process, his earlier pit stop having been marginally faster than Hill's. But the damage had been done and the race lost its edge.

Schumacher and Benetton were ultimately fined $25,000, a penalty which was considered inadequate since Schumacher had committed a cardinal sin by ignoring the black flag which calls for a driver to stop at the end of his next lap. Meanwhile, Damon Hill had scored an emotional victory at home by collecting a trophy which had eluded his father in seventeen attempts to win the British Grand Prix. Damon's mum and two sisters were there to see him do it, and you could tell by their choked expressions just how much this result meant.

The weather had been glorious, Silverstone looking at its best. As the sun beat a rich retreat later that evening, Hill took to a temporary stage in the grassy paddock and, guitar in hand, sang his heart out with a rock band. It was, he said, the end of a day made in heaven. After all he and the team had been through, no one begrudged him this moment of a lifetime. And, despite the bungling by Benetton and the officials, Hill had been as good as his angry word from three days before.

Frank, as usual, had kept his comments to the minimum. 'I'm not quite certain what Damon means,' he said, when responding to questions about Hill's earlier remarks. 'Of course we support Damon. His pole position was absolutely outstanding. Just when you are thinking that he had reached a certain level, he moves forward to find a new one. He was most impressive all weekend.'

The same could not be said of Schumacher and Benetton. The German driver was summoned before a special meeting of the FIA World Council, where he discovered that the original $25,000 fine had been increased to $500,000. Worse than that, he would be disqualified from the Silverstone result and suspended for two races. Fortunately for everyone concerned, an appeal would allow Schumacher to take part in his home Grand Prix at Hockenheim. Had he not been able to do so, the Williams team, and Hill in particular, would have been under serious threat from German race fans seeking revenge.

In the event, Schumacher's engine broke but Hill failed to make the most of it after tangling unnecessarily with a Tyrrell on the first lap, the subsequent stop for repairs dropping him out of the points. Damon finished second to Schumacher in Hungary, but Michael's run of good fortune would be brief. He was thrown out of first place in Belgium (on a technical infringement), Hill inheriting a victory which reduced Schumacher's championship lead to twenty-one points. By the time Schumacher made his return from the two-race suspension, the gap would be a single point thanks to impressive victories for Hill in Italy and Portugal. The momentum was with Hill and Williams as they moved on to Spain for the European Grand Prix. It would turn out to be a disaster.

The race started on the right note when Hill blasted past Schumacher's pole position Benetton. This upset Schumacher's plans straight away since he had been relying on a clean start in order to shoot into the lead and execute a three-stop strategy. Hill, planning to stop just twice, was looking good. When he held that advantage until the first round of stops, it seemed he had the race under easy control. Then the Williams plan went awry.

Due to a faulty valve inside the refuelling equipment which diverted fuel away from the collection chamber, Hill was sent out with insufficient to cover the next third of the race. Schumacher was now leading but, when it was time for his second stop, his advantage was only fourteen seconds, not enough to maintain his lead. Hill, oblivious to the earlier problem, took charge once more and fully expected to go some distance before having to make his second and final stop. He was astonished when the team called him in a few laps later, almost at half distance. He was even more surprised when they pumped ninety litres of fuel on board, enough to see him through to the finish. Schumacher, meanwhile, had around fifty-five litres in the Benetton. And he would have the benefit of another set of tyres at three-quarter distance.

Hill was history from that point on. Struggling with a 50 kg weight handicap, his tyres were badly abused within six laps. Furthermore, the extended braking distances and poor acceleration made him look hesitant in traffic. And, all the while, Hill was trying to figure out what on earth had gone wrong. Schumacher was slicing through the back-markers and pulling out half a second a lap, and Hill could do nothing about it. What made it even worse was the fact that there were twenty litres of fuel remaining in Hill's car at the finish. The original fault with the refuelling equipment may have been out of the team's hands, but Hill had some heavy questions to ask about the subsequent tactics and this unnecessary burden of additional fuel.

He felt, with some justification, that he should have won the race and yet he had appeared to fail miserably. Benetton, meanwhile, had run like clockwork and Schumacher's championship lead had extended to five points with two races to go. The fact was that, in a perfect world, Williams and Hill were not as uncompetitive as they had seemed and, conversely, Benetton should not have been as crushingly dominant as the results suggested. But history has no time for ifs and buts. The record books, however, were about to enshrine one of Hill's greatest drives as the season moved into its closing stages in Japan and Australia.

Hill's continuing unease was not helped by a bruising discussion with Patrick Head during practice at Suzuka. Damon felt his comments about the car were not receiving the attention they deserved and, in the ensuing debate, Head severely criticised Hill's ability by suggesting that everyone on the team found working with the Englishman to be difficult. It was interesting to note that at no stage did Hill turn to Frank for support. He knew what the answer would be: Frank would echo the views of his technical director, but in a more subtle manner.

While it was true that Hill occasionally needed to be prodded into action, such a forthright debate hardly seemed to be the best tactic at such a crucial stage. Hill was livid as he stormed out of the garage and brushed aside the waiting members of the British press. The debate with Patrick had merely fuelled Hill's long-held belief that, deep down, the Williams team did not consider him to be top-flight material.

On the other hand, if this had been Head's way of encouraging a bloody-minded determination in his driver, then his blunt address had been worthwhile, judging by Hill's superb efforts on race day. In truly appalling conditions, Hill chased Schumacher, the two of them being head and shoulders above the rest in a race that would be decided by a combination of luck, skill and the correct tactics in the rapidly changing circumstances. The conditions became so bad that the Safety Car was deployed after only eight laps. When the racing resumed, it was stopped almost immediately when a car spun off and broke a marshal's leg. Schumacher assumed the lead once more at the restart but lost it when he made a pit stop with just ten laps remaining. Hill, meanwhile, was running non-stop to the finish.

Schumacher drove flat out in an effort to catch Hill, both producing incredible performances in such treacherous conditions. Since the final result would be the aggregate of the two parts, Schumacher had 6.8 seconds in hand as a result of his lead when the race was stopped. It meant he would not need actually to overtake Hill on the road in order to regain the lead, the most difficult circumstances imaginable for Hill as he pushed himself to the limit against his unseen rival. Schumacher not only had the benefit of a fresh set of tyres, Hill was struggling with a car which did not handle as well as the Benetton. In addition, his mechanics had been unable to remove the right-rear wheel during the pit stop, which meant Hill was having to go the full distance on the same wet-weather tyre.

The gap as they went into the last lap was 2.4 seconds. Hill drove the lap of his life, the Williams teetering on the very limit of control. If he failed here, his championship would be as good as over. If he flew off the road, he would be forever branded as a loser – not least, one suspected, by certain members of the Williams team. On that lap, he actually extended his lead. But no one knew the truth until Schumacher crossed the line.

The delay while the computer flashed up the corrected final gap of 3.3 seconds seemed to take three minutes. It was the first time Hill had crossed the line first and then had to wait to find out if he had won. Not only had he collected maximum points, he was still in the running for the championship. The final winner-take-all shoot-out would be in Adelaide. And, just to make Frank's day, a stirring drive by Mansell into fourth place had helped to keep Williams at the top of the constructors' championship, a few points clear of Benetton.

Hill landed himself in trouble the minute he touched down in Australia. With the Suzuka verbal exchange still on his mind, he gave vent to his feelings at an impromptu press conference at the airport:

I have been in negotiation with the team about my contract. They have taken up their option on my services for next year, but I reckon I am a lot better than my contract says I am. This dispute is about the team recognising what you feel yourself to be worth. I have won nine Grands Prix. This year I have had to carry the role of number one driver in only my second season in Formula One. I'm only one point off the championship lead with one race to go.

Hill's £300,000 salary was a mere pittance for a driver fighting for the championship but, when all was said and done, Frank had given him the opportunity in the first place. Without Williams, Hill would be in the anonymous margins of the limelight and not centre stage. By the time he had reached the circuit and thought about his hasty words, Damon attempted to soften his views:

What I tried to get across was that, throughout the period since my option was taken up – and even before that – I have been trying to get some sort of reassurance that Williams have got the faith in me to do the job. What I want to know is whether I am going to get the financial recognition for the job that I think I'm doing. It's a question of endorsement, a show of faith, and I feel sometimes I have been left not too certain about where I stand. Maybe I am wrong, maybe I have misinterpreted the signals, but this is all new territory to me.

Frank refused to comment, saying his focus was on winning the championship. 1995 could wait.

Mansell, reigniting all his old flair, took a storming pole position with Schumacher joining the Englishman on the front row. Hill was third fastest, but off the required pace. Frank and Patrick doubted Damon could do it. But Hill had a surprise in store for his bosses. And, more to the point, for Schumacher.

The contenders both chose independently to go for a three-stop tactic. That ensured that they would run together, flat-out all the way. No one else would get a look-in. It was a superb contest, Hill summoning up reserves of bravado and audacity not seen before. Determined not to let Schumacher out of his grasp, Hill sat inches from the Benetton as they slashed through back-markers and took their cars to the limit. They happened to make their first stops on the same lap, rejoining together to continue this gripping encounter. Schumacher put on an extra spurt at the moment when Hill was detained briefly by a slower car as the race approached half distance. A season's work was about to distil into a microsecond of decision-making by both drivers.

In his desperation to escape Hill's clutches, Schumacher ran wide at the exit of one corner and brushed the wall. Hill rounded the corner and saw the Benetton coming off the grass and into the middle of the track. Assuming his rival had just had a brief moment on the narrow verge, Hill seized the opportunity to attack while Schumacher was still unsettled as they approached the next corner. If only Hill had arrived a second sooner, he would have realised that the Benetton had actually hit the wall, that there was no need to hurry. He could pick him off on the next straight. But Hill did not know that. This was the opportunity he had been waiting for. The Williams aimed for the gap inside the Benetton. Schumacher turned towards the corner. The two cars came together with a bump. Schumacher teetered on two wheels before crashing back onto the track, his race over.

Had Schumacher done it deliberately? Had he realised that his chance had gone, and the only tactic left was to take Hill with him? The argument will continue for as long as motor racing folk gather to chew over the sport's defining moments. But, whatever Schumacher's motives may have been, he was left in limbo as the Williams disappeared out of sight.

Hill continued down the back straight. If he could score just two points, the championship would be his. But he knew he was in trouble. He could see that the left-front suspension had been bent. Maybe, just maybe, it could be fixed. When he reached the pits, a quick glance by the mechanics told Damon that it was all over. The excited voice of the track commentator informed Michael Schumacher that he had just become the 1994 world champion. One of the most dramatic seasons in the history of the sport was over.

Not quite. The race was continuing and the result was backing towards Nigel Mansell. Hill and Schumacher had eliminated themselves and Gerhard Berger was about to spin his Ferrari out of the lead. Mansell's thirty-first and final Grand Prix victory would ensure that Williams won the constructors' championship by a comfortable margin.

The drivers' title had escaped them but to have come as close as they did after such a traumatic period was a tribute to the entire Williams team. In an end-of-season interview with Nigel Roebuck of *Autosport*, Frank summed up his feelings in typically direct and honest fashion: 'Enormous sadness is the overriding thing, of course. And I don't mean that in any trite sense. Everyone in the company was truly shattered by what happened at Imola. They all felt a certain responsibility, and it's still there on the minds of many people here. At the end of the day, the fact is that Ayrton Senna died in a Williams car, and that's an enormously important responsibility.'

Certain factions, mainly outside the sport, were determined not to let him forget it.

CHAPTER SEVENTEEN

The Boy Damon

The 1995 San Marino Grand Prix marked the first anniversary of something everyone would rather forget. Or, at least, not talk about. Imola was the third race of the season and, for once, no one looked forward to it. Walking through the gates at the far end of the long, narrow paddock brought back memories which produced a lump in the throat for most people. Particularly those working for Rothmans Williams-Renault.

The place was overrun with members of the media. Quite what they expected to find was difficult to say. To the outsider, it seemed that no one cared about events twelve months before. The teams were going about their business, preparing to fight another race. No one wanted to talk about 1994. But the bustle and industry, carried on in most cases with a deeper sense of purpose than before, was merely a front, a means of suppressing the terrible recollections which threatened to invade private thoughts at every turn.

Frank Williams treated the race like any other. There were no interviews on Senna, no comments. But that did not mean the subject was far from his mind. On the Saturday evening, after most people had left the circuit, the team went to a deserted Tamburello and paid their quiet respects.

It was a difficult moment but, for many, it was a necessary release of bottled-up emotion.

Underlying all of this, like some persistent sore, was the continual talk of an investigation into the accident and a trial before a local magistrate. The authorities had impounded Senna's car on the day of the crash and the investigating magistrate, Maurizio Passarini, had appointed a committee to examine every detail of the car, the circuit and the circumstances leading up to the moment of impact. There had been rumour and counter-rumour about the cause of the accident: the driver had made a mistake; he had run over some debris; the steering had broken; the Williams, with its tyre pressures too low after running behind the safety car for four slow laps, had simply bottomed out at 193 mph, leaving the driver helpless; the power steering had failed. Something had killed Ayrton Senna. But none of this was going to bring him back. The feeling seemed to be, if there is going to be a trial, then let's get it over and done with. There was little hope of that when, just a few weeks before the race on 30 April, Passarini requested another six months before issuing a report on the findings of the investigating committee. The best solution for Williams in the short term was to go to Imola and win the race.

Damon Hill had started the year with all guns blazing. An upbeat pre-season press conference had given the impression that here was a man who had come close in 1994, learned many lessons and was now at one with his team and ready to blow Michael Schumacher and Benetton away. That had seemed to be the way of it in Brazil when Hill led the opening race with convincing ease until his rear suspension broke. Victory went to Schumacher. Hill put matters right in Argentina when he had Schumacher beaten hands down. The latest Williams, FW17, did not miss a beat. Hill said he had never enjoyed a race as much. He was in the right frame of mind to return to Imola, deal with anticipated difficulties and then continue the winning momentum on the track.

Hill would be racing alongside David Coulthard. That may seem logical and straightforward, the Scotsman having been impressive during his first races with Williams, but the novice had already caused quite a stir. As 1994 had come to an end, Coulthard was being fought over by two teams. At the end of August, he had agreed to have Williams extend the team's option on his services until two days after the final race in Adelaide.

Prior to agreeing to the extension, Coulthard's performances had not been brilliant but, coincidentally, he suddenly got his act together and showed impressive form in the next three races. Then he was forced to stand down to make way for Mansell's return and, during that period, it became apparent to Williams that Coulthard had signed a contract with McLaren for 1995. The matter was finally resolved at the end of 1994 when the Contracts Recognition Board, established shortly before in order to deal with precisely this type of problem, ruled in favour of Williams. Frank took up his option, the side-effect of which was that Nigel Mansell, who had made it clear that he wanted to return to Formula One for a full season, would not be racing with his former employers. 'Nigel could see that we were trying to keep David,' said Williams. 'I had no problem with that. Nigel knew he had to live with the fact that he was being put on hold. Of course, he didn't take it very well – he's got an ego, but I don't belittle him for that.'

Mansell would later announce, with a suitable flourish, that he would be driving for McLaren. Then, during winter testing, he found that he did not fit the cockpit of the latest car, an embarrassing set-back for everyone concerned. He finally made his race debut for McLaren at Imola, where a lacklustre performance indicated that the relationship might be brief.

Certainly, Mansell was made to look second-rate by Hill. The same applied to the rest of the field. In conditions made extremely tricky by a damp but drying track, Hill remained calm while lying fourth in the early stages behind Schumacher's Benetton, Berger's Ferrari and Coulthard. Once the anticipated pit stops for slick tyres had taken place, Hill was third and ready to force Schumacher into a rare mistake as the Benetton crashed. When Berger later made another pit stop, Hill was unbeatable. Coulthard's race had been eventful, a spin being followed by a ten-second penalty for speeding in the pit lane. He would finish fourth. Hill was leading the world championship for the first time ever and Williams were in charge of the constructors' championship. It would be short-lived.

Roles were reversed in Spain, where Benetton suddenly found form and Williams struggled. Even so, Hill looked to be on course for a distant but comfortable second place behind Schumacher when, on the last lap, a hydraulics failure dropped the Williams to fourth. In Monaco, Hill actually managed to collect the points for second place, but he was even more unhappy than he had been in Barcelona. A brilliant pole position lap – one of the best of his career – appeared to have set the scene for a victory with a car which was working perfectly. It was a different story on race day, however, when a problem with the differential made the Williams very difficult to drive. A win for Schumacher and Benetton merely heightened the frustration.

In Canada, Benetton suffered a mechanical problem, but it was indicative of his run of luck that Schumacher should recover sufficiently to take a somewhat fortunate fifth on a day when neither Williams had finished. Coulthard had spun off on the second lap (making it the third race in succession in which he had failed to finish) and Hill had lost second place with a recurrence of the same problem which had cost him points in Spain. Both Hill and Williams continued to fall further behind in their respective championships when Schumacher won in France, Hill and Coulthard finishing second and third. As the teams headed for Silverstone, the pressure was on the favourites to produce at home.

In fact, part of the pressure was self-inflicted. Hill had been critical of the team's ability to prepare the cars properly; Head had intimated that Hill's second place at Monaco had little to do with the faulty differential (the inference being that the driver had not been quick enough) and, in the same interview, Patrick had made known his displeasure over Renault's announcement that they would provide engines to Benetton as well as Williams in 1996. Adrian Newey had been criticised for his part in what, with the benefit of hindsight, appeared to be a poor pit stop strategy in France. Then Michael Breen, a solicitor acting as Hill's manager, had fed ill-advised comments to the *Times* newspaper concerning the quality of the Williams cars. Frank, as ever, said nothing.

The media-led hype, generated by the need to provide stories from one of Britain's major sporting events, had raised the temperature. Hill was about to turn up the heat even further during a dramatic race.

A superb lap had given Damon pole position and he made the most of it as he shot into the lead. It was soon apparent that Williams had opted to stop twice whereas Schumacher, some way behind, would take on fuel and tyres just once. The race followed its predicted pattern, Hill losing the lead after his first stop, regaining it when Schumacher made his one and only visit. Damon had it all to do as he attempted to establish a big enough cushion to allow his final stop without falling behind the Benetton once more.

He failed by a matter of seconds. But, no matter, the Williams had fresh tyres whereas the Benetton did not. Hill closed rapidly on the leader. Sensing a wheel-to-wheel battle of dramatic proportions, the 90,000 crowd, memories of Adelaide as fresh as if it happened the day before, was on its feet, willing their man on. He responded with more than a little vigour.

As the leaders swept into the tight complex of corners behind the pits, Hill attempted an overtaking move which, to work successfully, would have required Schumacher to bend over backwards. Naturally, he was not about to oblige. In fact, he was surprised that Hill should have even thought about attempting a pass from so far back. The resulting collision sent both cars into the gravel trap and retirement.

Moving centre stage, Johnny Herbert and David Coulthard, in effect the substitutes at Benetton and Williams, took their turn to fight for the lead, but the battle was resolved when Coulthard was called into the pits for a ten-second penalty, the result of his speed limit device having failed during an earlier pit stop. But Coulthard would at least finish second.

His team-mate was contemplating zero points and heavy criticism in newspapers deprived of their anticipated tale of glory for Britain's championship hope. In fact, Frank would provide the copy writers with manna from heaven when he was wheeled into the Benetton pit to congratulate Herbert on his first win. According to the newspaper reports on Monday morning, Frank also apologised to the Benetton team for his driver having been 'a bit of a prat'. Frank later denied he had said it. But, by then, Hill had seen the story splashed across the back of every tabloid. He was no more impressed with his boss than Frank had been with him.

Matters would not improve in Germany when Hill spun

out of the lead at the start of the second lap. Williams would later issue a statement saying that subsequent inspection of the car had revealed a technical problem which might have contributed to the spin. But there were some who doubted that. Meanwhile, Coulthard was not in the team's good books. He had finished second but the feeling was he had done nothing about taking the fight to the winner – none other than Michael Schumacher. Hill was twenty-one points behind and Williams were wallowing in third place in the constructors' championship. Nothing less than a win would be acceptable in Hungary.

In the event, Hill produced a thoroughly convincing display as he led from pole position and was never challenged, the championship coming alight when Schumacher retired with four laps to go. Michael would take the initiative once more thanks to a win in Belgium, Hill very unhappy with his rival's driving tactics as they fought wheel to wheel in a race dominated by rain showers and the need to change tyres at precisely the right moment. Hill finished second but Coulthard was bitterly disappointed to have retired from the lead, his engine having lost its oil thanks to a pipe which had been broken by a thump from behind during the scramble through the first corner. His luck would not improve in Italy where, despite having taken pole position, Coulthard would lose the lead once more, this time thanks to a rare failure of a wheel bearing. Hill, meanwhile, was crashing his way into the headlines once more.

Running behind Schumacher as they disputed second place, Hill had misjudged his braking on the entry to a chicane. The matter had been complicated slightly as they lapped a dithering back-marker, but the result was embarrassingly straightforward: the Williams went into the back of the Benetton and both cars left the road. The fact that

Schumacher had not been hurt — at least, not physically — could be seen as marshals restrained the German as he leapt from the cockpit and remonstrated with his rival.

As a result of this latest argy-bargy, the points situation remained static but Hill's position became slightly worse in Portugal when he finished behind Schumacher, neither driver a match for Coulthard as he won his first Grand Prix in commanding style. Unfortunately for David, the late-season run of form had not come soon enough. He had been debilitated more than anyone had realised by tonsillitis earlier in the year and it was during this period that Frank had agreed to test Jacques Villeneuve. The Indycar champion had impressed everyone when he drove the Williams at Silverstone in early August. He was signed soon after and, when Hill agreed advantageous terms later in the month, it was clear that Coulthard could finally join McLaren.

Meanwhile, Hill was having one last shot at wrenching the championship from Schumacher's grasp as they returned to the Benetton driver's home patch for a race at the new Nurburgring. It was to be perhaps one of the most miserable days in Hill's career. The pressure appeared to be getting to him as he banged wheels and left the road more than once in an attempt to prevent Schumacher from putting the issue beyond doubt. In the end, Hill spun off for good and Schumacher, pumped up by the frenzied support from a crowd willing on a first world champion from Germany, produced his most stunning victory yet as he snatched the lead with two laps to go. The title was all but a formality, and Hill knew it as he emerged from behind the crash barriers to applaud the champion-elect. Naturally, one or two sports writers in Britain saw that as the action of a wimp. No one at Williams, least of all Frank, rushed to their man's defence.

In fact, they had little to say of any consequence about

either driver. Coulthard, who had claimed pole position, had kicked off in the worst possible manner by spinning while on his way to the grid. He took over the spare car and struggled home third. But if Frank and Patrick felt let down in Germany, they were to be completely dismayed at the second of two races in Japan. In fact, they would be appalled.

Schumacher duly clinched the championship at the first, the Pacific Grand Prix at Aida, when he took yet another peerless win, the combination of his driving and faultless pit stop tactics leaving the Williams drivers thrashing helplessly in his wake. But at least they had finished second and third. The Japanese Grand Prix a week later would make that result seem exceptional. Hill looked beaten before he started. He had got word of the increasingly vicious round of sniping by the media back home and he was at a loss to explain why his world seemed to be falling apart. All the more reason, then, to try to repeat his storming drive at Suzuka twelve months before.

The race started off promisingly enough as Williams carried out a highly efficient series of pit stops which helped Hill close on the leader, Schumacher. Then a light shower of rain, mixing with oil dropped by a competitor with a blown engine, made the surface lethal at Spoon Hairpin. Hill, given his luck, found it first, the Williams hitting the kerb a mighty thump before running across the gravel run-off area and out the other side. Fearing there might be damage to the nose of the car, he stopped at the pits for a replacement. Not long after, Coulthard went off at exactly the same place. He, too, rejoined, but the stones which had been scooped up by the radiator ducts suddenly shot onto the track and under Coulthard's wheels as he braked for the next corner. The Williams spun off and hit the barrier.

Frank Williams had been watching this pantomime on television as he sat in his usual place at the back of the garage. No sooner had he begun to come to terms with Coulthard having lost second place than the camera switched to another blue and white car which was going nowhere. To everyone's disbelief, Hill had gone off at the same corner as before. This time there would be no recovery. Frank remained staring at the screen. He didn't need anyone to tell him that Williams had failed to win the constructors' championship for the first time in four years. And his team had lost it good and proper. Frank was soon on his private plane, heading back to Britain.

If he was wondering what to say to Hill when next they met in Australia, he need not have worried. Hill turned up in Adelaide two weeks later refreshed and positive. His worries cast aside, he had reverted to his old self, dominating the last race of the season from start to finish. Frank remarked:

Damon went to Bali for a holiday before going to Australia. I don't know what he did there but when he turned up in Australia, he was a different man. There was no need to tell him he was the greatest, all that number that racing drivers sometimes need. He was entirely positive from the word go, and it was great that he won the race and took that memory into the winter. Schumacher had got the better of him in the war of words in 1995, but I think Damon had come to understand what it takes to beat Schumacher in a race, from a driving point of view.

While Hill may have got his act together, damage had been done which would have a far-reaching effect. Damon's problem was that he had grown up and matured with the team as he moved from test driver to number one. For all his impressive deeds on the track, it was as if he remained a lad in Frank's eyes. There was nothing like the respect which would be accorded to a driver who had proved himself elsewhere and had become 'desirable'. If anything, 'The Boy Damon' – as he was affectionately known in certain quarters – was a victim of the team's familiarity with him.

In the immediate aftermath of Senna's accident, Frank had approached Heinz-Harald Frentzen with a view to driving for Williams for the rest of 1994. Flattered by the offer, Frentzen nevertheless wished to remain loyal to Sauber, the team which had given him his F1 break. Frank, hard man that he is, was impressed by that. He said he would keep in touch. As Hill began to motor nowhere at the end of the 1995 season, the moment seemed right to place another call to Frentzen's agent. Williams and Frentzen discussed 1997 and something was signed. Whether it was an option or a firm contract would become a matter for serious debate among outsiders later in the season. But it is clear that an agreement of sorts was reached even before Hill and Villeneuve had begun a major test programme for 1996. When Hill said the next season would be 'now or never', he did not realise the expression had a fuller meaning than he at first thought. As things would turn out, 1996 would probably be the last serious shot he would ever have at the championship.

It did not seem that way when he won the first three races of the season. It was true that Villeneuve had laid down a marker when he claimed pole position at the opening round in Melbourne and led every lap until an oil leak forced a reduction in pace. But it was clear from the easy manner in which Hill had shadowed his partner that he had plenty in hand.

Villeneuve won his first race in Germany, and Hill looked like walking away with the Monaco Grand Prix until a rare failure of his Renault engine brought retirement. Villeneuve was not there to take over, the French-Canadian never at home on the street circuit. Even so, as the season went on, it seemed that the Williams drivers would have the run of the championship, Schumacher having left Benetton for Ferrari, where he was discovering that the reliability of the red cars left a lot to be desired. By the halfway point, Hill had won five of the eight races. It began to look as though he would wrap up the title by the end of August. Then his progress became less certain in every sense.

Frentzen's name was being mentioned with increasing regularity even though Frank refused to admit any connection with the German driver. In any case, it was Villeneuve's position which seemed to be under threat. His performances in the first half of the season had not been anything to write back to Canada about, but a win at Silverstone marked a change. As he settled in with the team and began to understand the car and the tactical skills necessary to get the best out of it, Villeneuve's confidence grew. He won in Hungary, despite never having been there before, and then claimed pole position under similar circumstances at Spa-Francorchamps in Belgium. He led that race until pit stop confusion for both Williams drivers allowed Schumacher through. Villeneuve finished second, with Hill an angry fifth. His championship lead had been reduced to thirteen points. There were four races left and it seemed anything could happen.

On the free weekend between the Belgian and Italian Grands Prix, Michael Breen called a press conference in London to announce that Damon had been informed that his services would not be required in 1997. Hill's lawyer said he had no idea why the negotiations had suddenly been terminated.

The sports writers went into overdrive. Memories were stirred of Piquet, Mansell and Prost, reigning champions who had left the team, sometimes under acrimonious circumstances. Pictures of Frank, headset in place, intense expression on an unsmiling face, were used to foster the impression that he was a 'hard bastard'. Alan Jones, watching developments from Australia, did not go along with that line of thinking:

My view of Frank is that he has always been extremely analytical rather than hard – and there is a difference. When I was driving for him, I knew the job I had to do and Frank knew what he had to do. I said at the time that if I killed myself, Frank would say: 'Jeez, that's a bit of a pity. He wasn't a bad old bloke, Alan.' A couple of minutes later and he would be up and down the pit road, looking for a replacement. But I accepted that. Likewise, I'd flick in quick-smart if he didn't give me the car or the money I wanted. We had this mutual respect.

Frank is very single-minded. He's unbelievably determined. He just eats and breathes motor racing and he never seems to tire of it. Plenty of times when I was racing, I would just want to go back to the motel and call it a day, but Frank would be there, still kicking on. I don't think he's changed a great deal.

During a packed press conference at Monza a few days after Breen's announcement, a stunned and saddened Hill could shed no further light on the decision. Not long before, Frentzen had announced that he would be joining Ville-neuve. Speculation over the reason why was allowed to run unchecked. Some said Frentzen had actually signed at the end of 1995. Other sources suggested that it was merely an option, one which Frank had decided to exercise after being forced to deal with Hill's agent rather than with Damon himself. If the latter is true, then it was an elementary failing on Hill's part since he had known Frank long enough to appreciate that talking face to face is the only way, particu-larly when Frank held most of the cards simply because there were few other options available to Hill if he wished to stay with a top team. Eddie Irvine, in his third season of Formula One, summed it up:

I have always felt that a driver needs to sit down and talk, one to one, with the team owner when important deals are being cut. He needs to be able to read the person he is in discussion with. It's too important a matter to leave to someone else. It is vital to maintain a good relationship with the team owner and Damon should have been doing everything possible to stay with Williams.

One of the rumours suggested that Damon, through his adviser, had been asking for more money. Whether that was the case or not, I don't know. But I certainly would not want to play a game of poker with Frank. He has always liked to prove that it is his car, rather than the driver, which does the winning, and I have to say he seems to have a point. Look at the hard facts. Frank got David Coulthard into his car in 1995 and David won races. Frank removed Coulthard at the end of the year and David stopped winning races. I think Damon might find it similar in 1997.

Irvine's prescient observation aside, Hill might also have been advised to listen to Peter Windsor on the subject of dealing with Frank and second-guessing his boss:

Frank was probably the most unpredictable person I have ever worked for in my life. It was impossible to predict what he was thinking or how he would react to any situation. I would say that 80 per cent of the time I got it wrong; there was always something that he would say or do or think that was so unexpected that you would never have even imagined that he would be thinking that way. Sometimes he would take those decisions just for the sake if it. But, a lot of the time, you'd think: 'Bloody hell, he's right! I never thought of it that way.' I've never met anyone like that before or since.

Hill probably thought the same thing as he tried to come to terms with the thunderbolt which had been delivered out of the blue. It was interesting to compare his dignified behaviour with the ranting of others who had found themselves in a similar position. One person who had first-hand evidence of this was Ann Bradshaw, the team's highly-respected press officer:

Damon was a gentleman all the way through. I was left a bit in the lurch because I wasn't party to all the things which had been going on and the news about Damon came out of the blue. But, as far as I was concerned, what was done was done and I had to deal with it.

People were saying that Frank was being mean. I'm not saying I agree with that but, as far as I'm concerned, he can be whatever he wants because he has every right. He got the team to where it is today. Patrick is a wonderful person and has played a major part in the team's success but, at the end of the day, Frank took the risks. He employs 250 people. He generates a lot of business. Everyone, at times like this, seems to think they have the right to tell him what to do. I think they have no right at all. He hires and fires. It's his choice.

Bradshaw, through her various roles in journalism and public relations, has known Williams for more than twenty years. Now the media director for the TWR motor sport group, Bradshaw can comment with impartiality and authority on a leading personality few people outside motor racing know anything about:

I think our relationship is different to most because I have known him for so long and, of course, because I am a woman in a man's world. But, even from my point of view, Frank has never been someone who engaged in social chit-chat. He is not someone you

would shoot the breeze with. He can be evasive – not indecisive –
but evasive until he has made up his mind. Then, once that is done,
you know where you stand.

Certainly, Hill was in no doubt about his position. The
one thing certain was that he would demonstrate to Frank
he had made a serious mistake by choosing Frentzen. On the
first lap of the Italian Grand Prix, Hill showed extraordinary
aggression as he took the lead from Jean Alesi's Benetton
and pulled away. No one could get close. Villeneuve had
touched a pile of tyres marking the apex of a corner and bent
his suspension. If Hill won this race, the championship was
his. Then, in yet another dramatic and unexpected development, Hill spun and stalled. He was out of the race. Damon
could not believe he had made such a small but costly error.

The championship fight was set to continue, at least to
Portugal. And from there it would go to Suzuka after
Villeneuve, in an inspired drive, had forged his way through
to win at Estoril, pushing Hill into second place in the
process. There were nine points between them, Hill remaining the clear favourite. But, in this topsy-turvy season, you
could make no firm predictions, count on nothing.

They shared the front row for this final race. Hill, who
had added to his problems throughout the season by making
poor starts, this time got away cleanly. The chips were down
and Hill produced an imperious drive. When Villeneuve lost
a wheel and retired after thirty-six of the fifty-two laps, Hill
could have parked and celebrated the championship. But he
pressed on, determined to win his last race for the team. It
was an emotional moment as he drove the final mile for
Williams Grand Prix Engineering. Typically, Hill felt not
the slightest inclination to show Frank the metaphorical
finger as he put on as near perfect a display as Williams

could wish for. He had brought a highly productive and at times turbulent chapter in his career to a superb close.

Frank had given Damon his chance and Hill had been through every emotion in the book. This was the best by far, making up for the unspeakable sadness of 1994 and the mind-crushing frustration of 1995. Finally, he was able to reflect openly on his time with Williams:

I'd go along with the suggestion that people are fond of Frank. I have a soft spot for him. But I also know he is capable of doing despicable things – despicable in my terms. It's a relative thing and I'm not prepared to enlarge on it any further.

I think he lives in a different world to most people. I didn't know him before the accident but I know enough people who tell me that he hasn't really changed at all. He's just become a little bit more . . . difficult to fathom, perhaps. But I'll say this: he can charm people and he knows that he can charm people and he knows that's one of his talents. I think you can be taken in by that if you're not careful.

But you can't ignore the fact that he has made himself whatever he is. It's a conscious thing. I'd like to have met Frank Williams, aged sixteen, just to see what you would have got there compared to what you've got now. I wonder if he spoke with a Geordie accent for example!

He's very different to the person that appears on television. He has this intense expression but, if you look at other team owners on the pit wall, they are the same. When I go on aeroplanes, I quite often get invited onto the flight deck. A lot of the pilots ask me about Frank. They'll say, 'What about that Frank Williams? He's a miserable looking bastard, isn't he?' They'll say that and I almost fall into the trap of defending him.

I know another side to him. There is a kid in there who just gets a big kick out of the whole thing. He loves the high stakes, and he loves the cars and, especially, he loves the deals and the winning in the chess game.

I do believe he gets a kick out of just dropping a driver. I came up with the theory – which perhaps gives him more credit than maybe he deserves and I'm being too lenient – that both he and Patrick are nice guys who don't want to appear to be soft. They compensate by doing the most appalling things, as if to say to everyone: 'Don't mess with us.' I sometimes think they don't do what they want to do; I think they do what they think they ought to do in order to appear tough enough for Formula One. They would never want to appear to go soft on a driver; that's soppy. In that sort of world, you cannot afford to appear to let emotion into your judgement. I sometimes felt Frank was trying to cultivate an image of mystique; the fewer questions he could answer, the better.

I don't feel bitter, or anything like that. But I think that I kept my mouth shut for too long about certain things and I should have said at the time what I was really thinking. I think I carried the can for a lot of things and I was frightened of putting the boot in – well, maybe not putting the boot in as such – but I was frightened of putting my side for fear of upsetting my relationship with Frank and Patrick. Don't forget, every year I was there, I was on a one-year deal. I didn't really have any authority. I didn't feel like I was ever in a position where I could speak out quite that freely, and I was always too reserved. I think I let them off the hook several times.

Now I am leaving, I feel I want to set the record straight on that part of it. I think I understand them. There's never been any grudges; there's not any bitterness. I put it down as an interesting experience.

I don't approve of the way Frank plays with people – but then I'm from a totally different background and upbringing. My principles are different to his. I could never do the things he does. You might ask who's more worthy and who's better. You can't do that. It's a different situation and you have to live your life the way you think best.

When you talk to some people, the conversation dovetails; you are on the same wavelength; you can talk and you can allude to things without explaining. When you talk to Frank, it's: 'What d'you mean?' If, say, you're talking about friendship, doing something for someone perhaps, he's not sure what you are on about. It's difficult for him to relate to what you are trying to say. I found it very difficult to talk to him at the race track and I know I am not the only driver to have felt that way.

But these are all very minor points. I can't have any regrets about my time with Williams. Frank gave me my chance and I have some wonderful memories.

CHAPTER EIGHTEEN

The trouble with speed

On 20 February 1997, almost three years since the death of Ayrton Senna, a judicial hearing opened in a makeshift courtroom in Imola. The permanent building was considered to be too small, an undeniable fact thanks to the Senna affair having become a *cause célèbre* which was in danger of turning into a circus.

In an unprecedented move in motor sport, six people were to be charged with manslaughter. Frank Williams, Patrick Head and Adrian Newey were to answer charges as manufacturers of the car. They would stand trial with Federico Bendinelli, representing SAGIS, the owners of Imola, Giorgio Poggi, the circuit director, and Roland Bruynseraede, the race director who sanctioned the circuit on behalf of the FIA, the sport's governing body.

The death of a racing driver raises emotional issues which tend to cloud the reality. When Senna crashed, he was doing his job to the best of his ability in a car which the Williams team had built to the best of their ability. It was a partnership which thrived under pressure. Neither side would have mentioned at any stage that death and injury could result. There was no need. The risks involved were obvious and the clamour from outside the sport which followed Senna's death was, ironically enough, the result of a comfortable vacuum created by massive strides in safety procedures.

The shock of his death, and its dramatic exposure on television, brought home the larcenous nature of a business which, in statistical terms, is safer than more leisurely pursuits such as fishing. But that did not – and should not – prevent the belief that motor racing can be made even more secure. The problem with the court case was that the Italian legal system gave the impression that fatalities could be eradicated completely, that Senna's death could somehow have been avoided.

In a perfect world, it could. But mistakes and misjudgements, while being few and far between, will always be made in top-level competition of any kind. As Max Mosley, the president of the FIA, pointed out, people should not be liable to prosecution for 'an ordinary, honest mistake which is part of the sport. You either ban the sport altogether or you say: "That's dangerous. Don't do it unless you accept that mistakes can be made which might result in injury or even death." This is fundamental to any number of sports, including skiing, motor cycle racing, mountain climbing and boxing. What we need is a form of Dangerous Sports Law.'

That would be for the future. In the meantime, the Senna case was not being allowed to rest, particularly after an Italian magazine claimed the entire affair was being swept under the carpet. That led to questions in the Italian Senate, a point from which there could be no return, thus ensuring the trial would have an exceptionally high profile.

Speculation continued to suggest that the steering broke. The Williams defence set out to prove that the fracture was the result rather than the cause of the subsequent collision with the concrete wall. The race officials defended the charge that the circuit safety facilities were inadequate and that the track had not been cleared properly following the accident on the start line, which precedes the Tamburello curve. On 16 February 1997, the *Sunday Times* published photographs which suggested that Senna was about to run over a piece of debris moments before he crashed. It looked suspiciously like a remnant from Lehto's Benetton following the start-line collision but, even if Senna had run over the debris, or swerved to avoid it, the location, just beyond the starting grid, was at least a couple of hundred yards before the point where he eventually lost control. Even so, the coverage given to this small and, at face value, irrelevant aspect illustrated the continuing interest in a court case which boiled down to motor racing paying due respect to Italian law, no matter how inappropriate that law seemed in relation to the sport.

The charge of manslaughter is commonplace in a country where the slightest degree of blame or negligence is regarded as a criminal offence. According to Mosley, the defendants were likely to be acquitted. In an interview on Radio 5 Live, Mosley, a former barrister, said: 'Nobody can be certain about these things. Good legal advice in Italy, having examined all the facts, is that they ought to be acquitted and I'm reasonably confident that they will be on the basis that what Williams say happened to the car and what the prosecutor says happened to the car are two different things and Williams are more likely to be right than the prosecutor.'

The Williams team had been granted no more than twenty minutes' inspection of Senna's car even though the wreckage had been examined in minute detail by Italian technicians. Mosley, who raced Formula Two cars in the late sixties, was aware that the intricacies of the Senna case were not unique. In 1961, Jim Clark's Lotus was involved in a collision with Wolfgang von Trips during the Italian Grand Prix at Monza. Von Trips and fourteen spectators were killed when his Ferrari spun off the track. It would be two years before Clark was cleared of any blame. In 1970, Jochen

Rindt suffered fatal injuries when he crashed his Lotus during practice at Monza. The inquest started straight away and lasted several years before charges against Lotus were dismissed. In each case, the Italian authorities impounded the wreckage. Clark's car was returned after a few years, but the British team never did receive Rindt's Lotus. During the prolonged Rindt case, Lotus continued to race in Italy although Colin Chapman, the team's founder, stayed away from the 1971 Italian Grand Prix and entered his cars under the name of Worldwide Racing – as opposed to Team Lotus – as a precaution against further action by the court.

Nothing has changed insofar as Italian law continues to call for an investigation into the death of a racing driver. In Senna's case, however, the matter had become public property thanks to media coverage which was unheard of at the time when von Trips and Rindt lost their lives. Senna's trial would reflect the overwhelming emotion attached to the loss of a sporting icon known the world over. Had it been anyone other than Senna at the wheel of the Williams, the existing courtroom would have been perfectly adequate, assuming there had been a public hearing at all.

It was an unavoidable fact which Williams and his team had to accept as they prepared a defence while continuing their customary detailed planning for the forthcoming season. In the midst of it all, Frank and Patrick were also involved in a tug-of-war over Adrian Newey as the chief designer attempted to join McLaren despite his Williams contract running until July 1999. Newey, who was reputed to have been offered £2m by McLaren, said money was not at issue. He was believed to have been unhappy with his status within the team. There had also been suggestions that Hill's dismissal had been a factor in his decision to leave, but that seemed unlikely given Newey's criticism of Hill's performances, particularly at the end of 1995.

Newey had been present throughout a period of impressive growth at Williams Grand Prix Engineering. The company's turnover had jumped from £12m to £36m, Williams having diversified into touring car racing by running a team on behalf of Renault in the British championship. Frank remained the major shareholder with Patrick Head holding the other 30 per cent. An operating profit of £6.6m had been registered for 1995, by which time the team was on the move again, this time to the former headquarters of a pharmaceutical company just outside the village of Grove in Oxfordshire. The thirty-two-acre site, on which would be built brand-new workshops, cost £6.7m and it required months of planning by specialists to organise the move of 224 full-time staff and their equipment without unnecessary disruption to the racing programme.

FW19 was the first car to be designed completely at Grove. The immediate concern was that it would be affected by Newey's enforced leave, which began in November 1996. By then, however, the important work on FW19 had been carried out. Williams took out a High Court writ to prevent Newey from working elsewhere, but the matter eventually reached an amicable conclusion. On 22 April, Williams and McLaren jointly announced that Newey would become McLaren's technical director on 1 August 1997.

By the time of the announcement, three races had been run and Villeneuve had won two of them. Frentzen, after a difficult start to the season, would score his maiden F1 victory at Imola, thus underscoring Williams's status as favourites to win the constructors' championship. As the season got into its stride, however, a combination of circumstances – including a disastrous tyre choice in the rain at Monaco – would allow Schumacher and Ferrari to become a consistent challenger.

The season followed a thrilling course as the championship see-sawed between the two teams, right up to the final race in Spain. For forty-seven laps, Villeneuve and Schumacher drove like men possessed, the Williams driver pulling a daring overtaking move which appeared to catch Schumacher by surprise. Repeating his action at Adelaide in 1994, Schumacher drove into his rival. This time it didn't work. The Williams continued, the Ferrari did not. Villeneuve was World Champion. Frank had already won the constructor's title for a record ninth time.

Schumacher's performances had confirmed Frank's early-season prediction – one which he makes every year, in fact – that nothing can be taken for granted. Although he would worry over where his next victory was coming from, the thrill of the chase had continued to be meat and drink to a man who remains a devoted fan of Formula One. 'Frank has got a complete, child-like enthusiasm for racing,' says Peter Windsor. 'It's infectious and it's wonderful. His eyes light up. When I worked there – and I'm sure it's the same now – the best moments of the day were between five and six in the evening. I used to go into his office, have a cup of tea and just talk about racing: the old days, the present, the future. Anything to do with racing. Those were the best moments.'

It was that love of racing, of going quickly, which almost killed Frank Williams. But the accident in 1986 seems to have heightened his enthusiasm for a business he has commanded with such quiet brilliance. He will deny any claims of managerial excellence, of course. 'I just love racing,' he will say. 'Watching the drivers do what they do in a racing car is brilliant. It turns me on. It always has. This business of going quickly in a car, that's been my trouble all along.'

Index

Aida, Japan *see* Pacific Grand Prix
Aitken, Jonathan, 74
Albilad company, 74, 80, 96, 98
Albilad-Williams Racing Team, 96
Alboreto, Michele, 140
Alesi, Jean, 187, 272
Alfa Romeo, 31, 114
Al Fawzan, Mohammed, 64, 68
Ambrozium (Swiss businessman), 45
Anderson, Ian, 101
Andretti, Mario, 71, 81, 85, 125
Argentina Grand Prix, 1980, 97
Arnoux, René, 92, 97, 100–2
Association of British Machine Tool
    Makers (ABMTM), 67
Aston Tirrold, Oxfordshire, 112
Australian Grand Prix: 1986, 163–5;
    1994, 253–5
Austrian Grand Prix: 1970, 36; 1979,
    95; 1980, 104; 1985, 145
Autocar, The (magazine), 6, 98, 119
Autocourse (annual), 102, 107
Autosport (magazine), 9–10, 20, 26,
    56, 68, 215, 217, 231, 256

Bailey, Len, 39
Barnard, John, 136
Baroom (steel and cement merchant),
    80
Barrichello, Rubens, 232, 234

Belgian Grand Prix: 1981, 116; 1982,
    127–8; 1985, 145; 1986, 156;
    1987, 171
Bell, Derek, 38
Bendinelli, Federico, 276
Benetton cars: Schumacher drives for,
    82, 229, 258; world
    championships, 82; 1989
    successes, 183; Patrese joins,
    216; 1994 successes, 231, 242,
    245, 250–1; fined in 1994
    British Grand Prix, 247–8; 1995
    season, 260, 262; Schumacher
    leaves, 268
Berger, Gerhard, 193, 196–8, 204,
    213, 240–1, 255, 260
Bin Laden company, 80
Blundell, Mark, 199
Boutsen, Thierry, 182, 185
Boxford House, near Newbury, 148,
    156, 179
Brabham BT24, 27, 108–10
Brabham BT26, 27, 29
Brabham cars: FW drives, 16–17, 20;
    BMW turbo engine, 126; 1982
    unreliability, 127; at Paul Ricard
    Circuit, 144
Brabham, Jack, 27, 30
Bradshaw, Ann, 271
Brands Hatch, Kent: FW races at, 11;

Courage wins at, 23; Race of
Champions (1969), 28–9; *see also*
British Grand Prix; Grand Prix
of Europe
Brawn, Ross, 82
Brazilian Grand Prix: 1978, 70; 1981,
114–15; 1986, 154; 1987,
170–1; 1994, 224
Breen, Michael, 261, 268–9
Bremner, Rory, 215
Bridges, Charles, 27
British Grand Prix: 1970 (Brand's
Hatch), 35; 1972 (Brand's
Hatch), 40; 1975 (Silverstone),
46; 1979 (Silverstone), 88–93;
1980 (Brand's Hatch), 102–3;
1981 (Silverstone), 116; 1985
(Silverstone), 103; 1986 (Brand's
Hatch), 158–61; 1987
(Silverstone), 144–5; 1990
(Silverstone), 172–3; 1991
(Silverstone), 185; 1992
(Silverstone), 192, 206; 1993
(Silverstone), 221–2; 1994
(Silverstone), 245–9
British Racing and Sports Car Club,
10
BRM team, 22, 24, 42
Brodie, Dave, 50–1, 58, 63
Brundle, Martin, 138, 216, 223
Bruynseraede, Roland, 276

Camel cigarettes, 189, 227
Campbell's Soup: FW works for, 11
Canadian Grand Prix, 1973, 44;
1977, 65; 1980, 107–11; 1985,
142; 1986, 156; 1989, 182;
1991, 191; 1992, 203–4; 1994,
244
Cane, Michael, 183
Canon company, 141, 189, 197, 227
Caserta, Italy, 21
Castrol oil company, 25
Challis, Alan, 130, 156
Champion company, 67

Chapman, Colin: designs, 81–2;
death, 141, 156; and Rindt case,
279
Cippenham, near Slough, 21, 23, 25,
39, 47
Clark, Jim, 278–9
Clarke, John, 43
Collins, Peter, 141–2
Colman, Sir Michael and Lady, 51
Contracts Recognition Board, 259
Cooper car: FW acquires and sells,
19–20
Cosworth Engineering, 48, 61, 89,
96; *see also* Ford-Cosworth engine
Coulthard, David: drives for FW,
243–4, 259–63, 265, 270; wins
first Grand Prix (Portugal 1995),
264
Courage, Lady Sarah ('Sally'; Piers's
wife), 22
Courage, Piers: friendship with FW,
9–10, 15, 21; sells 1955
Plymouth to Horsley, 16; drives
for FW, 21–5, 27–31, 85;
contracts and earnings, 30–1;
killed, 32–4, 104
Crichton-Stuart, Charles, 14–15, 18,
47, 73, 75, 77, 98, 117, 124, 130
Crumpler, Gary, 210
Crystal Palace circuit, London, 10
CSS Promotions (company), 131
Cunningham, Iain, 170, 178–9, 181,
238

Dallah Avco company, 80
Dallara, Gianpaolo, 53
Dallas Grand Prix, 1984, 136, 142
Daly, Derek, 125–6, 133–4
Dennis, Ron, 132
Depailler, Patrick, 99
Dernie, Frank, 82, 88, 124, 126, 150,
156
de Tomaso F1 car, 30–6, 53

Detroit *see* United States Grand Prix (East)

Didcot: Station Road premises, 62–4, 112; Williams move to Basil Hill Road, 137; new wind tunnel installed, 188, 200–1

Dijon, France, 127–8

Ducarouge, Gerard, 175

Duffeler, Pat, 42, 45

Dunlop company, 25, 27

Dutch Grand Prix: 1968, 24; 1970, 31–2; 1973, 44; 1980, 104–6

Ecclestone, Bernard, 40–1, 49, 61, 150–1, 159, 245

Eckersley, Wayne, 89–90

Ecurie Ecosse, 6

Elf company, 190, 200, 208, 210

Enna, Sicily, 30

European Grand Prix, Spain (1994), 250–1

Eva, P., 9

Evans, Bob, 26

F1 Racing Magazine, 132

Fahd, King of Saudi Arabia, 98

Fahd, Prince Muhammed bin *see* Muhammed bin Fahd, Prince

Faron, Eric, 207

Ferrari: and 1996 Grand Prix, 1; Courage declines offer from, 30; Brawn joins, 82; in 1979 Grands Prix, 95; and motor racing politics, 114; turbo engines, 126, 132; in 1982 season, 127; contract with Mansell, 177, 183, 185; sign up Prost, 185; Schumacher drives for, 268, 280; in 1997 season, 280

Ferrari, Enzo: congratulates FW on first Grand Prix victory, 94

FIA (Fédération Internationale de l'Automobile), 37, 218–19, 224, 240–2, 276–7

Fiat company, 188

FISA (Fédération Internationale de Sport de l'Automobile): conflict with FOCA, 100–1, 114, 126

Fittipaldi, Emerson, 123

FOCA (Formula One Constructors' Association): formed, 40–1; subsidies and benefits, 46, 55; FW loses membership, 61; Williams regain membership, 80; conflict with FISA, 100–1, 114, 126

Ford Europe, 48

Ford-Cosworth engines, 25, 43–4, 61, 86, 88, 96, 126, 133, 135; turbocharging, 132

Formula Three (*formerly* Formula Junior): racing, 12–19, 22–3

Formula Two championships, 23, 38

Frank Williams (Racing Cars) Ltd: set up, 21; advertises in *Autosport*, 26; absent from 1970 French Grand Prix, 35; moves to Reading, 39; changes to Walter Wolf Racing, 56

Fraser, Sir Hugh, 73

French Grand Prix: 1979, 87; 1980, 100–2; 1982, 127–8; 1994, 245

Frentzen, Heinz-Harald: replaces Damon Hill at Williams, 2–3, 267–9, 272, 280; pressure on, 133

Fruit of the Loom, 67

Galisteu, Adriane, 234–5

Galli, Nanni, 41–2, 44, 67

Ganley, Howden, 42, 44

German Grand Prix: 1979, 94; 1980, 104; 1981, 116–17

Giacomelli, Bruno, 108

Gomm, Maurice, 39

Goodyear company: sponsors motor racing, 27, 67, 70–1, 76, 163, 171; withdraws from racing, 114; returns to racing (1982), 128

Goring-on-Thames: Battle House, 113

INDEX

Grand Prix of Europe, Brand's Hatch, 1985, 145
Grand Prix (magazine), 165
Grove, Oxfordshire, 280
Guardian newspaper, 86

Hakkinen, Mika, 216, 230, 242
Hamilton, Maurice, 130, 143
Harris, Tony, 64
Harrison, Ian, 245
Hayes, Walter, 48
Hazel, Jeff, 110, 123
Head, Colonel Michael, 59
Head, Patrick: FW hires, 59–60, 62–5; friendship with Jones, 66, 77, 121; and FW06, 67–8, 72; interviews Oatley, 69; checking routines, 75–6, 82; and 1978 US Grand Prix bolt incident, 76–7, 79, 82; on 1978 successes, 79; adopts ground effect, 81; conservatism in design, 81–2; interviews Brawn, 82–3; on Jones at 1979 Monaco Grand Prix, 86; and 1979 British Grand Prix victory, 94–5; develops FW07B, 97; and 1980 French Grand Prix, 101; and Jones's defeat at 1980 Dutch Grand Prix, 105; 1980 success, 106; and Jones's departure (1981), 120; and FW08 car, 126; technical authority, 128; relations with press, 129; reluctance to adopt carbon fibre, 135; insists on FW's choosing 1984 driver, 138; relations with Rosberg, 146; and FW's road accident, 151–2; position after FW's accident, 157, 167; and FW12 engine, 177; avoids commercial side of company, 184; appoints Newey, 188; and Mansell, 192; and 1991 Portuguese mishap, 194; develops FW14B, 199; speaks to Patrese in 1992 season, 205–6; impressed by Damon Hill, 217; designs FW15, 219; on antipathy to Prost, 223; develops FW16 car, 228; and 1994 French Grand Prix, 245; and Hill's misfortune at 1994 Grand Prix practice, 246–7; criticises Hill, 251–2, 261; Hill's view of, 274; charged with manslaughter of Senna, 276, 279; company shareholding, 280
Henry, Alan, 34, 66–7, 118, 132, 225
Herbert, Johnny, 262
Herrick, Steve, 96, 131
Heseltine, Michael, 137
Hesketh 308C car *see* Wolf-Williams car
Hesketh, Alexander Fermor-Hesketh, 3rd Baron, 73
Hesketh team, 54
Hill, Damon: dismissed by FW, 1–4, 180, 268–72; birth, 8; FW introduces Jonathan Williams to, 12; test drives for Williams, 199, 216; drives Brabham in 1992 British Grand Prix, 206; contract with FW, 217–18, 226, 267; in 1993 season, 219–24; first Grand Prix victory (Hungary 1993), 223; on effect of new technical regulations and FW16 car, 228–9; 1994 season, 229–30, 243–5, 247–55; at Imola (1994), 235, 238; in 1994 Monaco Grand Prix, 241–2; and Senna's death and funeral, 242; 1994 British Grand Prix victory, 245–9; protests at lack of support, 246, 249, 251; criticised by Head, 251–2; discontent with Williams, 253–4, 262; 1995 season, 258–66; relations with FW, 266, 273–4; 1996 season and championship, 267, 272–3

Hill, Graham: and birth of Damon, 8; death, 217

Holmes, Francis, 7

Honda company: FW negotiates with, 132–3; powers Williams cars, 135–6, 142; Didcot workshops, 137; lacks belief in FW, 174–5; treatment of Mansell, 174; relations with Senna, 175; engines for McLaren, 204

Honda, Soichiro, 174

Horsley, Anthony ('Bubbles'), 15–18

Howe, Edward Richard Curzon, 6th Earl, 22

Hungarian Grand Prix: 1986, 162; 1993, 223

Hunt, James: with Hesketh team, 54, 57; drives for McLaren, 57; retires in 1977 Austrian Grand Prix, 66; in 1978 US Grand Prix West, 71; press support for, 102; retirement from racing, 123; popularity, 186; on Mansell in 1992 season, 205

ICI company, 141

Ickx, Jacky, 27, 54, 56–7

Imola: judicial inquiry into Senna's death, 276; *see also* San Marino Grand Prix

Irvine, Eddie, 270

Iso-Marlboro cars, 41

Iso-Rivolta company, 41–2, 45

Italian Grand Prix, Monza: 1961, 278; 1974, 45; 1977, 65; 1978, 76; 1981, 117; 1996, 1, 3

Jabouille, Jean-Pierre, 89–91, 104

Jackson, John, 89

Jaguar cars: success at Le Mans, 6

Japanese Grand Prix: 1987, 173; 1991, 197; 1994, 229–31; 1995, 265–6; *see also* Pacific Grand Prix

Jarama, Spain, 84

Jarier, Jean-Pierre, 92

Jarrow, 5

Jones, Alan: wins 1977 Austrian Grand Prix, 65–6; drives for FW, 66, 68, 70–2, 74–7, 79, 83–5, 87–90; and 1978 US Grand Prix incident, 76–9; criticises team after 1979 Spanish failure, 85–6; 1979 British Grand Prix breakdown, 89–91, 93; first wins for FW (1979), 94–5; 1980 season, 97, 99–111; loses 1980 Dutch Grand Prix, 105–6; wins world championship (1980), 111; in 1981 season, 114–20; disagreements with Reutemann, 115–17, 119–20; broken finger, 117–18; retirement, 117, 121; replacement for, 123; retains relationship with FW, 131; on FW's character, 269

Jones, Bernie, 122

Jones, Beverley, 91

Judd, John, 176–7

Kettlewell, Michael, 10, 21

Kinnill, Robin, 169–70, 239

Knutstorp, Sweden, 20

Labatts company, 190

Laffite, Bernadette, 52

Laffite, Jacques, 45–6, 52–3, 100, 102, 124, 134–5, 137, 160

Lamy, Pedro, 236

Larini, Nicola, 230

Las Vegas Grand Prix: 1981, 118–21; 1982, 128–30

Lauda, Niki: in 1975 British Grand Prix, 46; in 1978 Brazilian Grand Prix, 70; retires in 1978 US Grand Prix West, 72; negotiates with FW, 124; in 1982 season, 128

Lehto, J.J., 235–6, 278

Le Mans 24-Hour race, 6

Lennep, Gijs van, 44
Leyland Vehicles, 96, 126, 131
Leyton House team, 188
Ligier cars, 100–3, 111, 135
Lilly, Penny, 170
Lombardi, Lella, 52–3
London Hospital, 153–4
Long Beach, California see United
    States Grand Prix (West)
Longford, Tasmania, 24
Lotus cars, 42, 81–2, 127, 140–1,
    156, 175, 279
Lucas, Charles, 15, 22

McLaren, Bruce: killed, 32, 34
McLaren cars: financing, 42; Hunt
    drives for, 57; Oatley designs for,
    69; in 1982 season, 127;
    association with Porsche, 132;
    carbon fibre chassis, 135–6;
    turbo engines, 136, 145; adopt
    Honda engines, 176; sign up
    Senna, 176; Senna renews
    contract (1991), 187; in 1991
    season, 192, 198; in 1992 season,
    199; Senna leaves, 226; and
    Senna's death, 238; Mansell
    drives for, 259–60; Newey joins,
    279
McLaren Honda cars, 182
McLaren-TAG turbo, 145
McNally, Patrick, 32
Makepeace, John, 63
Mallory Park, Leicestershire, 9, 11, 38
Mansell, Nigel: leaves FW, 3, 268;
    drives for FW, 65, 139, 144–5;
    poor record, 140; increasing
    confidence, 141; mistake at 1985
    Portuguese Grand Prix, 141–2;
    accident at Paul Ricard, 142–4;
    first Grand Prix win (Brands
    Hatch 1985), 145; and FW's
    road crash, 150, 152; 1986
    season, 156, 158–66; 1986
    British Grand Prix victory,
160–1; rivalry with Piquet,
    160–3, 170, 172–4; 1987
    season, 170–2; crash in 1987
    Japanese Grand Prix, 173–4;
    dislikes FW12 car, 177; Ferrari
    contract, 177, 183; rejoins
    Williams (1991), 185, 187, 200;
    announces retirement (1990),
    186; earnings, 186, 200;
    popularity, 186, 223; 1991
    season, 190–3; mechanical
    failure in 1991 Canadian Grand
    Prix, 191–2; in 1991 Portuguese
    Grand Prix mishap, 194–6;
    conflict with Berger, 196;
    prickly character, 196–7, 200;
    1992 championship season, 198,
    199–207; rivalry with Patrese,
    201, 204, 206–8; reaction to
    Prost's Williams contract,
    208–9; announces retirement
    from Williams (1992), 211–15;
    Indycar racing, 215; in USA,
    223; returns to Williams (1994),
    243–6, 259; 1994 season,
    253–4; drives for McLaren
    (1995), 259–60
Mansell, Rosanne, 186
March Engineering, 37–40, 61, 64
Marlboro cigarette company, 41–2,
    44–5, 54, 57
Marriott, Andrew, 66–7
Mass, Jochen, 65, 87, 100
Merzario, Arturo, 44–6, 49, 54, 57
Mexican Grand Prix, 1992, 201
Mexico City, 36
Michelin tyre company, 70, 114, 128
Mobil company, 141
Monaco Grand Prix: 1969, 29; 1978,
    74; 1979, 86–7; 1981, 116–18;
    1983, 135; 1991, 191; 1992,
    202–3; 1994, 240–1; 1995, 263
Montreal see Canadian Grand Prix
Montreal Gazette, 204

Monza: Jonathan Williams drives at, 24; *see also* Italian Grand Prix
Morris, Alison, 63
Morris, Philip (company), 42
Mortimer, near Reading, 48
Mosley, Max, 37, 218–19, 277–8
Motor, The (magazine), 6
Motoring News, 118
Motul Oil, 38, 40
Muhammed bin Fahd, Prince, 73–5, 80, 93, 98
Muller, Johnny, 24

Nakajima, Satoru, 176
Neve, Patrick, 61, 64–5
New Zealand, 27
Newbury, 179–80; *see also* Boxford House
Newey, Adrian, 188, 200, 217, 219, 228, 261, 276, 279–80
Newman/Haas Indycar team, 215
Nottingham, 7–9, 11
Nurburgring, Germany: FW crashes at, 18
Nye, Doug: *Racers*, 70, 88

Oatley, Neil, 68–9, 78, 92, 112–13, 127, 137
Ojjeh, Akram, 75
Ojjeh, Mansour, 75, 95, 131–2
Ontario Motor Speedway, 84
Orriss, Viv, 42
Oulton Park, Cheshire: FW races at, 8, 10; Pescarolo races at, 38
Owen, H.R., 73

Pace, Carlos, 38, 40–1
Pacific Grand Prix, Aida (Japan): 1994, 229–31; 1995, 265
Page & Moy, 26
Paletti, Ricardo, 234
Passarini, Maurizio, 258
Patrese, Riccardo: FW approaches, 65; drives for FW, 177, 182, 185, 187, 190–3, 196, 200–2,

204–5, 214; rivalry with Mansell, 201, 204, 206–8; retires, 205; crashes in 1992 Portuguese Grand Prix, 213–14; joins Benetton, 216
Paul Ricard Circuit, 142, 148–9, 181–2
Penn, Francis, 9
Penske team (USA), 61
Personal (steering wheel manufacturer), 67
Pescarolo, Henri, 38, 40–1
Peterson, Ronnie, 65
Phoenix, Arizona *see* United States Grand Prix (East), 1991
Pinner Road, Harrow, 14–15
Piquet, Nelson: leaves Williams team (1987), 2, 172–3, 278; 1980 season, 99–100, 102–10; wins 1981 championship, 116–19; with Brabham, 124; 1985 season, 144; at Brands Hatch 1985 Grand Prix of Europe, 145; joins Williams, 148; and FW's road crash, 150, 152; 1986 season, 154, 158–66; rivalry with Mansell, 160–3, 170, 172–3, 197; wins 1987 championship, 170–3; joins Lotus, 176; 1991 season, 191; Imola crash, 237
Pironi, Didier, 100, 102, 108, 110–11, 124, 224; quits racing through injuries, 127
Poggi, Giorgio, 276
Politoys-Cosworth car, 39–41
Ponsonby, Sir Ashley, 122
Porsche company, 132
Portuguese Grand Prix: 1985, 141–2; 1991, 193–6
Postlethwaite, Harvey, 56, 58–9
Prost, Alain: leaves FW, 3, 268; drives for FW, 65, 208–9, 213, 215, 217, 219; 1982 season, 126; wins 1985 world

championship, 145; wins 1986 championship, 156, 158, 163–6; 1987 season, 171, 174; 1988 successes, 176; 1989 season, 183; Ferrari contract, 185; conflict with Mansell, 186; rivalry with Senna, 209, 221, 225; relations with Hill, 217; Mosley's objections to, 218–19; 1993 season, 220–5; dislike of wet driving, 224; retires, 225; FW praises, 226; record wins, 231

Rainier, Prince of Monaco, 29
Ratzenberger, Roland: killed, 233–4, 240–1
Reading (Bennet Road): Frank Williams (Racing Cars) Ltd moves to, 39, 47–8, 57
Redman, Brian, 35
Regazzoni, Clay: drives for FW, 83–5, 87, 94, 97; wins 1979 British Grand Prix, 90–3
Renault cars: 1979 French Grand Prix victory, 87–9; at 1979 British Grand Prix, 88–90; in 1980 season, 97, 104, 106; and motor racing politics, 114; turbo engines, 126, 132; 1982 unreliability, 127; partnership with Williams, 177, 182–3, 190, 200, 208; introduce V10 engine, 183, 200; support Mansell, 210–11; supply engines to Benetton, 261
Reutemann, Carlos: wins 1975 British Grand Prix, 46; in 1978 Grands Prix, 70, 72; drives for FW, 97–100, 102, 106, 111, 114, 125, 158; team arrangements with Jones, 115–16; in 1981 season, 116–20; retirement from racing, 125
Reynolds, R.J. (company), 227
Rider, Steve, 165

Rindt, Jochen, 279
Roebuck, Nigel, 215, 256
Rosberg, Kiejo ('Keke'): drives for FW, 65, 123–30, 133–5; wins 1982 world championship, 130–1; on difficulties of Honda engine, 136; in 1984 season, 137; relations with Mansell, 140, 146; in 1985 season, 142–6; retires in 1985 Portugese Grand Prix, 142; leaves FW, 146; relations with FW, 146; on FW's road accident, 154; final Grand Prix (Australia 1986), 163–4
Rothmans company, 227
Rushen, Dennis, 49

St Joseph's boarding school, Dumfries, 5
San Marino Grand Prix, Imola, 1980, 106–7; 1982, 126; 1987, 171; 1994, 231, 232–6; 1995, 257
Sauber team, 267
Saudia airline, 64, 66–8, 72–4, 80, 96
Saudia-Leyland Williams cars, 96
Saudia-Williams team, 75, 88
Saudi Arabia, 73–4, 80–1, 86, 95, 132, 141
Sawyer-Hoare, Charles, 47
Scheckter, Jody, 58, 70–1, 75, 87, 95, 123
Schenken, Tim, 35–6
Schumacher, Michael: drives for Benetton, 82, 229, 258; 1994 championship season, 229–31, 242–5; and Senna's death, 235–7; penalised at 1994 British Grand Prix, 248–9; rivalry with Hill, 255, 258, 263–6; 1995 championship season, 258, 260–1, 263–6; drives for Ferrari, 268, 280
Senna, Ayrton: death at Imola (1994), 2, 171, 234–9, 241, 256;

Rushen appreciates, 49; drives for FW, 65, 138; qualities, 138, 142; successes, 142; at 1985 Brands Hatch Grand Prix of Europe, 145; 1987 season, 171–3; attacked by Mansell in 1987 Belgian Grand Prix, 171; Honda and, 175; joins McLaren, 176; dominates 1989 season, 183; earnings, 186; 1991 season, 192–3, 196–8; disputes with Mansell, 197, 205, 214; 1992 season, 202–4, 214; rivalry wth Prost, 209, 221–2, 225; 1993 season, 220–4; FW seeks to sign up, 224–5; contract with Williams, 226; 1994 season, 229–31, 233; drives FW16 car, 229; funeral, 242; suspects Schumacher's car, 245; judicial inquiry into death of, 276–9

Senna, Leonardo, 235

Sicily, 16–17

Silverstone: International Trophy: 1969, 28–9; 1975, 53–4; see also British Grand Prix

Sindhi, Sheikh Kamal, 68

Skarpnack, Sweden, 20

South African Grand Prix: 1969, 28; 1974, 45; 1978, 71; 1981, 114; 1983, 135; 1985, 146

Spanish Grand Prix: 1969, 29; 1977, 64; 1979, 84; 1980, 99–100; 1991, 196; 1992, 201

Speedwell Conversions, 8

Stanley, Louis, 33

Stewart, Jackie, 28–9, 31, 33–4, 38

Stoke Mandeville hospital, 156

Stubbs, David, 156

Stuck, Hans, 65

Sultan bin Salman, Prince, 73

Sunday Times, 278

Surtees team, 41

TAG see Techniques d'Avant Garde

TAG Turbo (Porsche), 136

TAG Williams team, 131

Tanaka, Masahiro, 227

Tasman series (races), 23, 25, 27

Tauranac, Ron, 36

Techniques d'Avant Garde (TAG), 75, 131–2

Thatcher, Margaret (Baroness), 137, 153

Thynne, Sheridan, 10–11, 113, 131, 156–7, 167, 184, 210, 215

Toleman team, 138

Tomaso, Alessandro de, 30, 36

Torrie, Bob, 62, 122

Trips, Wolfgang von, 278

Tyrrell, Ken, 28, 46

Tyrrell team, 46, 125

United States Grand Prix (East): Watkins Glen, 1969, 29; 1975, 52–3; 1978, 76–8, 82; 1980, 107, 111; Detroit, 1985, 142; Phoenix, Arizona, 1991, 191

United States Grand Prix (West), Long Beach: 1978, 71–2; 1979, 84; 1980, 96–9; 1981, 114–15; 1982, 125

Vallelunga, Italy, 30

Villeneuve, Gilles, 72, 74, 87, 95, 116, 124; killed, 127

Villeneuve, Jacques: in 1996 Grand Prix contest, 2; drives for FW, 264, 267–8, 272, 280

Vincentelli, Dr, 152

Walter Wolf Racing (company), 56, 123

Ward, T.W. (company), 26, 40–1, 45, 63, 67

Warr, Peter, 58, 82

Watkins Glen see United States Grand Prix (East)

Watkins, Professor E.S. (Sid), 150–3,

174, 234, 237; *Life at the Limit*, 151

Watson, John, 71, 124, 128–30

Weaver, John, 153

Wendlinger, Kurt, 241

Williams, Claire (FW's daughter), 91, 148

Williams, Frank: dismisses Damon Hill, 1–4, 268–74; idiosyncratic behaviour, 4; injured in 1986 road crash, 4, 98, 149–56; upbringing and education, 5–8, 11; early interest in cars and racing, 6–11; early career and jobs, 8–9, 11; full name (Francis Owen Garbett Williams), 8; early racing crashes, 9–10, 18, 20; as Jonathan Williams's 'mechanic', 12–14; lacks technical knowledge, 12, 36; early financial problems, 14–18; wins bet by appearing naked, 15; buying and selling, 19; as entrant and team owner, 20; Formula Two racing, 23, 30, 38; Monza Formula Two victory (1968), 24; wins commercial sponsorship for Grand Prix racing, 25–6, 28; association with de Tomaso, 30–1; and death of Piers Courage, 32–9; enthusiasm, 36–7, 50, 281; builds own cars, 39–40; charm and appeal, 42–3, 183–4, 273; marriage to Virginia, 47, 50–1; home in Mortimer, 48; birth of son (Jonathan Piers), 51; rents home on Colman estate, 51–2; running, 53, 112–13, 148; relations with Wolf, 56, 58–9; hires Head, 59–60; independence from Wolf, 60–1; introduces FW06 car, 66–8; success in 1978 Grands Prix, 79; first Grand Prix victory

(Silverstone 1979), 91–3; 1980 constructors' and driver's successes, 106, 111; moves to Goring-on-Thames, 113; relations with Jones, 120–1; interest in tyres, 128; supervises races, 129–30; flying, 132–3, 184; human relations, 146–7, 195–6; moves to Boxford House, 148; hospital treatment, 151–2; quadriplegia, 155, 157; returns to work and racing, 157, 159, 162, 166–7; reaction to physical condition, 166–70, 178, 196; Hill's view of, 173–4; alienation from Honda, 175; awarded CBE, 176; disabled equipment and aids, 178; fastidiousness, 179; in Newbury house, 179–80; cruel streak, 180; spending, 180; revisits crash scene, 181; view of accident, 182; and 1991 Portuguese Grand Prix mishap, 194–5; on Mansell, 200; on Mansell's retirement, 211–14; conflict with FIA in 1993, 218; relations with Senna, 226–7; and Senna's death, 237–9, 256–7; attitude to Hill, 266; charged with manslaughter of Senna, 276, 278–9; as major company shareholder, 280

Williams FW06 car, 66–72, 74, 81, 84, 95

Williams FW07 car, 81, 84–6, 97

Williams FW07B car, 97

Williams FW07C car, 114

Williams FW08 car, 126

Williams FW09 car, 136

Williams FW10 car, 137–8

Williams FW12 car, 177

Williams FW13B car, 183

Williams FW14 car, 190

Williams FW14B car, 199, 207, 219

Williams FW15 car, 219

Williams FW16 car, 227–9, 233, 243
Williams FW17 car, 258
Williams FW19 car, 280
Williams Grand Prix Engineering:
    FW's commitment to, 4; Thynne
    becomes commercial director,
    11; formed, 60; Didcot premises,
    61–3; bank support for, 63;
    workforce, 63; two-car policy,
    80; wins 1980 constructors'
    championship, 106; wins 1981
    constructors' championship, 122;
    wins Queen's Award for Export
    Achievement, 122; expansion
    and reorganisation, 123; wins
    1986 constructors'
    championship, 161, 163; Honda
    terminate arrangements with,
    175–6; partnership with
    Renault, 177, 182; expansion,
    189; and new technical
    regulations, 229; and pit-stop
    tactics, 230; wins 1994
    constructors' championship, 255;
    fails to win constructors'
    championship (1995), 266; and
    inquiry into death of Senna, 278;
    annual turnover and profits, 280;
    move to Grove, 280; in touring
    car racing, 280
Williams, Jaime (FW's son), 148
Williams, Jonathan: friendship with
    FW, 9–14; Formula Junior
    driving, 12–14; FW works for as
    mechanic, 12–13; financial
    problems, 14; at Crichton-
    Stuart's, 15; on Horsley, 18; and
    Piers Courage, 22; wins for FW
    at Monza, 24
Williams, Jonathan Piers (FW's son),
    51, 94, 148
Williams, Owen Garbett (FW's
    father), 5
Williams, Mrs Owen Garbett (FW's
    mother), 5, 12

Williams, Ted, 26, 40–1, 63
Williams, Virginia (FW's wife;
    Ginny): marriage, 47–8, 51;
    birth of children, 50–1, 91;
    home on Colman estate, 51–2;
    and FW's salary with Wolf, 56;
    finds new Oxfordshire premises,
    61; at 1979 British Grand Prix
    victory, 91, 93; moves house to
    Goring-on-Thames, 113; moves
    to Boxford House, 148; and
    FW's road accident and
    hospitalisation, 151–2, 155–6;
    and FW's moves to recovery,
    157, 159, 170; accepts
    constructors' trophy (1986),
    161; leaves Boxford House,
    179–80
Williams-Ford cars, 46
Windsor, Peter: race reports, 98, 119;
    as Williams team manager, 98,
    193; and FW's ambitions, 103;
    with FW in road crash, 149–50,
    152; and FW's hospital
    treatment, 153; position at
    Williams after FW's accident,
    156; revisits crash scene with
    FW, 181; and Portuguese pit-
    stop mishap, 193–5; on
    Mansell's leaving Williams, 213;
    on FW's character, 270, 281
Wolf, Walter: agreements with FW,
    53–6, 59–60; working relations
    with FW, 57–8; transporter
    damaged, 64
Wolf-Williams car (formerly Hesketh
    308), 56–7, 59

Yate, Paul, 153
York, Sarah, Duchess of (née
    Ferguson), 32
Young, Mike, 10

Zandvoort see Dutch Grand Prix